# HUMAN RIGHTS FIFTY YEARS ON

MANCHESTER
UNIVERSITY PRESS

# Human rights fifty years on
# A reappraisal

*edited by Tony Evans*

Manchester University Press
MANCHESTER AND NEW YORK

*distributed exclusively in the USA by St. Martin's Press*

Copyright © Manchester University Press 1998

While copyright in the volume as a whole is vested in Manchester University Press, copyright in individual chapters belongs to their respective authors, and no chapter may be reproduced wholly or in part without the express permission in writing of both author and publisher.

Published by Manchester University Press
Oxford Road, Manchester M13 9NR, UK
and Room 400, 175 Fifth Avenue, New York, NY 10010, USA

Distributed exclusively in the USA by
St. Martin's Press, Inc., 175 Fifth Avenue, New York, NY 10010, USA

Distributed exclusively in Canada by
UBC Press, University of British Columbia, 6344 Memorial Road,
Vancouver, BC, Canada V6T 1Z2

British Library Cataloguing-in-Publication Data
A catalogue record for this book is available from the British Library

Library of Congress Cataloging-in-Publication Data applied for


ISBN   0 7190 5102 9   hardback
       0 7190 5103 7   paperback


First published 1998

05  04  03  02  01  00  99  98      10  9  8  7  6  5  4  3  2  1

Typeset in Monotype Bell by Carnegie Publishing, Chatsworth Rd, Lancaster
Printed in Great Britain by Biddles Ltd, Guildford and King's Lynn

# CONTENTS

# ACKNOWLEDGEMENTS

The editor would like to thank all of the contributors to this volume for their industry and patience. Thanks also go to Jan Hancock, of the Department of Politics, University of Southampton, for his support in preparing the final manuscript. Special thanks must go to Annie Taylor for her unfailing support and encouragement.

# CONTRIBUTORS

**Christine Chinkin** is Professor of international law at the London School of Economics, author of *Third Parties in International Law*, Oxford, Oxford University Press, 1993 and a number of articles on the guarantee of women's human rights under international law.

**Noam Chomsky** is Institute Professor in the department of linguistics and philosophy at Massachusetts Institute of Technology. He has published widely on human rights issues, as well as on social, political and contemporary affairs. His most recent books are *World Orders Old and New*, London, Pluto, Press, 1994 and *Powers and Prospects*, London, Pluto Press, 1996.

**Tony Evans** is Lecturer in global politics at the University of Southampton. His recent publications include *US Hegemony and the Project of Universal Human Rights*, Basingstoke, Macmillan, 1996 and Democratization and human rights in A. McGrew (ed.), *The Transformation of Democracy? Globalization and Territorial Democracy*, Cambridge, Polity Press, 1997.

**Johan Galtung** is Professor of peace studies; Granada, Ritsumeikan, Tromsö, Witten/Herdecke universities; Director, TRANSCEND: A Peace and Development Network. He has published widely on human rights and development. Among his most recent books is *Human Rights in Another Key*, Cambridge, Polity Press, 1994.

**Norman Lewis** is Co-ordinator for Globalisation and Power 2001, The Centre for the Study of Globalisation and Regionalisation, University of Warwick. Recent publications include Introduction to the republication of V. I. Lenin, *Imperialism: the Highest Stage of Capitalism*, London and Chicago, Pluto Press, 1996 and with Andrew Linklater, International relations – a case of one step forward, two steps back, in S. Chan and J. Wiener (eds), *Theorising in International Relations*, New York, Edwin Mellen Press, 1997.

**Tony McGrew** is Senior Lecturer in international relations at the Open University. He is currently engaged in research on globalization and its consequences for western states. His most recent publications include an edited volume, *The Transformation of Democracy? Globalization and Territorial Democracy*, Cambridge, Polity Press, 1997.

**Laura Parisi** is a PhD candidate in the department of political science at the University of Arizona and a visiting lecturer in the department of political science at Virginia Polytechnic Institute and State University. Recent publications include L. Parisi and Andrea K. Gerlak, An umbrella of international environmental policy: the global environment facility at work, in Dennis L. Soden and Brent S. Stee (eds), *Environmental Policy and Administration in Three Worlds: Developing, Industrial, and Post-industrial*, New York, Marcel Dekker, 1997.

**V. Spike Peterson** is Associate Professor, in the department of political science (with affiliations in women's studies, comparative cultural and literary studies, and international studies). She edited and contributed to *Gendered States: Feminist (Re)Visions of International Relations Theory* (1992) and was co-author (with Anne Sisson Runyan) of *Global Gender Issues* (1993) (second edition forthcoming).

Fiona Robinson is Assistant Professor of politics at Carleton University, Ottawa, Canada. Her publications include articles in *Alternatives* and *Review of International Political Economy* on ethics, feminist theory and international relations theory. She is the author of *Globalizing Care*, Boulder, Westview (forthcoming).

Caroline Thomas lectures in global politics at Southampton University. Her main research interest is in human security in the era of globalization. Recent publications include C. Thomas and P. Wilkin (eds), *Globalization and the South*, London, Macmillan, 1997 and C. Thomas and P. Wilkin (eds), *Critical Security in a Global Economy*, London, Lynne Reinner, 1998.

# ABBREVIATIONS

| | |
|---|---|
| ABA | American Bar Association |
| ACLU | American Civil Liberties Union |
| AFL | American Federation of Labour |
| AFTA | ASEAN Free Trade Area |
| AI | Amnesty International |
| APEC | Asian Pacific Economic Cooperation |
| ASEAN | Association of South East Asian Nations |
| CEDAW | Convention on the Elimination of All Forms of Discrimination Against Women |
| CEO | Chief executive officer |
| CERDS | Charter of Economic Rights and Duties of States |
| CGAP | Consultative Group to assist the poorest |
| CIA | Central Intelligence Agency |
| CRS | Congressional Research Service |
| CSCE | Conference on Security and Cooperation in Europe |
| EBRD | European Bank for Reconstruction and Development |
| EC | European Community |
| ECHR | 1) European Commission on Human Rights; 2) European Court of Human Rights |
| ECOSOC | United Nations Economic and Social Council |
| EEC | European Economic Community |
| EU | European Union |
| FDI | Foreign Direct Investment |
| GA | General Assembly |
| GAOR | General Assembly Official Records |
| GATT | General Agreement on Tariffs and Trade |
| HRW | Human Rights Watch |
| ICCPR | International Covenant on Civil and Political Rights |
| ICESCR | International Covenant on Economic, Social and Cultural Rights |
| ICJ | 1) International Commission of Jurists; 2) International Court of Justice |
| IFC | International Finance Corporation |
| IFI | International Financial Institution |
| IGO | Intergovernmental Organization |
| ILO | International Labour Organization |
| IMF | International Monetary Fund |
| INGO | International Non-Governmental Organization |
| LDC | Less Developed Country |
| MAI | Multilateral Agreement on Investment |
| MIGA | Multilateral Investment Guarantee Agency |
| MNC | Multi-National Corporation |
| NAFTA | North American Free Trade Agreement |
| NATO | North Atlantic Treaty Organization |
| NGO | Non-Governmental Organization |
| OAS | Organization of American States |
| ODA | Overseas development aid |
| OECD | Organization for Economic Cooperation and Development |

| | |
|---|---|
| PAMSCAD | Programme of Actions to Mitigate the Social Costs of Adjustment |
| RFSTNRP | Research Foundation for Science, Technology and Natural Resource Policy |
| SAP | Structural Adjustment Programme |
| SC | Security Council |
| TC | Trilateral Commission |
| TNC | Transnational Corporation |
| TNO | Transnational Organization |
| UDHR | Universal Declaration of Human Rights |
| UN | United Nations |
| UNAMIR | UN Assistance Mission for Rwanda |
| UNCED | United Nations Conference on Environment and Development |
| UNDP | United Nations Development Programme |
| UNGA | United Nations General Assembly |
| UNHCR | United Nations Commission on Human Rights |
| UNICEF | United Nations Children's Fund |
| UNO | United Nations Organization |
| UNPROFOR | United Nations Protection Force in the Former Yugoslavia |
| UNTS | United Nations Treaty Series |
| USAID | United States Agency for International Development |
| WTO | World Trade Organization |

# Power and human rights

# Introduction: power, hegemony and the universalization of human rights

*Tony Evans*

It is inevitable that several publications will mark the fiftieth anniversary of the Universal Declaration of Human Rights (UDHR). As with the twentieth, thirtieth and fortieth anniversaries, many of these will celebrate the great 'progress' made in protecting human rights throughout the world. Following Jeremy Bentham's view that 'right is the child of law, from real laws come real rights' (Bentham cited in Cranston 1967, 44), 'progress' in these publications is usually measured by a detailed examination of international law and formal methods of implementation. Subsequently, it is common to see claims of 'revolutionary' or 'amazing' progress in guaranteeing human rights (Opsahl 1989, 33), though the widely reported political facts suggest that this is an exaggeration.

This failure to explain the disjuncture between the theory and practice of human rights reveals that the literature has much to say about utopian visions and legal solutions but little to say about the social and political context in which violations take place. Although an analysis of legal texts, institutional processes and organizational practices may tell us much about the abstract elegance of the law, legal method and organizational theory, it has little to tell us about how to protect people's (and peoples') rights. Noting this many years ago, John Vincent called those who think and write in narrow legal and organizational terms 'notoriously wishful thinkers' (Vincent 1986).

The contributors to this volume adopt a less sanguine view than that taken by mainstream writers on human rights. We take seriously the continually reported, inconvenient facts of torture, genocide, structural deprivation, disappearances and all manner of other violations. Our aim is not to reject the purpose of human rights, which is to create the conditions for individuals and peoples to lead a dignified life. Nor do we argue that those actively engaged in protecting human right are misguided. Rather, our aim is to interrogate the modern manifestation of human rights and to question the political, social and economic role of rights at the end of the twentieth century. Our central contention is that any assessment of the dominant idea of human rights must include an analysis of interests, power and hegemony.

Unless politics and power are added to the debate, our understanding of the status of human rights in the past and future eras remains incomplete.

This chapter begins with some remarks on the relationship between human rights, power and hegemony. This is followed by an examination of the post-war context of the human rights project, which provided the context for the Universal Declaration. Since the Declaration remains the most widely known statement of universal human rights, an understanding of this early period is invaluable in gaining an insight into the present and future context of rights talk. A third section will examine universal human rights and hegemony under conditions of globalization and attempt to draw some conclusions. A final section will speculate on some of the issues concerned with the future of human rights.[1]

## Power and human rights

The project to place human rights at the centre of global politics, first begun with the Universal Declaration of Human Rights fifty years ago, has had limited impact on the lives of those in most need of rights. For the most part, the theory and practice of human rights is conducted in the language of legal and philosophical reason; the former focusing on international law and methods of implementation and the latter on the meaning, source and justification for rights claims (Evans 1996, 3–6). When questions of power are mentioned in the third, political facet of the human rights debate, these are framed around conventionally conceived concepts of sovereignty, domestic jurisdiction and non-intervention, either in the tradition of power politics (Kennan 1985) or international society (Vincent 1986). All three facets of the debate are conducted largely within a liberal framework, leaving little space for questions concerned with power and interests. Which groups benefit from the dominant idea of rights? What exclusionary practices are sustained by the dominant idea of human rights? What role does the dominant idea of human rights play in processes of legitimation? Such questions are rarely confronted.

The unselfconscious separation of the human rights debate into three facets reflects a widely held assumption that the age of human rights marks the triumph of reason over politics; as though, after two centuries of struggle, the truth of human rights is at last universally accepted. Placed at the centre of such thinking is, of course, the Universal Declaration, which represents the symbolic moment of 'arrival' when all humankind came to acknowledge the reason of rights (Raphael 1967). Supported in the post-cold war period by euphoria over the 'end of history' thesis (Fukuyama 1989), this approach denies the possibility of any further social or political dynamism, and confines the 'political' to disagreements *within* the dominant world order. In this view, all that is left of the human rights debate are technical issues to do with international law, implementational procedures and the re-articulation of liberal theories of rights (Robinson, chapter 3 in this volume). Power and interests are no longer an issue.

Consequently, much of the theory and practice of human rights leads to conclusions of 'optimism or hope, almost invariably expressed in the passive voice in order to increase its apparent authority' (Watson 1979). These conclusions reveal a failure of mainstream theory and practice to take account of the social and political construction of rights. Given the political context of both the French and American revolutions, which are widely understood as the starting point of the modern human rights movement, this seems a strange omission. In the wake of these momentous revolutions, what was once thought of as the natural order – the divine right of kings, a duty to the crown, the authority of the established church – was rejected in favour of a new order – the people as sovereign, the rights of the citizen and the authority of civil government. The old order, which for centuries was accepted as defining the legitimate limits of social and political action, was now seen as oppressive and tyrannical, while the new offered the conditions of human dignity and freedom.

The conclusion to be drawn from these revolutions is that rights are concerned with establishing and maintaining the moral claims that legitimate particular interests. Put succinctly by Neil Stammers, 'ideas and practices concerning human rights are *created* by people in particular historical, social, and economic circumstances' (Stammers 1995, 488). Following the success of the American and French revolutions, the emergent bourgeoisie sought to legitimate their alternative order through the inclusive language of natural rights rather than the divisive language of interests and dominance. The separation of private (economic) from public (political) life, which is central to natural rights, was presented as a moral imperative in the interests of all citizens, not the outcome of new power relationships that served the specific interests of the bourgeoisie. Natural rights did not reveal 'any universal truths about the relationship between individuals, society and the state' (Stammers 1993, 74). Rather, natural rights provided the 'moral high ground' that justified overturning the old order while simultaneously legitimating the interests of the dominant group in the new.

This account of power suggests two different approaches to human rights. The first, traditional view, sees human rights as empowering people in the fight against persecution and injustice. The second, alternative view, sees human rights as power over people, expressed in exclusionary practices that deny the full participation of those who fail to support the interests of the dominant group. Exclusion is justified either on the grounds that these groups have neither the rational nor moral capacity to engage in decision-making processes (Hindess 1992) or, more simply, that they are 'mad' (Keeley 1990). The invisibility of women from the human rights debate offers an example of this type of exclusion (Peterson and Parisi, chapter 6 in this volume). Similarly, many less developed countries suffer exclusion and demonization for the failure to implement rights that support a liberal agenda (Thomas, chapter 7 in this volume; Furedi 1997).

## Human rights and post-war hegemony

The post-Second World War theory and practice of human rights is no different from previous periods with respect to power. Within the tradition of international political realism that occupied the minds of academics and world leaders for much of the period since the Second World War, hegemony has implied the existence of a single, dominant state possessing both the material capability and will to maintain world order in its own interests. Social and political control is maintained with a system of formal and informal rules that serve the interests of the hegemon. In cases where lesser states fail to comply, the hegemon must resort to force. In this context, universal claims like human rights seem an unnecessary distraction from the business of maintaining a world order based on the principles of sovereignty, non-intervention and domestic jurisdiction. However, as in the case of the French and American revolutions, an emergent hegemon seeks to promote new moral foundations that distinguish it from the previous order.

To explain this need demands a more subtle approach to hegemony; one that takes account of the hegemon's need for legitimacy in the exercise of power and leadership. In recent years, many scholars have turned to the works of Antonio Gramsci as the starting point for developing this account.

To the realist conception of hegemony as dominance through 'coercive force', Gramsci adds the notion of hegemony maintained through consensus and the legitimation of 'intellectual and moral leadership' (Gramsci 1971, 57–8). In this formulation, hegemony is exercised in two ways: *externally* by influencing behaviour and choice through rewards and punishment and *internally* by shaping personal beliefs, opinions and values that reflect prevailing interests. In this sense, hegemony is achieved and maintained by developing a widely accepted order characterized by a 'common social-moral language' that expresses a singular version of reality, 'informing with its spirit all forms of thought and behaviour' (Femia 1987, 24). The legitimate right to exercise social and political control achieves its highest aims when the hegemon's moral claims are afforded the epithet 'common sense' (Gramsci 1971, 419–25). This implies that secondary groups undergo processes of socialization, binding the ruler and the ruled in a consensual order that legitimates power (Ikenberry and Kupchan 1990, 287). In short, the hegemon enhances control based on might with that based on right.

This understanding of hegemony offers an insight into the post-war politics of rights, particularly the role of the USA as global hegemon and leader of the human rights project. The United States emerged from the conflict with material capabilities far in excess of any other country. US interests possessed 70 per cent of global financial assets and maintained a high rate of industrial production, nearly doubling manufacturing output during the war years (*UN Statistical Yearbook* 1948). High levels of productivity presented a historic opportunity to devote resources to establishing a stable world order safe for American exports of goods and capital (Cafruny 1989, 116). This was as much a necessity as an aspiration, for unless the USA took full advantage of its new global position, post-war overproduction and the demobilization of troops threatened a period of high unemployment, economic depression and social unrest (Chomsky 1994, 100–6). The first concern of policy-makers and capital in 1945 was to secure the USA's dominant economic position and to exploit it.

To achieve this aim required strategies that protected access to natural resources, cheap labour and, most important, markets (Robinson 1996; Rupert 1995). It was therefore important that the USA did not return to its historic policy of isolation, which had informed US foreign policy during the inter-war years. Promoting human rights as a universal principle, as a symbol of solidarity related to ideas of individualism, freedom and *laissez-faire* economics, offered the potential to avoid the consequences of the inter-war years by mobilizing public support for a global US economic and political role (Loth 1988, ch. 1).

To resolve the contradictions between isolationism and global expansion, policy-makers drew upon popular images of being an American, particularly those associated with migration and the early settlers (Augelli and Murphy 1988). On the one hand, migrants were expressing the *freedom from* an old, oppressive order and celebrating the creation of a new, emancipatory regime that respected human rights and freedoms. If the old (European) order subsequently decayed, that was of no interest to Americans. Their destiny lay in the New World, isolated from an order that once served them badly. On the other hand, migrants were also expressing the *freedom to* exercise their own initiative and imagination, including engaging in economic life unrestrained by government. Both approaches to freedom find expression in the language of civil and political rights, which anyone can claim by virtue of being human. Thus, to be an American,

> it follows that one can remain indifferent to appeals that are premised upon claims of general rights only with difficulty: were one not to acknowledge, in some manner, that those demands were legitimate, then the definition of being an American would also be threatened. In some sense, being an American means that everyone has a potentially legitimate claim on you. Reciprocally, anyone is entitled, in some sense, to make demands on Americans and America, simply by being human. (Strong 1980, 51)

Thus, as E. H. Carr observed, although in the immediate post-war period international moral scepticism achieved 'the status of professional orthodoxy in both academic and political circles', for the United States it was 'a most implausible view, especially in a culture conscious of itself as an attempt to realize a certain moral ideal in its domestic political life' (Carr 1962, 15).

In the language of human rights – more accurately civil and political rights associated with the freedom of the individual – policy-makers sought to appeal to a historically and culturally grounded image that attracted public support for US global engagement. In short, human rights became a metaphor for being an American and a justification for projecting an American conception of rights across the globe. Thus, by invoking human rights, policy-makers appealed to a central tenet of American culture as a way of avoiding the 'vicious circle of isolation, depression, and war'.[2] Americans were not asked to make great personal sacrifices in support of those devastated by fascism, but for the survival of human freedom itself.

From the earliest days of preparing for a post-war order, the USA claimed the moral high ground by promoting universal human rights. Americans had a duty to remain engaged in world politics and to defend the universal human rights of all people everywhere (Hoffmann 1977, 9). But the project to promote universal human rights must also be seen as integral to the logic of hegemony (Falk 1980). Promoting the American conception of human rights was part of a strategy intended to extend US sphere of influence over a much wider area, including gaining access to world markets (Chomsky, chapter 2 in this volume). As self-proclaimed protector of universal human rights, the USA sought to legitimate its role as leader of the new world order and to justify intervention wherever and whenever it was necessary. Crucially, the success of the project rested upon gaining popular approval for a set of civil and political rights associated with liberalism, or more explicitly, those rights already found in the Constitution of the United States of America.

## Resistance to US hegemony and the project of universal human rights

There is an obvious tension between promoting universal values and the exercise of state hegemony. Constraints on state power designed to protect universal human rights are constraints on all states, even the hegemon. To avoid this difficulty, the hegemon must sustain a view of human rights that demands little change to existing social practices. As discussions for the Universal Declaration began in the UN Commission on Human Rights, policy-makers found it increasingly difficult to maintain an agenda that supported US interests. Two consequences followed from this: first, domestic interests turned against further US support for promoting universal values negotiated at the UN; and second, the USA's claim to legitimate moral leadership was increasingly questioned by other members of the international community.

During the early days of the United Nations, the feeling of solidarity found in victory sustained the belief that all humankind was embarking on a 'Great Adventure' to place human rights at the centre of world politics (Humphry 1984). However, the USA soon discovered that the values associated with 'being an American' did not describe the full spectrum of human rights promoted by others. Although the virtue of tolerance was widely accepted as an integral characteristic of civil and political rights, tolerance did not extend to alternative visions of the future that prioritized collective, economic and social rights. Nor did tolerance extend to a conception of universal human rights that obliged component parts of a federal system to abandon existing social practices − for example, racist and segregationist policies such as those still thriving in the southern states of the USA.

Although disagreement over the appropriate conception of human rights emerged very early in the discussions for creating the United Nations (UN), these were not confronted until the Commission on Human Rights convened. It was the socialist states that mounted the early resistance to a liberal conception of rights. These states shared a view of history that understood the post-war world as an era of transition from a capitalist to a socialist order. From this it followed that any durable international agreement on human rights should reflect the values of a future social order, not those of the past. These values included economic and social rights like the right to work and social security. As discussion for the Declaration and Covenants continued, the socialist states repeatedly highlighted their own 'progressive' approach and denigrated that of the USA, which they claimed clung conservatively to outmoded values. In the view of the socialist states, human rights should express a 'new and bright future for the individual in the vast field of social rights',[3] not one that paralleled the French Declaration of the Rights of Man and the Citizen, which, they argued, represented a reactionary attempt to legitimate outdated, middle-class, bourgeois values.[4] In short, the socialist states argued that human rights should be determined by the forces of history, not by western minds ignorant of those forces (Kudryartsev 1986).

Joining the socialist states, a small group of less developed countries also presented a challenge to the USA's favoured approach. These states took issue with the USA on three general fronts. The first alarmed both the West and the socialist states. Less developed countries argued that the UN Charter placed human rights at the centre of world politics, reforming the principles of sovereignty and, notwithstanding Article 2(7), permitting intervention on humanitarian grounds. According to less developed states, further additions to international law were unnecessary, likely to confuse the new definition of sovereignty legitimated by the Charter and make the protection of human rights more difficult.[5] Second, and in line with the socialist states, less developed states supported a view of human rights that included economic, social and cultural rights. Third, and of particular importance for the USA, less developed states took the principle of self-determination at face value, including permanent sovereignty over natural wealth and resources.[6] This was interpreted by international business and financial interests based in the USA as a threat to legitimate nationalization, the state control of industry and the expropriation of capital.

In the face of the alternative conceptions of rights offered by the socialist and less developed states, the US found it increasingly difficult to sustain domestic support for full engagement in the human rights debate. In particular, 'So-called economic and social rights' (letter from the American Bar Association (ABA) undated) were targeted by American conservatives and isolationists as the greatest potential threat to the Constitution. These groups argued that negotiations on human rights promised 'socialism by treaty' and the destruction of the 'American Way' (Eisenhower 1963, 287)). In the atmosphere of the emerging cold war, conservatives saw any proposal to include economic and social rights in a binding agreement as an attempt to ensnare the United States in a complex international and legal system that sought to penetrate, influence and finally bring down the traditional social and political freedoms for which America stood (Tananbaum 1988, ch. 3). Although the conservative lobby failed to remove all references to economic and social rights in the Declaration, conservatives assumed that the USA would refuse to ratify any binding agreement that included this set of rights (Ransom 1946). At the same time, conservatives sought to insist on a 'federal clause' that allowed constituent parts of a federal system the option to accede independently of the federal government (Dept of State 1951). No binding agreement on human rights that extended federal authority was acceptable to conservatives.

Since the early 1930s, conservatives had expressed concern over incremental changes to the US Constitution, which they saw as an inevitable outcome of New Deal politics. Conservatives argued that the federal government's increasing interest in the civil rights and social welfare of citizens eroded the constitutional rights of the states. During the war, and immediately afterwards, these fears were exacerbated by policies that saw the racial integration of troops, a report by the Commission on Civil Rights that threatened to outlaw certain racist policies and a growing concern in Washington over segregated education. Conservatives saw the federal structure of the USA as the only bulwark against a federal government intent on imposing a programme of civil rights that challenged state laws on inter-racial marriage, the ownership of property and education (Kaufman and Whiteman 1988).

Domestic resistance to human rights took three forms. First, under the Constitution, international treaties are enforceable throughout the country. Ratifying a human rights treaty had the potential of challenging the separate law-making powers of the states and overturning existing laws that discriminated on grounds of sex, race, colour, language, property, birth or political opinion. The American Bar Association argued, for example, that a binding agreement on human rights would outlaw existing state laws relating to women, miscegenation and membership of the communist party. Second, conservatives argued that ratifying any agreement on human rights would lead to the annulment of United States' immigration and naturalization laws, forfeiting the right to determine who should or should not enter the country and encouraging a 'multitude' of Chinese, Indians and Indonesians to leave their 'already over-populated countries' (Holman 1952; Holman 1953). Third, conservatives argued that any human rights agreement would empower the federal government to enact certain civil rights laws and other legislation that would not be enacted without such an agreement (Tananbaum 1988).

The strength of both domestic and international resistance to the hegemon's conception of human rights left the federal government with a dilemma. On the one hand, following the invocation of human rights during the war years, the USA felt an obligation to fulfil expectations it had itself generated. On the other hand, competing conceptions of human rights made it less possible for the hegemon to promote a version of human rights that supported its own domestic and economic interests. To add to this complexity, the principle of self-determination and rapid decolonization promised to erode the West's majority in the General Assembly, adding further to the number of states that supported economic and social rights. Although the Declaration caused the USA some anxiety, the vagueness of its language and its non-binding status presented few threats. However, once attention turned to binding agreements, the USA sought to degrade the importance of the formal human rights debate (Evans 1995). Instead, the USA attempted to use its privileged position as the new hegemon to assert a conception of human rights that supported its own international ambitions and the interests of capital.

For most of the last fifty years, the formal human rights debate lacked the support of the hegemon and 'largely pirouetted around a missing centre' (Moskovitz 1974, 16). The singular conception of human rights promoted by the USA could not be sustained. Alternative conceptions promoted by the socialist and less developed states soon became the object of the growing cold war ideological struggle over who held the moral high ground. These competing conceptions formed the basis for the two parallel debates on human rights: first, the formal/legal debate at the UN, which generated an impressive array of international law; second, an informal/political debate, promoted by the USA, which emphasized only those rights that served the interests of the hegemon.

The conflict over differing conceptions of human rights offered a focus for cold war rhetoric that dominated international politics for over four decades. As the USA sought to legitimate its own claim to global leadership by promoting its 'superior' record of civil and political rights, and castigating the USSR and its allies for their poor records, so the socialist states countered by promoting their 'superior' record of economic and social rights. For superpowers often engaged in a cold war struggle to win the support of less developed countries, the issue of economic and social rights was of particular importance.

Although the amount of international law generated at the UN is often claimed as evidence of wide agreement on human rights, the continued expansion of global capital, particularly US capital, ensured that the West's commitment was limited to a liberal conception of rights. With the end of the cold war that commitment is less challenged.

## Human rights in the post-cold war era

The end of the cold war has brought to a close the ideological struggle over human rights, leaving the USA as the unmatched superpower. Symbolic of this superiority is the USA's ratification of the International Covenant on Civil and Political Rights (ICCPR), following years of procrastination. At first sight this may suggest that the USA has lifted at least some of its historic objections to accepting human rights as developed at the UN, and that there is now a willingness to give hegemonic support to protect those rights. However, the US ratification includes many reservations, declarations and understandings, which suggest that little has changed. Importantly, the federal government declares that the Covenant does not come into effect until Congress adopts the necessary legislation, thus avoiding old arguments about the treaty-making powers of the executive and the imposition of social norms on the states.

The Lawyers Committee on Human Rights has argued that ratifying the Covenant subject to important limitations only reinforces the USA's historic view that 'one set of rules applies to the United States and another set to the rest of the world'. Accordingly, the USA is guilty of 'hypocrisy' (Lawyers Committee 1992). Similarly, Louis Henkin accuses the USA of seeking moral legitimacy by ratifying the Covenant while avoiding any international obligations. Henkin concludes that the US ratification signals that human rights 'conventions are for other states, not the United States' (Henkin 1995, 433). At the UN, the Human Rights Committee expressed concern for reservations that 'essentially render ineffective all Covenant rights which would require any changes to national law to ensure compliance' so that 'no real international rights or obligations have been accepted'.[7] If the USA did ever move to ratify the International Covenant on Economic, Social and Cultural Rights (ICESCR) then it would certainly suffer from similar or, more likely, greater limitations.

Although the ratification of the ICCPR may be interpreted as indicative of US power, many scholars argue that today it is a mistake to understand hegemony in terms of a single dominant state. Instead, the literature on globalization suggests a new global order concerned with powerful processes of cultural, social, economic and political change, which challenge past beliefs about the nature of sovereignty, society and the wider international political community. According to this argument, hegemony no longer resides with the state but with a global complex of transnational core-periphery relations, creating new patterns of economic growth and consumption that are beyond state control (Cox 1994, 108). In short, the global organization of production and finance means that the state no longer initiates policy but, rather, reacts to global social forces against which it can mount limited resistance (McGrew, chapter 8 in this volume).

Globalization makes it tempting to conclude that the state is in terminal decline, although such a conclusion is rejected by most writers on globalization. Instead, globalization assumes that the state continues to play an integral role as an administrative unit for creating and orchestrating the conditions of globalization. Rather than being the central actors in global politics, states are 'the authors of a regime that defines and guarantees, through international treaties and constitutional affect, the global and domestic rights of capital' (Panitch 1995, 85). Decisions made at the national level may temporarily disrupt patterns of globalization, but states cannot escape its processes. According to the United Nations Development Programme (UNDP),

> [E]verywhere the imperative to liberalize has demanded a shrinking of state involvement in national life, producing a wave of privatizations of public enterprises and, generally, job cuts. And everywhere the opening of financial markets has limited governments' ability to run deficits – requiring them to slash health spending and food subsidies that benefit poor people. (UNDP 1997, 88)

If the argument presented here is correct, that human rights claims are the outcome of power relations, then in the current era all issues must be subordinated to the imperatives of globalization. Seen in this light, the USA's ratification of the ICCPR is little more than the formal legitimation of a set of rights that supports the interests associated with global economic growth and development. But as in the early days of the human rights debate, guarantees of freedom do not extend to those who challenge free market principles or resist the imperative of liberal processes for economic growth and development. The often acknowledged tensions between sovereignty and individual rights are replaced by those between globalization and individual rights (Chinkin, chapter 5 in this volume).

Examples of prioritizing the imperatives of globalization over human rights are not hard to find. Twenty years ago Gormley noted the link between human rights abuses and economic development in Latin America, observing that 'governments have undertaken a policy of systematic genocide, in order to clear forest regions for farming, the building of roads, or industrial sites' (Gormley 1976, 19). Barber and Grainne observe that 'thirty to forty percent of the ten million people who have been resettled to make way for large dams in China since the 1950s are still impoverished and lack adequate food and clothing' (Barber and Grainne 1993, 24). The massacre of at least fifty East Timorese by Indonesian troops in 1991 led to threats from donor countries to discontinue economic aid, but the importance of keeping stable trade with Indonesia soon took precedence over human rights considerations (Robinson 1993).

The plea for tolerance over human rights by many leaders of less developed states further reflects the imperative of economic growth and development. Many less developed countries argue that their attitude to human rights is conditioned by two considerations peculiar to their status as young nations. The first concerns the problem of building a nation, given the territorial boundaries and institutions of the colonial legacy. This demands the application of a 'stability' test when thinking about human rights: does the application of a right help or hinder the process of nation-building and the move from a post-colonial to a mature state? Second, if the long-term stability and security of a nation are assumed to depend upon economic growth and development, traditional values must not be allowed to stand in the way. The suppression and coercion of those who attempt to resist change are therefore legitimate. Economic growth and development is in the interests of future generations, the nation at large and prior to implementing human rights (Tamilmoran 1992).

Patterns of systematic abuse of human rights lead Johnson and Button to conclude that 'development processes (trade agreements, national economic development strategies, and so forth), individuals, organisations (multilateral lenders, multinational and national corporations), and governments, all deny human rights' (Johnson and Button 1994, 213). Similarly, the UNDP Human Development Report concludes that 'human development over the past 30 years is a mixed picture of unprecedented human progress and unspeakable human misery' (UNDP 1996, 17).

During the cold war, those who dealt with repressive regimes defended their actions with the 'greater good' argument: human rights must take second place to the defeat of communism. Now that this argument is no longer available, it might be assumed that a major barrier to taking action for securing human rights has been lifted. However, in recent years a new, more subtle defence for continuing 'business as usual' has emerged. Political, business and financial leaders have turned increasingly to the language of democracy rather than that of human rights, promoting the assumption that 'if democracy then human rights' (Carothers 1994). Legitimate aid and trade relations can then continue unhindered by moral considerations provided there is evidence of democratic institutions (Chomsky, chapter 2 in this volume). When this assumption is questioned, economic interests can still look to the old arguments associated with Richard Cobden and George Washington that trade 'civilizes' and promotes the growth of democracy (Vincent 1986, 133–4).

However, while establishing the formal institutions of democracy may be a necessary condition for claiming human rights, it is not a substitute for them. Many states are democratic in formal–institutional terms only. These states do not provide for the reform of social and legal systems that are essential for maintaining the conditions for human rights, including a reduction of inequality, land reform, a free press and access to public office. Trade unions are weak, wages are depressed below a level to sustain a dignified life, legislation on environmental security, health and safety never reaches the statute books and all movements that seek social justice are labelled anti-democratic and quashed (Burbach 1993). Promoting an institutional form of democracy that pays little attention to human rights outcomes – characterized by Gills, Rocamora and Wilson as 'low intensity democracy' (Gills, Rocamora and Wilson 1993) – may have more to do with providing a moral defence for engaging in a global economic system where structural violations of human rights go almost unnoticed (Galtung 1994; Salmi 1993; Kothari 1994).

Moreover, the change of emphasis from human rights to democracy, without regard for the institutions of globalization, is of little significance to people when the activities of transnational corporations, multinational banks and global and regional trading organizations play a greater part in shaping their social lives. With the realization that the global rather than the national economy exercises the greater influence on economic well-being, the state loses its significance as a centre of authority through which people can express their preferences and claim their rights. Instead, attention is focused on international institutions and organizations. These institutions and organizations assume the task of providing the rules for action. Although national governments continue to engage in international politics, governance is conducted by what Cox has called the *nébuleuse* (Cox 1995), a group of formal and informal organizations without democratic pretensions. Included in the *nébuleuse* are organizations like the World Bank, the World Trade Organization (WTO), the Trilateral Commission (TC) and the Group of Eight (G8, until recently the G7) who determine the norms and rules of conduct that emphasizes 'efficiency, discipline, and confidence; economic policy credibility and consistency; and limitations of democratic decision-making processes' (Gill 1995, 412). The rules and norms for social behaviour are set at a global level, favouring the interests of global capital and without regard for multiculturalism (Lewis, chapter 4 in this volume). Thus the link between government and governed is weakened but not replaced with new forms of democracy related to global institutions (Haymans 1995). As Sir Shridath Ramphal has observed:

> More and more the G7 is looking – and acting – like a self-appointed presidium. We need to convince these leaders of major western democracies that the democracy idea has a larger reach than national frontiers. Democracy at the national level but authoritarian in the global homeland – these are contradictions in terms. (Ramphal 1992, 82)

Structural Adjustment Programmes (SAP) typify the redistribution of structural decision-making powers away from states and into global economic institutions, such as the World Bank and the International Monetary Fund (IMF) (Thomas, chapter 7 in this volume). Targeting primarily social programmes, SAPs typically demand dramatic cuts in government expenditure as a prerequisite for further loans. In this way, the Bank assumes responsibility for the economic coordination of the state, subject to strict conditionality criteria, and largely ignores economic and social rights. Thus SAPs deny 'human rights to food, education, work and social assistance' and render such claims meaningless (Tomasevski 1993, 61).

The maintenance of a global order in which the governed play little part ensures that people become more accountable to remote centres of authority, rather than those centres being accountable to people (McGrew 1997; Held 1995). This is the process of 'distanciation' where 'locales are thoroughly penetrated by and shaped in terms of social influences quite distant from them' (Giddens 1990). Distanciation ensures that the relationship between international institutions and populations is not concerned with human rights, human values, the quality of life or human dignity, but with technical issues to do with maintaining an order that supports free market principles. For example, arguments over intellectual property rights focus on the rights of ownership, capital and the commodification of life rather than human rights issues concerned with the 'privatization of life forms' (Gill 1995).

Furthermore, the 'common sense' of liberal approaches to economic growth and development allows governments to conflate the interests of people with those of corporate and financial interests. The fanfares and triumphalism that inevitably accompany the start of new investment programmes – perhaps to build a dam or construct a chemical plant – overlook the human misery that follows as people are displaced, their physical environment degraded and their cultural heritage destroyed. The Narmada Dam project and the activities of Shell Oil in Nigeria offer good examples here. What is presented as in the national interest is often in '[t]he interests of global financial and corporate institutions', which 'are privileged over that of popular, national or redistributive goals' (Gills 1995). As Galtung has observed, '[t]here may well be situations when the state can do without popular consent, but not without corporations in general and the banks in particular' (Galtung 1994, 149).

Achieving the conditions for human rights seem less certain than ever under the hegemony of a global order based on free-market principles. Whereas in the cold war era economic and social rights were at least part of the human rights agenda, today that agenda is dominated by widespread acceptance that the way to secure human rights is through the free market. The *Economist* conclusion that 'the best hope for political freedom in some countries lies in opening them up through trade' is now the language of 'common sense' (*Economist* 1993). Those who do not share free-market assumptions over achieving human rights are met with incredulity. For the increasing number of people living in poverty in particular, the end of the cold war ideological struggle will mean that claims for economic rights remain unheard.

The prospect for achieving civil and political rights is no better under the new global hegemony. Civil and political rights are supported only in as far as satisfying them further promotes the primary aim of all governments, which is rapid economic growth and development. Civil and political rights are for those who accept the economic aims of globalization, not for those who seek the freedom to protest against these aims.

## Conclusion: the future of human rights

The status of universal human rights is uncertain in the current era. Globalization suggests that even if we could implement most of the rights agreed at the UN, many millions would still have to struggle with the misery of poverty. As the state and the inter-state system struggles to respond to increasing international pressures and changing domestic expectations, the old institutions of governance are strained. Whatever changes have already taken place, or are likely in the future, the content of human rights and the rights debate will need constant re-examination. Whether this means moving towards new ideas of global citizenship, as argued by Johan Galtung (Galtung, chapter 9 in this volume), or some other means of creating the conditions of democracy and political participation remains to be seen. Whatever the course of action taken, this final section attempts to raise some issues that are central to our present and future understanding of human rights.

At the centre of all human rights talk is the cardinal role given to the individual, both as a claimant and violator of rights. As a claimant, civil and political rights are prerequisites for innovation, endeavour and enterprise in the free-market world order, which supports the conditions for globalization. As a violator, the individual is wholly responsible for his or her actions, an assumption that reflects the Judaeo-Christian notion of sin. The significance of social, political and economic structures in which action takes place is of only peripheral concern when attempting to explain violations or apportion blame. This is convenient for those who most benefit from existing social and economic practices, for it deflects attention from violations that are the cause of much human misery.

Recognition of this does not deny individual responsibility for some human rights violations, but it does beg questions about current approaches to implementing human rights. Since the structures and practices of globalization are the cause of most violations of human rights, reliance on a legal system that seeks to apportion blame and punish individuals seems misplaced. As Johan Galtung has pointed out, structures cannot be juridical persons with intentions and capabilities nor can they be arrested, brought to trial and punished (Galtung 1994, 64). For example, to address the international torture network, Galtung highlights the need to identify torture production and trading systems, training practices and the torture research structures based increasingly on electronic specialization. Such issues are overlooked by a simple focus on the individual as the perpetrator of violations (Galtung 1994, 133). Similarly, Tomasevski argues that international law applies only to identifiable actions rather than social institutions and practices, which provide the context for action. International law may be capable of redressing consequences, but it cannot address causes (Tomasevski 1993, 181; Chinkin chapter 5 in this volume). The recent interest in creating a permanent International Criminal Court, following the experience of tribunals for the former Yugoslavia and Rwanda, may therefore have little impact on protecting human rights (*International Criminal Court Monitor* 1996).

Furthermore, even if we overlook the structural causes of violations, implementational methods like tribunals remain political tools, often used selectively and inconsistently. Are we not justified in asking, for example, why a tribunal was set up to prosecute those responsible for crimes against humanity in the former Yugoslavia but not for those who ordered the bombing of defeated and retreating troops on the road to Basra at the end of the Gulf War? Moreover, enthusiasm for existing tribunals seems less than full. Although the Dayton directive on the former Yugoslavia permits the 'arrest if encountered' of indicted individuals, this has been widely interpreted as 'avoid encountering at all costs' (Robinson 1997). General Mladic and Radovan Kardzic still 'roam freely in the Republika Srbska despite the fact that it is patrolled by NATO troops' (Daly 1997, 17). A further example of indifference is the British government's refusal to release evidence gathered by the intelligence services during the war in the former Yugoslavia that would assist in preparing cases against those accused of war crimes and crimes against humanity.

The consequences of the dominant conception of human rights, including the inconsistencies pointed to above, have not gone unnoticed, particularly by the leaders of countries currently enjoying a rapid rise in global economic power. The most recent resistance to the dominant conception of human rights is that voiced by Asian countries. The growing assertiveness of many Asian countries on human rights issues – particularly those of South-East Asia – reflects a growing confidence founded on rapid economic growth. These countries argue that national security, social stability and public order provided the foundations for the impressive levels of economic development achieved during the 1980s and early 1990s. According to Asian leaders, coercion played little part in sustaining a social order attractive for international business and finance. More important were traditional Asian values that emphasized community and duty rather than individualism and rights (Kausikan 1993). The West's conception of rights, which 'glorified' in a 'destructive' and 'gross individualism' during the 1980s, are not appropriate for Asian values and culture (Muzaffar 1995, 8). Instead, for the good of the community, Asians accept the necessity for strong leadership, including a limitation on personal freedoms, in exchange for public order, greater economic growth and the preservation of social and religious values (Chan 1995).

For Asian states, the imposition of those rights prioritized by the West is more concerned with the 'preservation of self-interest and the perpetuation of dominance' (Muzaffar 1995, 8), rather than a real concern to create the conditions for human dignity. If Asian states accepted the prioritization of rights favoured by the West, current practices concerning trade unions, civil liberties and social order would have to be abandoned, past progress in alleviating poverty would be reversed and competitiveness would decline. More importantly, the impressive advances in social and economic rights in many Asian countries would be reversed by the imposition of the West's conception of human rights (UNDP 1996).

Asian leaders have lost no opportunity to articulate their resistance to the dominant idea of human rights. At the 1993 Vienna Conference on Human Rights, for example, Asian leaders resisted the 'cultural imperialism' of western values, and accused the West of attempting to retain colonial control by imposing a conception of rights that did not reflect Asian culture. Asian leaders rejected all ideas for legitimating humanitarian intervention, stressed the importance of national sovereignty and reaffirmed the principle of non-interference in domestic affairs. Furthermore, Asian leaders rejected the use of human rights as an instrument of political and economic conditionality (Boyle 1995). By emphasizing the moral, social and cultural differences between Asian and western countries, Asian leaders sought to promote an alternative vision of human rights that supported Asian economic interests. Furthermore, Asian leaders sought to avoid western criticism of their current human rights practices (Caballero-Anthony 1995).

The defence of 'situational uniqueness' put forward by the countries of South-East Asia may be strengthened following the financial crisis in the region in late 1997. If the West's conception of human rights was thought inappropriate during the time of economic expansions, it seems unlikely to be embraced in times of crisis and contraction. For example, many countries in the region are planning to repatriate millions of guest workers forcibly – 1.5 million to Burma and Bangladesh from Thailand, 270,000 to the Philippines and Nepal from South Korea and a million to Indonesia and the Philippines from Malaysia. For many guest workers this will mean returning to repressive regimes from which they have previously fled. Those forced to return to Burma include members of ethnic minorities who have already suffered from a government campaign to relocate entire villages in the effort to quell autonomy-seeking rebels (*Guardian* 1998, 1). Although the outcome of such policies is well known, the 'special circumstances' plea is likely to be tolerated.

Another form of resistance to universal human rights is seen in the rise of nationalism. The collapse of the USSR was followed by the creation of a number of independent and secessionist movements, many of which sought to express their cultural uniqueness through nationalist images based on claims of historic continuity. These activities stimulated immense interest in a wide range of political and social questions, including those concerned with self-determination, citizenship and human rights. The context of the cold war meant that the opportunity for public debate on such questions was often denied. Concepts like nationalism and self-determination often conjured images more appropriately associated with pre-Second World War, if not nineteenth-century politics, international relations and statehood. The new nationalism within Eastern Europe is emerging at the interface of social identity found in past ideas of community and new ideas concerned with sovereignty (Zinginis 1993). In contrast to the debate on new conceptions of sovereignty developing in Western Europe, which is conducted in the language of integration, interdependence and globalization, east European countries are more concerned with difference, separation and their own exceptionalism. For those who do not fit the prevailing definition for membership of the national community the human rights consequences are immense.

While the former Yugoslavia provides the most recent example of nationalism as a rationale for violating human rights, it is hardly the only one. The attempt by Chechnya to secede from Russia has seen both sides violate human rights. The rise of neo-fascist nationalist movements in Western Europe, particularly in Germany and Austria, has brought many attacks on guest workers. In these examples nationalists have attempted to define their community by branding certain groups sub-human and therefore not qualified to make legitimate rights claims (Donnelly 1994). The practice of 'ethnic cleansing', a repugnant euphemism for genocide that has recently entered the language, offers the most striking example of this.

On the fiftieth anniversary of the Universal Declaration it is fitting to reflect upon the changing context of power and hegemony in which human rights claims and counter-claims are made. The often repeated argument that we have moved from the era of standard-setting to one more concerned with implementation may have little foundation, given the changing economic and political environment of globalization. If power and rights are as closely linked as argued here, and we live in a world characterized by a new hegemony, the idea that human rights standards are already decided seems misplaced. As the nature of sovereignty becomes less certain, states find it increasingly difficult to achieve either civil and political or economic, social and cultural rights for their people. Globalization also challenges the institutions that international society has created for protecting human rights and national democracy seems less able to provide the necessary conditions for people to lead a dignified life.

The challenge of globalization forces us to rethink many treasured concepts of the past, including international relations, democracy and human rights. If we fail to respond to changing times, we may come to look back on the Declaration's fiftieth anniversary as the zenith of our human rights achievements. The first step to avoiding this is to clarify the role of human rights in the current era. This volume is intended to go some way towards this goal.

## Notes

1 The author would like to thank Jan Hancock for providing additional material in this chapter.
2 Statement by Secretary of State Stettinius, *Department of State Bulletin*, 12:301, 3 June 1945, 1,007–13.
3 General Assembly Official Records (GAOR), Yugoslavia, 3rd Session, Com. III. 015).
4 GAOR, Czechoslovakia, 3rd Session, Com. III, 69.
5 GAOR, 3rd Session, Com. III, 43.
6 UN Doc. E/CN. 4/L. 24.
7 Human Rights Committee, 52nd Meeting, November 1994, Doc. CCPR/C/21/rev. 1/add. 6.

## References

American Bar Association (undated), Letter and ABA report and recommendations on human rights to Eleanor Roosevelt, Roosevelt Library, Hyde Park, box no. 5487, undated.
Augelli, E. and C. Murphy (1988), *America's Quest and the Third World*, London, Pinter Publishers.
Barber, M. and R. Grainne (eds) (1993), *Damning the Three Gorges*, 2nd edn, London, Earthscan.
Boyle, K. (1995), Stock taking on human rights: the World Conference on Human Rights, Vienna 1993, *Political Studies*, 43, 79–95.

Burbach, R. (1993), The tragedy of American democracy, in B. Gills, J. Rocamora and R. Wilson (eds), *Low Intensity Democracy: Power in the New World Order*, London, Pluto.

Caballero-Anthony, M. (1995), Human rights, economic change and political development, in J. T. H. Tang (ed.), *Human Rights and International Relations in the Asia Pacific*, London, Pinter.

Cafruny, A. W. (1989), Economic conflicts and the transformation of the Atlantic order, in S. Gill (ed.), *Atlantic Relations: Beyond the Reagan Era*, New York, St. Martin's Press.

Carothers, T. (1994), Democracy and human rights: policy allies or rivals?, *Washington Quarterly*, 17:3, 109–21.

Carr, E. H. (1962), *The Twenty Years' Crisis*, London, Macmillan.

Chan, J. (1995), The Asian challenge to universal human rights: a philosophical appraisal, in J. T. H. Tang (ed.), *Human Rights and International Relations in the Asia Pacific*, London, Pinter.

Chomsky, N. (1994), *World Orders Old and New*, London, Pluto.

Cox, R. W. (1994), The crisis in world order and the challenge of international organization, *Conflict and Cooperation*, 29:2, 99–114.

Cox, R. W. (1995), A perspective on globalization, in J. H. Mittelman (ed.), *Globalization: Critical Reflections*, Boulder, Lynne Rienner.

Cranston, M. (1967), Human rights: real and supposed, in D. D. Raphael (ed.), *Political Theory and the Rights of Man*, London, Macmillan.

Cranston, M. (1983), Are there human rights?, *Daedalus*, 112:4, 1–18.

Daly, E. (1997), Time for justice to be done, *Independent on Sunday*, 6 July.

Department of State (1951), Instructions to Delegates, *Foreign Relations of the United States – 1951*, Washington, US Government Printing Office, 734–5.

Donnelly, J. (1994), Human rights and the new world order, *World Policy Review*, 9:2, 249–77.

*Economist* (1993), The red and the blue, 8 May, 22.

Eisenhower, D. D. (1963), *The White House Years: Mandate for Change – 1953–56*, London, Heinemann.

Evans, T. (1995), US hegemony, domestic politics and the project of universal human rights, *Statecraft and Diplomacy*, 6:3, 314–41.

Evans, T. (1996), *US Hegemony and the Project of Universal Human Rights*, Basingstoke, Macmillan.

Falk, R. (1980), Theoretical foundations of human rights, in R. P. Newburg (ed.), *The Politics of Human Rights*, New York, New York University Press.

Femia, J. (1987), *Gramsci's Political Thought: Hegemony, Consciousness and the Revolutionary Process*, Oxford, Clarendon Press.

Fukuyama, F. (1989), The end of history, *The National Interest*, Summer, 3–18.

Furedi, F. (1997), The moral condemnation of the South, in C. Thomas and P. Wilkin (eds), *Globalization and the South*, Basingstoke, Macmillan.

Galtung, J. (1994), *Human Rights in Another Key*, Cambridge, Polity Press.

Giddens, A. (1990), *The Consequences of Modernity*, Cambridge, Polity Press.

Gill, S. (1995), Globalization, market civilization and disciplinary neoliberalism, *Millennium: Journal of International Studies*, 24:3, 399–423.

Gills, B. K. (1995), Wither democracy? Globalization and the new Hellenism, British International Studies Association, Annual Conference, University of Southampton.

Gills, B., J. Rocamora and R. Wilson (eds) (1994), *Low Intensity Democracy: Power in the New World Order*, London, Pluto.

Gormley, W. (1976), *Human Rights and the Environment*, Leyden, Sijthoff.

Gramsci, A. (1971), *Selections from Prison Notebooks*, in Q. Hoare and G. Howell (eds and trans.), London, Lawrence and Wishart.

*Guardian* (1998) Misery for migrant million, January 7.

Held, D. (1995), *Democracy and the Global Order*, Cambridge, Polity Press.

Henkin, L. (1995), US ratification of human rights conventions: the ghost of Senator Bricker, *American Journal of International Law*, 89:2, 341–50.

Hindess, B. (1992), Power and rationality: the western conception of political community, *Alternatives*, 17, 149–63.

Hoffmann, S. (1977), The hell of good intentions, *Foreign Policy*, 29, 3–26.

Holman, F. E. (1952), Giving America away, *Vital Speeches of the Day*, 16, 1 October, 748–53.

Holman, F. E. (1953), The greatest threat to our American heritage, *Vital Speeches of the Day*, 24, 15 September, 711–17.

Humphrey, J. (1984), *Human Rights and the United Nations: The Great Adventure*, Dobbs Ferry, Transnational Publishers.

Huymans, J. (1995), Post-cold war implosion and globalization: liberalism running past itself, *Millennium: Journal of International Studies*, 24:3, 471–87.

Ikenberry G. J. and C. A. Kupchan (1990), Socialization and hegemonic power, *International Organization*, 44:3, 283–315.

*International Criminal Court Monitor* (1996), Newsletter of the NGO coalition for an international criminal court, July/August.

Johnson, B. R. and G. Button (1994), Human environmental rights issues and the multi-national corporation: industrial development in the free trade zone, in B. R. Johnson (ed.), *Who Pays the Price?*, Washington, Island Press.

Kaufman, N. H. and D. Whiteman (1988), Opposition to human rights treaties in the United States: the legacy of the Bricker amendment, *Human Rights Quarterly*, 10:3, 309–37.

Kausikan, B. (1993), Asia's different view, *Foreign Affairs*, 92, 24–41.

Keeley, J. F. (1990), Towards a Foucauldian analysis of international regimes, *International Organization*, 44:1, 83–105.

Kennan, G. (1985), Morality and foreign policy, *International Affairs*, 64:2, 205–18.

Kothari, S. (1994), Global economic institutions and democracy: a view from India, in J. Cavanagh, D. W. and M. Arrunda (eds), *Beyond Bretton Woods*, London, Pluto.

Kudryartsev, U. N. (1986), Human rights and the Soviet Constitution, in *The Philosophical Foundations of Human Rights*, New York, UNESCO.

Lawyers Committee for Human Rights (1992), Letter to Senator Claiborne Pell, *Human Rights Law Journal*, 14, 3–4.

Loth, W. (1988), *The Division of the World – 1941–45*, London, Routledge.

McGrew, A. (1997), *The Transformation of Democracy*, Cambridge, Polity Press.

Moskovitz, M. (1974), *International Concern with Human Rights*, Dobbs Ferry, Oceana Publications.

Muzaffar, C. (1995), From human rights to human dignity, *Bulletin of Concerned Asian Scholars*, 27:4, 6–8.

Opsahl, T. (1989), Instruments of implementation of human rights, *Human Rights Law Journal*, 10:1, 13–33.

Panitch, L. (1995), Rethinking the role of the state, in J. H. Mittelman (ed.), *Globalization: Critical Reflections*, Boulder, Lynne Reinner.

Ramphal, S. (1992), Globalism and meaningful peace: a new world order rooted in international community, *Security Dialogue*, 32:3, 82.

Ransom, W. (1946), Letter to Eleanor Roosevelt, Roosevelt Library, Hyde Park, box no. 4587, 4 May.

Raphael D. D. (1967), Human rights, old and new, in D. D. Raphael (ed.), *Political Theory and the Rights of Man*, London, Macmillan.

Robinson, G. (1997), Britain's blind eye to inhumanity, *The Times*, 8 May, 20.

Robinson, M. (1993), Will political conditionality work?, *IDS Bulletin*, 21:1, 58–66.

Robinson, W. (1996), *Promoting Polyarchy: Globalization, US Intervention and Hegemony*, Cambridge, Cambridge University Press.

Rupert, M. (1995), *Producing Hegemony: The Politics of Mass Production and American Global Power*, Cambridge, Cambridge University Press.

Salmi, J. (1993), *Violence and the Democratic State*, London, Zed Books.

Stammers, N. (1993), Human rights and power, *Political Studies*, 41, 70–82.

Stammers, N. (1995), A critique of social approaches to human rights, *Human Rights Quarterly*, 17:3, 488–508.

Strong, T. B. (1980), Taking the rank with what is ours: American political thought, foreign policy, and the question of rights, in P. R. Newburg (ed.), *The Politics of Human Rights*, London, Macmillan.

Tamilmoran, V. T. (1992), *Human Rights in Third World Perspective*, New Delhi, Har-Anand Publications.

Tananbaum, D. (1988), *The Bricker Amendment Controversy: A Test of Eisenhower's Political Leadership*, Ithaca, Cornell University Press.

Tomasevski, K. (1993), *Development Aid and Human Rights Revisited*, London, Pinter Publishers.

*UN Statistical Yearbook* (1948), New York, United Nations.

UNDP (1996), *Human Development Report*, Oxford, Oxford University Press.

UNDP (1997), *Human Development Report*, Oxford, Oxford University Press.

Vincent, J. R. (1986), *Human Rights and International Relations*, Cambridge, Cambridge University Press.

Watson J. S. (1979), Legal theory, efficacy and validity in the development of human rights norms in international law, *University of Illinois Law Forum*, 3, 609–41.

Zinginis, A. D. (1993), Nationalism and the reality of the nation state: the case of Greece and Turkey in relation to the European orientation in the two countries, unpublished Ph.D. thesis, Essex University.

# 2

# The United States and the challenge of relativity

## Noam Chomsky

The adoption of the Universal Declaration of Human Rights on 10 December 1948 constituted a step forward in the slow progress towards protection of human rights.[1] The overarching principle of the Declaration is universality. Its provisions have equal standing. There are no moral grounds for self-serving 'relativism', which selects for convenience; still less for the particularly ugly form of relativism that converts the Declaration into a weapon to wield selectively against designed enemies.

The fiftieth anniversary of the Declaration provides a welcome occasion for reflection on such matters, and for steps to advance the principles that have been endorsed, at least rhetorically, by the nations of the world. The chasm that separates words from actions requires no comment; the annual reports of the major human rights organizations provide more than ample testimony. And there is no shortage of impressive rhetoric. One would have to search far to find a place where leadership and intellectuals do not issue ringing endorsements of the principles and bitter condemnation of those who violate them – notably excluding themselves and their associates and clients.

I will limit attention here to a single case: the world's most powerful state, which also has the most stable and long-standing democratic institutions and unparalleled advantages in every sphere, including the economy and security concerns. Its global influence has been unmatched during the half century when the Declaration has been in force. It has long been as good a model as one can find of a sociopolitical order in which basic rights are upheld. And it is commonly lauded, at home and abroad, as the leader in the struggle for human rights, democracy, freedom and justice. There remains a range of disagreement over policy: at one extreme, 'Wilson idealists' urge continued dedication to the traditional mission of upholding human rights and freedom worldwide, while 'realists' counter that America may lack the means to conduct these crusades of 'global meliorism' and should not neglect its own interests in the service of others. By 'granting idealism a near exclusive hold on our foreign policy', we go too far, high government officials warn, with the agreement of many scholars and policy analysts (Fromkin, *NYT*, 4 May 1997; Friedman, *NYT*, 12 January 1992). Within this range lies the path to a better world.

To discover the true meaning of principles that are proclaimed, it is of course necessary to go beyond rhetorical flourishes and public pronouncements, and to investigate actual practice. Examples must be chosen carefully to give a fair picture. One useful approach is to take the examples chosen as the 'strongest case', and to see how well they withstand scrutiny. Another is to investigate the record where influence is greatest and interference least, so that we see the operative principles in their purest form. If we want to determine what the Kremlin meant by human rights and democracy, we pay little heed to *Pravda*'s denunciations of racism in the United States or state terror in its client regimes, even less to protestation of noble motives. Far more instructive is the state of affairs in the 'peoples' democracies' of Eastern Europe. The point is elementary, and applies generally. For the USA, the Western hemisphere is the obvious testing ground, particularly the Central America–Caribbean region, where Washington has faced few external challenges for almost a century. It is of some interest that the exercise is rarely undertaken, and when it is, it is castigated as extremist or worse.

Before examining the operative meaning of the Declaration, it might be useful to recall some observations of George Orwell's. In his preface to *Animal Farm*, Orwell turned his attention to societies that are relatively free from state controls, unlike the totalitarian monster he was satirizing. 'The sinister fact about literary censorship in England', he wrote, 'is that it is largely voluntary. Unpopular ideas can be silenced, and inconvenient facts kept dark, without any need for any official ban.' He did not explore the reasons in any depth, merely noting the control of the press by 'wealthy men who have every motive to be dishonest on certain important topics', reinforced by the 'general tacit agreement', instilled by a good education, 'that "it wouldn't do" to mention that particular fact'. As a result, 'Anyone who challenges the prevailing orthodoxy finds himself silenced with surprising effectiveness.'

As if to illustrate his words, the preface remained unpublished for thirty years (Crick, *TLS*, 15 September 1972).

## The prevailing orthodoxy

In the case under discussion here, the prevailing orthodoxy is well summarized by the distinguished Oxford–Yale historian Michael Howard: 'For 200 years the United States has preserved almost unsullied the original ideals of the Enlightenment ... and, above all, the universality of these values', though it 'does not enjoy the place in the world that it should have earned through its achievements, its generosity, and its goodwill since World War II' (Howard 1985). The record is unsullied by the treatment of 'that hapless race of native Americans, which we are exterminating with such merciless and perfidious cruelty' (John Quincy Adams in Weeks 1992, 192) or the fate of the slaves who provided cheap cotton to allow the industrial revolution to take off – not exactly through market forces; by the terrible atrocities the US was once again conducting in its 'backyard' as the praises were being delivered; or by the fate of Filipinos, Haitians, Vietnamese and a few others who might have somewhat different perceptions.

The favoured illustration of 'generosity and goodwill' is the Marshall Plan. That merits examination, on the 'strongest case' principle. The inquiry again quickly yields facts 'that "it wouldn't do" to mention'. For example, the fact that 'as the Marshall Plan went into full gear the amount of American dollars being pumped into France and the Netherlands was approximately equalled by the funds being siphoned from their treasuries to finance their expeditionary forces in South East Asia', to carry out terrible crimes (Kahin and Kahin 1995, 30; Saville 1993; Curtis 1995). And that under US influence Europe was reconstructed in a particular mode, not quite that sought by the anti-fascist resistance, though fascist and Nazi collaborators were generally satisfied.

Nor would it do to mention that the generosity was largely bestowed by American taxpayers upon the corporate sector, which was duly appreciative, recognizing years later that the Marshall Plan 'set the stage for large amounts of private US direct investment in Europe' (Wachtel 1990, 44), establishing the basis for the modern transnational corporations, which 'prospered and expanded on overseas orders ... fuelled initially by the dollars of the Marshall Plan' and protected from 'Negative developments' by 'the umbrella of American power' (*Business Week*, 7 April 1975). Furthermore, 'Marshall Plan aid was also crucial in offsetting capital flight from Europe to the United States,' a matter of which 'American policy makers were in fact keenly aware', preferring that 'wealthy Europeans' send their money to New York banks because 'cooperative capital controls had proven unacceptable to the American banking community'. 'The enormity of Marshall Plan aid thus did not so much reflect the resources required to rebuild Europe ... but rather the volume of funds that were needed to offset the "mass movement of nervous flight capital" predicted by leading economists, a flow that apparently "exceeded" the Marshall Plan aid provided by American taxpayers' – effectively, to 'wealthy Europeans' and New York banks (Helleiner 1994, 58–62).

It is, again, of some interest that thoughts of that nature were 'silenced with surprising effectiveness' during the fiftieth anniversary celebration of this unprecedented act of generosity and goodwill, the strongest case put forth by admirers of the 'global meliorism' of the world's most powerful state, hence of direct relevance to the question being addressed here.

The 'prevailing orthodoxy' has sometimes been subjected to explicit test, on the obvious terrain. Lars Schoultz, the leading academic specialist on human rights in Latin America, found that US aid 'has tended to flow disproportionately to Latin American governments which torture their citizens ... to the hemisphere's relatively egregious violators of fundamental human rights' (Schoultz 1981). More wide-ranging studies by economist Edward Herman found a similar correlation worldwide, also suggesting a plausible reason: aid is correlated with improvement in the investment climate, often achieved by murdering priests and union leaders, massacring peasants trying to organize, blowing up the independent press, and so on. The result is a secondary correlation between aid and egregious violation of human rights. It is not that US leaders prefer torture; rather, it has little weight in comparison with more important values. These studies precede the Reagan years, when the questions are not worth posing (Chomsky and Herman 1979, ch. 1; Herman 1982).

By 'general tacit agreement', such matters too are 'kept dark', with memories purged of 'inconvenient facts'.

The natural starting point for an inquiry into Washington's defence of 'the universality of [Enlightenment] values' is the Universal Declaration. It is accepted generally as a human rights standard. US courts have, furthermore, based judicial decision on 'customary international law, as evidenced and defined by the Universal Declaration of Human Rights'.[2]

The Declaration became the focus of great attention in June 1993 at the World Conference on Human Rights in Vienna. A leading headline in the *New York Times* reads: 'At Vienna talks, US insists rights must be universal', Washington warned 'that it would oppose any attempt to use religious and cultural traditions to weaken the concept of universal human rights', Elaine Sciolino reported. The US delegation was headed by Secretary of State Warren Christopher, 'who promoted human rights as Deputy Secretary of State in the Carter Administration'. A 'key purpose' of his speech, 'viewed as the Clinton Administration's first major policy statement on human rights', was 'to defend the universality of human rights', rejecting the claims of those who plead 'cultural relativism'. Christopher said that 'the worst violators are the world's aggressors and those who encourage the spread of arms', stressing that 'the universality of human rights set[s] a single standard of acceptable behavior around the world, a standard Washington would apply to all countries'. In his own words, 'This United States will never join those who would undermine the Universal Declaration' and will defend its universality against those who hold 'that human rights should be interpreted differently in regions with non-Western cultures', notably the 'dirty dozen' who reject elements of the Declaration that do not suit them (Sciolino, *NYT*, 15 June 1993).

Washington's decisiveness prevailed. Western countries 'were relieved that their worst fears were not realized – a retreat from the basic tenets of the 1948 Universal Declaration of Human Rights. The 'challenge of relativity' was beaten back, and the conference declared that 'The universal nature of these rights are freedoms is beyond question' (Riding, *NYT*, 26 June 1993).

A few questions remained unasked. Thus, if 'the worst violators are the world's aggressors and those who encourage the spread of arms', what are we to conclude about the world's leading arms merchant, then boasting well over half the sales of arms in the Third World, mostly to brutal dictatorships, policies accelerated under Christopher's tenure at the State Department with vigorous efforts to enhance the publicly-subsidized sales, opposed by 96 per cent of the population but strongly supported by high-tech industry (Hartung 1994; Hartung, *Nation*, 30 January 1995)?[3] Or its colleagues Britain and France, who had distinguished themselves by supporting Indonesian and Rwandan mass murders, among others?[4] The subsidies are not only for 'merchants of death'. Revelling in the new prospects for arms sales with NATO (North Atlantic Treaty Organisation) expansion, a spokesman for the Aerospace Industries Association observes that the new markets (ten billion dollars for fighter jets alone, he estimates) include electronics, communications systems, etc., amounting to 'real money' for advanced industry generally. The exports are promoted by the US government with grants, discounts loans and other devices to facilitate the transfer of public funds to private profit in the US, while diverting the economies of the 'transition economies' of the former Soviet empire to increased military spending rather than the social spending that is favoured by their populations (the US Information Agency reports). The situation is quite the same elsewhere (Gerth and Weiner, *NYT*, 29 July 1997).

And if aggressors are 'the worst violators' of human rights, what of the country that stands accused before the International Court of Justice for the 'unlawful use of force' in its terrorist war against Nicaragua,[5] contemptuously vetoing a Security Council resolution calling on all states to observe international law and rejecting repeated General Assembly pleas to the same effect (*NYT*, 29 October 1996: *Boston Globe*, 4 November 1996; *Extra!*, December 1987)? Do these stern judgements hold of the country that opened the post-cold war era by invading Panama, where, four years later, the client government's Human Rights Commission declared that the right to self-determination and sovereignty was still being violated by the 'state of occupation by a foreign army', condemning its continuing human rights abuses?[6] I omit more dramatic examples, such as the US attack against South Vietnam from 1961–62, when the Kennedy Administration moved from support for a Latin American-style terror state to outright aggression, facts that it still 'wouldn't do' to admit into history.[7]

Further questions are raised by Washington's (unreported) reservations concerning the Declaration of the Vienna Conference. The US was disturbed that the Vienna Declaration 'implied that any foreign occupation is a human rights violation' (Assistant Secretary of State for Human Rights, John Shattock, quoted in Wronka 1997). That principle the US rejects, just as, alone with its Israeli client, the US rejects the right of peoples 'forcibly deprived of [self-determination, freedom and independence] ... particularly peoples under colonial and racist regimes and foreign occupation or other forms of colonial domination ... to struggle to [gain these rights] and to seek and receive support [in accordance with Charter and other principles of international law]' – facts that also remain unreported, though they might help clarify the sense in which human rights are advocated.[8]

Also unexamined was just how Christopher had 'promoted human rights under the Carter Administration'. One case was in 1978, when the spokesperson for the 'dirty dozen' at Vienna, Indonesia, was running out of arms in its attack against East Timor, then approaching genocidal levels, so that the Carter Administration had to rush even more military supplies to its bloodthirsty friend (Chomsky and Herman 1979; Chomsky 1992; Taylor 1991). Another arose a year later, when the Administration sought desperately to keep Somoza's National Guard in power after it had slaughtered some 40,000 civilians, finally evacuating commanders in planes disguised with Red Cross markings (a war crime), to Honduras, where they were reconstituted as a terrorist force under the direction of Argentine neo-Nazis. The record elsewhere in the regions was arguably worse (Kornbluh 1987, ch. 1; LaFaber 1983, 239).[9] Such matters too fall among the facts 'that it "wouldn't do" to mention'.

The high-minded rhetoric at, and about, the Vienna conference was not besmirched by inquiry into the observance of the resulting Declaration by its leading defenders.[10] These matters were, however, raised in Vienna in a Public Hearing organised by non-governmental organizatons (NGOs). The contributions by activists, scholars, lawyers and others from many countries provided a detailed review of 'Alarming evidence of massive human rights violations in every part of the world as a result of the policies of the international financial institutions', the 'Washington consensus' among the leaders of the free world. This 'neoliberal' consensus is based on what might be called 'really existing free market doctrine': market discipline is of great benefit to the weak and defenceless, though the rich and powerful must shelter under the wings of the nanny state. They must be allowed to persist in 'the sustained assault on [the free trade] principle' that is deplored in a scholarly review of the post-1970 ('neoliberal') period by GATT (General Agreement on Tariffs and Trade) secretariat economist Patrick Low (now director of economic research for the WTO (World Trade Organization)), who estimates the restrictive effects of Reaganite measures at about three times those of other leading industrial countries, as they 'presided over the greatest swing toward protectionism since the 1930s', shifting the USA from 'being the world's champion of multilateral free trade to one of its leading challengers', the journal of the council on Foreign Relations commented in a review of the decade (Low 1993, 271; Islam 1989–90).

It should be added that such analyses omit the major forms of market interference for the benefit of the rich: the transfer of public funds to advanced industry that underlies virtually every dynamic sector of the US economy, often under the guise of 'defence'. These measures were escalated again by the Reaganites, who were second to none in extolling the glories of the free market – for the poor at home and abroad. The general practices were pioneered by the British in the eighteenth century and have been a dominant feature of economic history ever since, and a good part of the reason for the contemporary gap between the First and the Third World (growing for the past thirty years along with the growing gap between the rich and poor sectors of the population worldwide).[11]

The Public Hearing at Vienna received no mention in mainstream US journals, to my knowledge, but citizens of the free world could learn about the human rights concerns of the vast majority of the world's people from its report, published in an edition of 2,000 copies in Nepal.[12]

## The Universal Declaration in US politics and society

### CIVIL AND POLITICAL RIGHTS

The provisions of the Declaration are not well known in the United States, but some are familiar. The most famous is Article 13(2), which states that 'Everyone has the right to leave any country, including his own'. This principle was invoked with much passion every year on Human Rights Day, 10 December, with demonstrations and indignant condemnations of the Soviet Union for its refusal to allow Jews to leave. To be exact, the words just quoted were invoked, but not the phrase that follows: 'and to return to his country'. The significance of the omitted words was spelled out on 11 December 1948, the day after the Declaration was ratified, when the General Assembly unanimously passed Resolution 194, which affirms the right of Palestinians to return to their homes or receive compensation, if they chose not to return, reaffirmed regularly since. But there was a 'general tacit agreement' that it 'wouldn't do' to mention the omitted words, let alone the glaringly obvious fact that those exhorting the Soviet tyrants to observe Article 13, to much acclaim, were its most dedicated opponents.

It is only fair to add that the cynicism has finally been overcome. At the December 1993 UN session, the Clinton Administration changed US official policy, joining with Israel in opposing Resolution 194, which was reaffirmed by a vote of 127 to 2. As is the norm, there was no report or comment. But at least the inconsistency is behind us; the first half of Article 13(2) has lost its relevance, and Washington now officially rejects its second half (Kagian, *MEI*, 17 December 1994; Kagian, *MEJN*, Febuary/March 1994; Mallison and Mallison 1996, ch. 4).

Let us move on to Article 14, which declares that 'Everyone has the right to seek and to enjoy in other countries asylum from persecution'. Haitians, for example, including the eighty-seven new victims captured by Clinton's blockade and returned with scant notice, as the Vienna conference opened (Reuters, *BG*, 18 June 1993). The official reason was that they were fleeing poverty, not the rampant terror of the military junta, as they claimed. The basis for this insight was not explained.

Reporting on the Vienna conference a few days earlier, Sciolino had noted that 'some human rights organizations have sharply criticized the Administration for failing to fulfill Mr Clinton's campaign promises on human rights' the 'most dramatic case' being 'Washington's decision to forcibly return Haitian boat people seeking political asylum'. Looked at differently, the events illustrate Washington's largely rhetorical commitment to 'the universality of human rights', except as a weapon used selectively against others (Sciolino, *NYT*, 15 June 1993).

The USA has upheld Article 14 in this manner since Carter (and Christopher) 'promoted human rights' by shipping miserable boat people back to torment under the Duvalier dictatorship, a respected ally helping to convert Haiti to an export platform for US corporations seeking supercheap and brutalized labour – or to adopt the terms preferred by USAID (United States Agency for International Development), to convert Haiti into the 'Taiwan of the Caribbean'. The violations of Article 14 were ratified formally in a Reagan–Duvalier agreement. When a military *coup* overthrew Haiti's first democratically elected President in September 1991, renewing the terror after a brief lapse, the Bush Administration imposed a blockade to drive back the flood of refugees to the torture chamber.[13]

Bush's 'reprehensible ... illegal and irresponsible refugee policy' (Americas Watch 1993) was bitterly condemned by candidate Bill Clinton, whose first act as President was to make the illegal blockade still harsher, along with other measures to sustain the junta, to which we return.

Again, fairness requires that we recognize that Washington did briefly depart from its rejection of Article 14 in the case of Haiti. During the few months of democracy (February to September 1991), the Bush Administration gained a sudden and short-lived sensitivity to Article 14 as the flow of refugees declined to a trickle – in fact, reversed, as Haitians returned to their country in its moment of hope. Of the more than 24,000 Haitians intercepted by US forces from 1981 through to 1990, Washington allowed 28 claims for asylum as victims of political persecution, granting 11 (in comparison with 75,000 out of 75,000 Cubans). During Aristide's seven-month tenure, with violence and repression radically reduced, 20 claims were allowed from a refugee pool one fiftieth the scale. Practice returned to normal after the military *coup* and the renewed terror (Chomsky 1993, ch. 8; Wilentz, *The New Republic*, 9 March 1992).

The contempt for Article 14 is by no means concealed. A front-page story

in the Newspaper of record on harsh new immigration laws casually records
the fact and explains the reasons:

> Because the United States armed and financed the army whose brutality sent
> them into exile, few Salvadorans were able to obtain the refugee status
> granted to Cubans, Vietnamese, Kuwaitis and other nationalities at various
> times. The new law regards many of them simply as targets for deportation
> [through they were fleeing] a conflict that lasted from 1979 until 1992,
> [when] more than 70,000 people were killed in El Salvador, most of them
> by the American-backed army and the death squads it in turn supported,
> [forcing] many people here to flee to the United States. (Rohter, *NYT*, 19
> April 1997)

The same reasoning extends to those who fled Washington's other terrorist
wars in the region.

The interpretation of Article 14 is therefore quite principled: 'worthy
victims' fall under Article 14, 'unworthy victims' do not. The categories are
determined by the agency of terror and prevailing power interests. But the
facts have no bearing on Washington's role as the crusader defending the
universality of the Universal Declaration from the relativist challenge. The
case is among the many that illustrate an omission in Orwell's analysis: the
easy tolerance of inconsistency, when convenient.

ECONOMIC, SOCIAL AND CULTURAL RIGHTS

Articles 13 and 14 fall under the category of civil and political rights. The
Universal Declaration also recognizes a second category: economic, social
and cultural rights. These are largely dismissed in the West. UN Ambassador
Jeane Kirkpatrick described these provisions of the Declaration as 'a letter
to Santa Claus ... Neither nature, experience, nor probability informs these
lists of "entitlements", which are subject to no constraints except those of
the mind and appetite of their authors'. They were dismissed in more
temperate tones by the US representative to the UN Commission on Human
Rights, Ambassador Morris Abram, who emphasized in 1990 that civil and
political rights must have 'priority', contrary to the principle of universality
of the Declaration (Wronka 1992).

Abram elaborated while explaining Washington's rejection of the Report
of the Global Consultations on the Right to Development, defined as 'the
right of individuals, groups, and peoples to participate in, contribute to, and
enjoy continuous economic, social, cultural and political development, in which
all human rights and fundamental freedoms can be fully realized'. 'Development is not a right', Abram informed the Commission. Indeed, the proposals
of the Report yield conclusions that 'seem preposterous', for example, that
the World Bank might be obliged 'to forgive a loan or to give money to build
a tunnel, a railroad, or a school'. Such ideas are 'little more than an empty

vessel into which vague hopes and inchoate expectations can be poured', Abram continued, and even a 'dangerous incitement'.[14] Closely paraphrasing Abram's thesis, we may understand the fundamental error of the alleged 'right to development' to be its tacit endorsement of the principle that:

> Everyone has the right to a standard of living adequate for the health and well-being of himself and his family, including food, clothing, housing and medical care and necessary social services, and the right to security in the event of unemployment, sickness, disability, widowhood, old age or other lack of livelihood in circumstances beyond his control. (UDHR Art. 25)

If there is no right to development, as defined, then this statement too is an 'empty vessel' and perhaps even 'dangerous incitement'. Accordingly, this principle too has no status: there are no such rights as those affirmed in Article 25 of the Declaration, just quoted.

The US alone vetoed the Declaration on the Right to Development, thus implicitly vetoing Article 25 of the Declaration as well (Wronka 1995).

It is unnecessary to dwell on the status of Article 25 in the world's richest country, with a poverty level twice that of any other industrial society, particularly severe among children. Almost one in four children under six fell below the poverty line by 1995 after four years of economic recovery, far more than other industrial societies (Mishel *et al.* 1997). Though Britain is gaining ground, with 'One in three British babies born in poverty', the press now reports, as 'child poverty has increased as much as three-fold since Margaret Thatcher was elected' and 'up to two million British children are suffering ill-health and stunted growth because of malnutrition'. Thatcherite policies reversed the trend to improve child health and led to an upswing of childhood diseases that had been controlled, while public funds were used for such purposes as illegal projects in Turkey and Malaysia to foster arms sales by state-subsidized industry (*Observer*, 12 January 1997; *Independent*, 24 and 25 November 1996; *Guardian Weekly*, 5 January 1997; *Observer*, 19 January 1997). In accord with 'really existing free market doctrine', public spending after seventeen years of Thatcherite gospel was the same 42.25 per cent of GDP that it was when she took over.

In the USA, subjected to similar policies, thirty million people suffered from hunger by 1990, an increase of 50 per cent from 1985, including twelve million children lacking sufficient food to maintain growth and development (before the 1991 recession). Forty per cent of children in the world's richest city fell below the poverty line. In terms of such basic social indicators as child mortality, the US ranks well below any other industrial country alongside of Cuba, which has less than 5 per cent of the GNP per capita of the United States and has undergone many years of terrorist attack and increasingly severe economic warfare at the hand of the hemispheric super-power (Chomsky 1996 and 1996a; UNICEF 1997).

Given its extraordinary advantages, the USA is in the leading ranks of relativists who reject the universality of the Declaration by virtue of Article 25 alone.

The same values guide the international financial institutions that the USA largely controls. The World Bank and the International Monetary Fund (IMF) 'have been extraordinarily human rights averse', the chairperson of the UN committee on Economic, Social and Cultural Rights, Philip Alston, observed with polite understatement in his submission to the Vienna counter-session. 'As we have heard so dramatically at this Public Hearing', Nouri Abdul Razzak of the Afro-Asian People's Solidarity Organization added 'the policies of the international financial institutions are contributing to the impoverishment of the world's people, the degradation of the global environment, and the violation of the most fundamental human rights', on a mind-numbing scale.

In the face of such direct violations of the principles of the Declaration, it is perhaps superfluous to mention the refusal to take even small steps towards upholding them. The United Nations Children's Fund (UNICEF) estimates that every hour, 1,000 children die from easily preventable disease, and almost twice that many women die or suffer serious disability in pregnancy or childbirth for lack of simple remedies and care. To ensure universal access to basic social services, UNICEF estimates, would require a quarter of the annual military expenditures of the developing countries, about 10 per cent of US military spending (UNICEF 1996). As noted, the USA actively promotes military expenditure in the developing countries; its own remain at cold war levels, although increasing, while social spending is being severely cut. Also declining sharply in the 1990s is US foreign aid, already the most miserly among the developed countries, and virtually non-existent if we exclude the rich country that is the primary recipient (Washington's Israeli client).[15]

In his 'Final Report' to the UN Commission on Human Rights, Special Rapporteur Leandro Despouy cites the World Health Organization's characterization of 'extreme poverty' as 'the world's most ruthless killer and the greatest cause of suffering on earth': 'No other disaster compared to the devastation of hunger which had caused more deaths in the past two years than were killed in the two World Wars together.' The right to a standard of living adequate for health and well-being is affirmed in Article 25 of the Declaration, he notes, and in the International Covenant on Economic, Social, and Cultural Rights, 'which places emphasis more particularly on the fundamental right of everyone to be free from hunger'.[16] But from the highly relativist perspective of the West, these principles of human rights agreements have no status though they are officially endorsed.

There are other differences of interpretation concerning Article 25. The UN Commission of Human Rights was approached by Third World countries seeking means 'to stem the huge flow of dangerous substances' to poor countries, concerned that 'dumping toxic products and wastes threatened the basic rights to life and good health' guaranteed by the Universal Declaration. The UN investigator determined that the rich countries send 'masses of toxic waste' to the Third World and now, the former Soviet domains. She said information she gathered shows 'serious violations of the right to life and health', the press reported, and in some cases 'had led to sickness, disorders, physical or mental disability and even death'. Her information was limited, however, because she had 'little cooperation from developed countries or corporations', and none at all from the USA, which is moving to terminate her mission (Olsen, *NYT*, 5 April 1998).

Article 23 of the Declaration declares that 'Everyone has the right to work, to free choice of employment, to just and favourable conditions of work and to protection against unemployment', along with 'remuneration ensuring for himself and his family an existence worthy of human dignity, and supplemented, if necessary, by other means of social protection'. We need not tarry on Washington's respect for this principle. Furthermore, 'Everyone has the right to form and to join trade unions for the protection of his interests.'

The latter right is technically upheld in the United States, though legal and administrative mechanisms ensure that it is largely observed in the breach. By the time the Reaganites had completed their work, the US was so off the spectrum that the International Labour Organization (ILO), which rarely criticizes the powerful, issued a recommendation that the US conform to international standards, in response to an AFL–CIO (American Federation of Labor and Congress of Industrial Organisation) complaint about strike-breaking by resort to 'permanent replacement workers' (Hoerr 1992; Chomsky 1993, ch. 11). Apart from South Africa, no other industrial country tolerated these methods to ensure that Article 23 remains empty words; and with subsequent developments in South Africa, the USA may stand in splendid isolation in this particular respect, though it has yet to achieve British standards, such as allowing employers to use selective pay increases to induce workers to reject union and collective bargaining rights (Harper, *Guardian*, 24 May 1994).

Reviewing some of the mechanisms used to render Article 23 inoperative, *Business Week* reported that from the early Reagan years, 'US industry has conducted one of the most successful anti-union wars ever, illegally firing thousands of workers for exercising their rights to organize'. 'Unlawful firings occurred in one-third of all representation elections in the late '80s, vs. 8% in the late '60s.' Workers have no recourse, as the Reagan Administration converted the powerful state they nurtured to an expansive welfare state for the rich, defying US law as well as the customary international law enshrined in the Declaration. Management's basic goal, the journal explains, has been to cancel the rights 'guaranteed by the 1935 Wagner Act', which brought the US into the mainstream of the industrial world (*Business Week*, 24 May 1994). That has been a basic goal since the New Deal provisions were enacted, and although the project of reversing the victory for democracy and working people was put on hold during the war, it was taken up again when peace arrived, with great vigour and considerable success (Fones-Wolf 1994).[17] One index of the success is provided by the record of ratification of ILO conventions guaranteeing labour rights. The USA has far the worst record in the Western hemisphere and Europe, with the exception of El Salvador and Lithuania. It does not recognize even standard conventions on child labour and the right to organize (*World Labour Report* 1994).

'The United States is in arrears to the ILO in the amount of $92.6 million', the Lawyers Committee for Human Rights notes. This withholding of funds 'seriously jeopardizes the ILO's operations'; Washington plans for larger cuts in ILO funding 'would primarily affect the ILO's ability to deliver technical assistance in the field', thus undermining Article 23 still further, worldwide (Lawyers Committee for Human Rights 1996). This is only part of the huge debt to international organizations that the USA refuses to pay (in violation of treaty obligations). Unpaid back dues to the UN are estimated at $1.3 billion, 'Our doors are kept open', Secretary General Kofi Annan writes, 'only because other countries in essence provide interest-free loans to cover largely American shortfalls – not only NATO allies ... but also developing countries like Pakistan and even Fiji' (*NYT*, 9 March 1998). A few weeks later, still refusing to pay, the Senate voted 90 to 10 that the UN 'thank the United States for its contributions', lower its obligations, 'and publicly report to all member nations how much the United States has spent supporting Security Council resolutions since 1 January 1990' (*NYT*, 27 March 1998).

The illegal attack on unions in violation of Article 23 has many effects. It contributes to undermining health and safety standards in the workplace, which the government chooses not to enforce, leading to a sharp rise in industrial accidents in the Reagan years (*Business Week*, 23 May 1994). It also helps to undermine functioning democracy, as people with limited resources lose some of the few methods by which they can enter the political arena. And it accelerates the privatization of aspirations, dissolving the sense of solidarity and sympathy, and other human values that were at the heart of classical liberal thought but are inconsistent with the reigning ideology of privilege and power. More narrowly, the US Labour Department estimates that the weakening of unions accounts for a large part of the stagnation or decline in real wages under the Reagonites, 'a welcome development of transcendent importance', as the *Wall Street Journal* described the fall in labour costs from the 1985 high to the lowest in the industrial world (UK aside) (*WSJ*, 13 September 1994; Mishel and Bernstein 1994; Mishel, Bernstein and Schmitt 1997).

Testifying before the Senate Banking Committee in February 1997, Federal Reserve Board Chair Alan Greenspan was highly optimistic about 'sustainable economic expansion' thanks to 'atypical restraint on compensation increases [which] appears to be mainly the consequences of greater worker insecurity', plainly a desideratum for a good society and yet another reason for Western relativists to reject Article 25 of the Declaration, with its 'right to security'. The February 1997 Economic Report of the President, taking pride in the Clinton Administration's achievements, refers more obliquely to 'changes in labour market institutions and practices' as a factor in the 'significant wage restraint' that bolsters the health of the economy (*Multinational Monitor*, March 1997, editorial).

The 'free trade agreements', as they are commonly mislabelled (they include significant protectionist features and are 'agreements' only if we discount popular opinion), make further contributions to these ends. Some of the mechanisms of these benign changes are spelled out in a study commissioned by the Labor Secretariat of the North American Free Trade Agreement (NAFTA) 'on the effects of the sudden closing of the plant on the principle of freedom of association and the right of workers to organize in the three countries'. The study was carried out under NAFTA rules in response to a complaint by telecommunications workers on illegal labour practices by Sprint. The complaint was upheld by the US National Labor Relations Board, which ordered trivial penalties after years of delay, the standard procedure. The NAFTA study, by Cornell University labour economist Kate Bronfenbrenner, has been authorized for release by Canada and Mexico, but not by the Clinton Administration. It reveals a significant impact of NAFTA on strike-breaking. About half of union organizing efforts are disrupted by employer threats to transfer production abroad, for example, by placing signs reading 'Mexico Transfer Job' in front of a plant where there is an organizing drive. The threats are not idle. When such organizing drives nevertheless succeed, employers close the plant in whole or in part. Current figures show that closures are three times higher than those in pre-NAFTA years. Plant-closing threats are almost twice as high in more mobile industries (for example manufacturing as opposed to construction) (Bronfenbrenner, *MN*, March 1997).

These and other practices reported in the NAFTA study are illegal, but that is a technicality, as the Reagan Administration had made clear, outweighed by the contributions to undermining the right to organize that is formally guaranteed by Article 23 – or in more polite words, bringing about 'changes in labour market institutions and practices' that contribute to 'significant wage restraint' thanks to 'greater worker insecurity' within an economic model offered with great pride to a backward world, and greatly admired among privileged sectors.

A number of other devices have been employed to nullify the pledge 'never [to] join those who would undermine the Universal Declaration' (Christopher) in the case of Article 23. The further dismantling of the welfare system, sharply reduced from the 1970s, drives many poor women to the labour market, where they will work at or below the minimum wage, with limited benefits, and an array of government subsidies to induce employers to prefer them to low-wage workers. The likely effect is to drive down wages at the lower end, with indirect effects elsewhere. A related device is the increasing use of prison labour in the vastly expanding system of social control. Thus Boeing, which monopolizes US civilian aircraft production (thanks to massive state subsidy for sixty years), not only transfers production facilities to China, but also to prisons a few miles from its Seattle offices, one of many examples (Wright 1997). Prison labour offers many advantages. It is disciplined, publicly subsidized, deprived of benefits, and 'flexible' – available when needed, left to government support when not.

Reliance on prison labour also draws from a rich tradition. The rapid industrial development in the southeastern region a century ago was based heavily on black convict labour, leased to the highest bidder. These measures reconstituted much of the basic structure of the plantation system after the abolition of slavery, but now for industrial development. The practices continued until the 1920s, until the Second World War in Mississippi. Southern industrialists pointed out that convict labour is 'more reliable and productive than free labour' and overcomes the problem of labour turn-over and instability. It also 'remove[s] all danger and cost of strikes', a serious problem at the time, resolved by state violence that virtually destroyed the labour movement. Convict labour also lowers wages for 'free labour', much as in the case of 'welfare reform'. The US Bureau of Labour reported that 'mine owners [in Alabama] say they could not work at a profit without the lowering effect in wages of convict-labor competition' (Lichtenstein 1994).

The resurgence of these mechanisms is quite natural as the superfluous population is driven to prisons on an unprecedented scale.

The attack on Article 23 is not limited to the USA. The International Confederation of Free Trade Unions reports that 'unions are being repressed across the world in more countries than ever before', while '[P]overty and inequality have increased in the developing countries, which globalization has drawn into a downward spiral of ever-lower labour standards to attract investment and meet the demands of enterprises seeking a fast profit', as governments 'bow to pressure from the financial markets rather than from their own electorates', in accord with the 'Washington consensus' (Taylor, *FT*, 13 June 1997). These are not the consequences of 'economic laws' or what 'the free market has decided, in its infinite but mysterious wisdom' (Cassidy, *NY*, 16 October 1995), as commonly alleged. Rather, they are the results of deliberate policy choices under really existing free-market doctrine, undertaken during a period of 'capital's clear subjugation of labor', in the words of the business press (Liscio, *Barron's*, 15 April 1996).

Contempt for the socio-economic provisions of the Declaration is so deeply engrained that no departure from objectivity is sensed when a front-page story lauds Britain's incoming Labour government for shifting the tax burden from 'large businesses to working people and the middle classes', steps that 'set Britain further apart from countries like Germany and France that are still struggling with pugnacious unions, restrictive investment climates, and expensive welfare benefits' (Ibrahim, *NYT*, 3 July 1997). Industrial countries never struggle with huge profits, starving children, or rapid increase in chief executive officer (CEO) pay (under Thatcher, double that of second-place USA) (Mishel and Bernstein 1994); a reasonable stand, under the 'general tacit agreement' that the 'country' equals 'large businesses', along with doctrinal conventions about the health of the economy – the latter a technical concept, only weakly correlated with the health of the population (economic, social or even medical).

The ability to nullify unwanted human rights guaranteed by the Declaration should be considerably enhanced by the Multilateral Agreement on Investment (MAI) that is now being forged by the Organization for Economic Cooperation and Development (OECD). If the plans outlined in draft texts are implemented, the world should be 'locked into' treaty arrangements that provide still more powerful weapons to undermine social policies and to restrict the arena of democratic politics, leaving policy decisions largely in the hands of private tyrannies that have ample means of market interference as well.[18] The efforts may be blocked at the World Trade Organization (WTO) because of protests of 'developing countries' that are not eager to become wholly-owned subsidiaries of great foreign enterprises. But the OECD version may fare better, to be presented to the rest of the world as a *fait accompli*, with the obvious consequences. Apart from Canada, all of this proceeds in a 'veil of secrecy', in the words of Sir Anthony Mason, former Chief Justice of the Australian High Court, condemning his government's decision to remove from public scrutiny the negotiations over 'an agreement which could have a great impact on Australia if we ratify it (*The Age* (Melbourne), 4 March 1998).[19] The business world was intimately involved from the start, but Congress and the public were kept in the dark; wisely, in the light of public attitudes towards such arrangements, well understood by political and media leaders and 'opinion makers'.

Washington's rejection of the economic, social and cultural rights guaranteed by the Declaration does receive occasional mention (Riding, *NYT*, 26 June 1993; Stephens, *NYT*, 28 April 1993), but the issue is generally ignored in the torrent of self-praise, and if raised, elicits mostly incomprehension.

To take some typical examples, *Times* correspondent Barbara Crossette reports that 'The world held a human rights conference in Vienna in 1993 and dared to enshrine universal concepts', but progress was blocked by 'panicked nations of the Third World'. American diplomats are 'frustrated at the unwillingness of many countries to take tough public stands on human rights', even though '[d]iplomats say it is now easier to deal objectively with human rights abusers, case by case', now that the cold war is over and 'developing nations, with support from the Soviet bloc', no longer 'routinely pass resolutions condemning the United States, the West in general or targets like Israel and apartheid South Africa'. Nonetheless, progress is difficult, 'with a lot of people paying lip service to the whole concept of human rights in the Charter, in the Universal Declaration and all that', but no more, UN Ambassador Madeleine Albright (now Secretary of State) observed (Crossette, *NYT*, 28 April 1996). On Human Rights day, *Times* editors condemned the Asian countries that reject the Declaration and call instead for 'addressing the more basic needs for people for food and shelter, medical care and schooling' – in accord with the Declaration (*NYT*, 10 December 1995, editorial).

The reasoning is straightforward. The USA rejects these principles of the Declaration, so they are inoperative. By calling for such rights the Asian countries are therefore rejecting the Declaration.

Puzzling over the contention that 'human rights extend to food and shelter', Seth Faison reviews a 'perennial sticking point in United States–China diplomacy, highlighting the contrast between the American emphasis on individual freedom and the Chinese insistence that the common good transcends personal rights'. China calls for a right to 'food, clothing, shelter, education, the right to work, rest, and reasonable payment', and criticizes the USA for not upholding these rights – which are affirmed in the Declaration, and are not a matter of 'the common good' but are 'personal rights' that the USA rejects.

Again, the reasoning is straightforward enough, once the guiding ideas are internalized (Faison, *NYT*, 5 March 1997).

## US sanctions for human rights abuses

As an outgrowth of the popular movements of the 1960s, Congress imposed human rights conditions on military aid and trade privileges, compelling the White House to find various modes of evasion. These became farcical during the Reagan years, with regular solemn pronouncements about the 'improvements' in the behaviour of client murderers and torturers that elicited much derision from human rights organizations, but no policy change. The most extreme examples, hardly worth discussing, involved US clients in Central America. There are other less egregious cases, beginning with the top recipient of US Aid (Israel) and running down the list. The leading human rights organizations have regularly condemned Israel's 'systematic torture and ill-treatment of Palestinians under interrogation' (Human Rights Watch 1994), along with apparent extrajudicial execution; legalization of torture; imprisonment without charge, for as long as nine years for some of those kidnapped in Lebanon, now declared 'legal' by the high courts as a 'card to play' for hostage exchange (*Ha'aretz*, 5 March 1998),[20] and other abuses. US aid to Israel is therefore illegal under US law, as HRW (Human Rights Watch) and AI (Amnesty International) have insistently pointed out (as is aid to Egypt, Turkey, Colombia and other high-ranking recipients) (AI 1996). In the most recent of its annual reports on US military aid and human rights, AI observes – once again – that 'Throughout the world, on any given day, a man, woman or child is likely to be displaced, tortured, killed or 'disappeared', at the hands of governments or armed political groups. More often than not, the United States shares the blame, a practice that 'makes a mockery of [congressional legislation] linking the granting of US security assistance to a country's human rights record' (*ibid.*).

Such contentions elicit no interest or response in view of the 'general tacit agreement' that laws are binding only when power interests so dictate.

The US also resorts regularly to sanctions, allegedly to punish human rights violations and for 'national security' reasons. Of 116 cases of sanctions used since the Second World War, 80 per cent were initiated by the USA alone, measures that have often received international condemnation, particularly those against Cuba since 1961, which are by far the harshest (Sommers, *CSM*, 3 August 1993; Devin and Fausey 1995). The popular and congressional human rights programmes from the early 1970s also sometimes called for sanctions against severe human rights violators; South Africa was the primary target outside of the Soviet sphere. The pressures, which were worldwide, had an impact. In 1976, the UN General Assembly called on the IMF to 'refrain forthwith from extending credits to South Africa'. The next day, at US/UK initiative, South Africa was granted more IMF funding than all of the rest of black Africa, in fact more than any country in the world apart from Britain and Mexico. The incoming Carter Administration attempted (in vain) to block congressional efforts to impose human rights conditions on IMF funding to South Africa (claiming that it opposed 'non-economic factors', which it introduced under fraudulent pretexts to block loans to Vietnam) (*Inquiry*, 17 April 1978). After much delay and evasion, sanctions were finally imposed in 1985 and (over Reagan's veto) in 1986, but the Administration 'created glaring loopholes' that permitted US exports to increase by 40 per cent between 1985 and 1988 while US imports increased 14 per cent in 1988 after an initial decline. 'The major economic impact was reduced investment capital and fewer foreign firms' (McDougall and Knight 1990; Garfield *et al.* 1995).

The role of sanctions is perhaps most dramatically illustrated in the case of the voice of the 'dirty dozen', Indonesia. After the failure of a large-scale

CIA (Central Intelligence Agency) operation to foment a rebellion in 1958, the USA turned to other methods of overthrowing the Sukarno government. Aid was cut off, apart from military aid and training. That is standard operating procedure for instigating a military *coup*, which took place in 1965, with mounting US assistance as the new Suharto regime slaughtered perhaps half a million or more people in a few months, mostly landless peasants. There was no condemnation on the floor of Congress, and no aid to the victims from any major US relief agency. On the contrary, the slaughter (which the CIA compared to those of Stalin, Hitler and Mao) aroused undisguised euphoria in a very revealing episode, best forgotten (Chomsky 1993, ch. 5). The World Bank quickly made Indonesia its third largest borrower. The USA and other Western governments and corporations followed along.

There was no thought of sanctions as the new government proceeded to compile one of the worst human rights records in the world, or in the course of its murderous aggression in East Timor, which, incidentally, has somehow not entered the growing literature on 'humanitarian intervention' – rightly, because there is no need for intervention to terminate the decisive diplomatic and military contribution of the USA and its allies. Congress did however ban US military training after the Dili massacre in 1991. The aftermath followed the familiar pattern. Delicately selecting the anniversary of the Indonesian invasion, Clinton's State Department announced that 'Congress's action did not ban Indonesia's purchase of training with its own funds', so it can proceed despite the ban, with Washington perhaps paying from some other pocket. The announcement received scant notice (Reuters, *NYT*, 23 June 1993). Under the usual 'veil of secrecy' Congress expressed its 'outrage', reiterating that 'it was and is the intent of Congress to prohibit US military training for Indonesia' (House Appropriations Committee): 'we don't want employees of the US Government training Indonesians', a staff member reiterated forcefully, but without effect (Wu, *FEER*, 30 June 1994).[21] Rather than impose sanctions, or even limit military aid, the US, UK, and other powers have sought to enrich themselves by participating in Indonesia's crimes.

Indonesian terror and aggression continue unhampered, along with harsh repression of labour in a country with wages half those of China. With the support of Senate Democrats, Clinton was able to block labour and other human rights conditions on aid to Indonesia. Announcing the suspension of review of Indonesian labour practices, Trade Representative Mickey Kantor commended Indonesia for 'bringing its labour law and practice into closer conformity with international standards', a witticism that is in particularly poor taste (*Economist*, 2 April 1994; *Counterpunch*, 15 February and 15 March 1994).

Also revealing is the record of sanctions against Haiti after the military *coup* of September 1991 that overthrew its first democratically elected government after a seven-month in office. The USA had reacted to President Aristide's election with alarm, having confidently expected the victory of its own candidate, World Bank official Mark Bazin, who received 14 per cent of the vote. Washington's reaction was to shift aid to anti-Aristide elements, and as noted, to honour asylum claims for the first time, restoring the norm after the military junta let loose a reign of terror, killing thousands. The Organization of American States (OAS) declared an embargo, which the Bush Administration quickly undermined by exempting US firms – 'fine tuning' the sanctions, the press explained, in its 'latest move' to find 'more effective ways to hasten the collapse of what the Administration calls an illegal Government in Haiti' (Crossette, *NYT*, 5 February 1992). US trade with Haiti remained high in 1992, increasing by almost half as Clinton extended the violations of the embargo, including purchases by the US government, which maintained close connections with the torturers and killers; just how close we do not know, since the Clinton Administration refuses to turn over to Haiti 160,000 pages of documents seized by US military forces – 'to avoid embarrassing revelations' about US government involvement with the terrorist regime, according to Human Rights Watch (Roth, *NYT*, 12 April 1997 (letter); Chomsky 1996). President Aristide was allowed to return after the popular organizations which swept him to power were subjected to three years of terror, and after he had pledged to adopt the extreme neoliberal programme of Washington's defeated candidate.

Officials of the US Justice Department revealed that the Bush and Clinton administrations had rendered the embargo virtually meaningless by authorizing illegal shipments of oil to the military junta and its wealthy supporters, informing Texaco Oil Company that it would not be penalized for violating the presidential directive of October 1991 banning such shipments. The information, prominently released the day before US troops landed to 'restore democracy' in 1994, had yet to reach the general public, and is an unlikely candidate for the historical record (Chomsky 1994, citing Solomon). These were among the many devices adopted to ensure that the popular forces that brought Aristide to power would have little voice in any future 'democracy'. The Clinton Administration advertises this as a grand exercise in 'restoring democracy', the prize example of the Clinton doctrine[22] – to general applause, apart from those who see us as sacrificing too much in the cause of 'global meliorism'. None of this should surprise people who have failed to immunize themselves from the inconvenient facts.

The operative significance of sanctions is articulated honestly by the *Wall Street Journal*, reporting the call for economic sanctions against Nigeria. 'Most agree, Nigeria sanctions won't fly' the headline reads: 'Unlike in South Africa, embargo could hurt West,' (Kamm and Greenberger 1995). In brief, the commitment to human rights is instrumental. Where some interest is served, they are important, even grand ideals; otherwise the pragmatic criterion prevails. That too should come as no surprise. States are not moral agents; people are, and can impose moral standards on powerful institutions. If they do not, the fine words will remain weapons; furthermore, lethal weapons.

US economic warfare against Cuba for thirty-five years is a striking illustration. The unilateral US embargo against Cuba, the longest in history, is also unique in barring food and medicine. When the collapse of the USSR removed the traditional security pretext and eliminated aid from the Soviet bloc, the US responded by making the embargo far harsher, under new pretexts that would have made Orwell wince: the 1992 Cuban Democracy Act, initiated by liberal Democrats, and strongly backed by President Clinton at the same time he was undermining the sanctions against the mass murderers in Haiti. A year-long investigation by the American Association of World Health found that this escalation of US economic warfare had taken a 'tragic human toll', causing 'serious nutritional deficits' and 'a devastating outbreak of neuropathy numbering in the tens of thousands'. It also brought about a sharp reduction in medicines, medical supplies and medical information, leaving children to suffer 'in excruciating pain' because of lack of medicines. The embargo reversed Cuba's progress in bringing water services to the population and undermined its advanced biotechnology industry, among other consequences. These effects became far worse after the imposition of the Cuban Democracy Act, which cut back licensed sales and donations of food and medical supplies by 90 per cent within a year. A 'humanitarian catastrophe has been averted only because the Cuban government has maintained' a health system that 'is uniformly considered the preeminent model in the Third World' (Washington Association for World Health 1997).

These do not count as human rights violations; rather, the public version is that the goal of the sanctions is to overcome Cuba's human rights violations.

The embargo has repeatedly been condemned by the United Nations. The Inter-American Commission on Human rights of the OAS condemned US restrictions on shipments of food and medicine to Cuba as a violation of international law. Recent extensions of the embargo (the Helms–Burton Act) were unanimously condemned by the OAS. In August 1996, its judicial body ruled unanimously that the Act violated international law.

The Clinton Administration's response is that shipments of medicine are not literally barred, only prevented by conditions so onerous and threatening that even the largest corporations are unwilling to face the prospects (huge financial penalties and imprisonment for what Washington determines to be violations of 'proper distribution', banning of ships and aircraft, mobilization of media campaigns, etc.). And while food shipments are indeed barred, the Administration argues that there are 'ample suppliers' elsewhere (at far higher cost), so that the direct violation of international law is not a violation. Supply of medicines to Cuba would be 'detrimental to US foreign policy interests', the Administration declared. When the European Union complained to the WTO that the Helms–Burton Act, with its wide-ranging punishment of third parties, violates the WTO agreements, the Clinton Administration rejected WTO jurisdiction, as its predecessors had done when the World Court addressed Nicaragua's complaint about US international terrorism and illegal economic warfare (upheld by the Court, irrelevantly). In a reaction that surpasses cynicism, Clinton condemned Cuba for ingratitude 'in return for the Cuban Democracy Act', a forthcoming gesture to improve US–Cuba relations (Garfield *et al.* 1995; Smith, *ITT*, 9 December 1996; Kirkpatrick, *Lancet*, 258:9040, 10 November 1996 and *CU*, winter, 1997; Marcus, *BG*, 12 April 1997; Morici, *CH*, February 1997; Cameron, *FF*, winter/spring, 1996).

The official stand of the Clinton Administration is that Cuba is a national security threat to the US, so that the WTO is an improper forum: 'bipartisan policy since the early 1960s (is) based on the notion that we have a hostile and unfriendly regime 90 miles from our border, and that anything done to strengthen that regime will only encourage the regime to not only continue its hostility but, through much of its tenure, to try to destabilize large parts of Latin America' (Morley and McGillion 1997). That stand was criticized by historian Arther Schlesinger, writing 'as one involved in the Kennedy Administration's Cuban policy'. The Clinton Administration, he maintained, had misunderstood the reasons for the sanctions. The Kennedy Administrations's concern had been Cuba's 'troublemaking in the hemisphere' and 'the Soviet connection', but these are now behind us, so the policies are anachronism (letter, *NYT*, 26 February 1997).

In secret, Schlesinger had explained the meaning of the phrase 'trouble-making in the hemisphere' – in Clintonite terms, trying to 'destabilize' Latin America. Reporting to incoming President Kennedy on the conclusions of the Latin American Mission in early 1963, he described the Cuban threat as 'the spread of the Castro idea of taking matters into one's own hands', a serious problem, he added, when '[t]he poor and underprivileged, stimulated by the example of the Cuban revolution, are now demanding opportunities for a decent living'. Schlesinger also explained the threat of the 'Soviet connection': 'Meanwhile, the Soviet Union hovers in the wings, flourishing large development loans and presenting itself as the model for achieving modernization in a single generation' (*Foreign Relations of the United States*, 1961–63).

The USA officially recognizes that 'deliberate impeding of the delivery of food and medical supplies' to civilian populations constitutes 'violations of international humanitarian law', and 'reaffirms that those who commit or order the commission of such acts will be held individually responsible in respect of such acts'.[23] The reference is to Bosnia–Hercegovina. The President of the United States is plainly 'individually responsible' for such 'violations of international humanitarian law'. Or would be, were it not for the 'general tacit agreements' about selective enforcement, which reign with such absolute power among Western relativists that the simple facts are virtually unmentionable.

Unlike such crimes as these, the Administration's regular contortions on human rights in China are a topic of debate. It is worth noting, however, that many critical issues are scarcely even raised: crucially, the horrifying conditions of working people, with hundreds, mostly women, burned to death locked into factories, over 18,000 deaths from industrial accidents in 1995 according to Chinese government figures, and other gross violations of international conventions (Smith 1997). China's labour practices have been condemned, but narrowly: the use of prison labour for exports to the USA. At the peak of the US–China confrontation over human rights, front-page stories reported that Washington's human rights campaign had met with some success: China had 'agreed to a demand to allow more visits by American customs inspectors to Chinese prison factories to make sure they are not producing goods for export to the United States', and also accepted US demands for 'liberalization' and laws that are 'critical elements of a market economy', all welcome steps towards a 'virtuous circle' (Friedman, *NYT*, 21 and 23 January 1993).

The conditions of 'free labour' do not arise in this context. They are, however, causing other problems: 'Chinese officials and analysts' say that the doubling of industrial deaths in 1992 and 'abysmal working conditions', 'combined with long hours, inadequate pay, and even physical beatings, are stirring unprecedented labor unrest among China's booming foreign joint ventures'. These 'tensions reveal the great gap between competitive foreign capitalists lured by cheap Chinese labor and workers weaned on socialist job security and the safety net of cradle-to-grave benefits'. Workers do not yet understand that as they enter the free world, they are to be 'beaten for producing poor quality goods, fired for dozing on the job during long work hours' and other such misdeeds, and locked into their factories to be burned to death. But apparently the West understands, so China is not called into account for violations of labor rights; only for exporting prison products to the United States.

The distinction is easy to explain. Prison factories are state-owned industry, and exports to the USA interfere with profits, unlike beating and murder of working people and other means to improve the balance sheet. The operative principles are clarified by the fact that the rules allow the United States to export prison goods. As China was submitting to USA discipline on export of prison-made goods to the US, California and Oregon were exporting prison-made clothing to Asia, including speciality jeans, shirts, and a line of shorts quaintly called 'Prison Blues'. The prisoners earn far less than the minimum wage, and work under 'slave labor' conditions, prison rights activists allege. But their production does not interfere with the rights that count (in fact, enhances them in many ways, as noted). So it passes unnoticed (Tefft, *CSM*, 22 December 1993; Erlich, *CSJ*, 9 February 1994; Wright 1997).

## Law and legitimacy

As the most powerful state, the USA makes its own laws, using force and conducting economic warfare at will. It also threatens sanctions against countries that do not abide by its conveniently flexible notions of 'free trade'. Washington has employed such threats with great effectiveness (and GATT approval) to force open Asian markets for US tobacco exports and advertising, aimed primarily at the growing markets of women and children. The US Agriculture Department has provided grants to tobacco firms to promote smoking overseas. Asian countries have attempted to conduct educational anti-smoking campaigns, but they are overwhelmed by the miracles of the market, reinforced by US state power through the sanctions threat. Philip Morris, with an advertising and promotion budget of close to nine billion dollars in 1992, became China's largest advertiser. The effect of Reaganite sanction threats was to increase advertising and promotion of cigarette smoking (particularly of US brands) quite sharply in Japan, Taiwan, and South Korea, along with the use of these lethal substances. In South Korea, for example, the rate of growth in smoking more than tripled when markets for US lethal drugs were opened in 1988. The Bush Administration extended the threats to Thailand, at exactly the same time that the 'war on drugs' was declared; the media were kind enough to overlook the coincidence, even suppressing the outraged denunciations by the very conservative Surgeon-General, Everett Koop. Oxford University epidemiologist Richard Peto estimates that among Chinese children under twenty today, fifty million will die of cigarette-related diseases, an achievement that ranks high even by twentieth-century standards (Shenon, *NYT*, 15 May 1994; Tefft and Rahman, *CSM*, 25 May 1994; Chaloupka and Laixuthai 1996; Chomsky 1991, especially chs 4–5).

While state power energetically promotes the substance abuse in the interests of agribusiness, it adopts highly selective measures in other cases. In the context of the war against drugs, the USA has played an active role in the vast atrocities conducted by the security forces and their paramilitary associates in Colombia, the leading human rights violator in Latin America, and the leading recipient of US aid and training, increasing under Clinton, consistent with traditional practice, noted earlier. The war against drugs is 'a myth', Amnesty International reports, agreeing with other investigators. Security forces work closely with narco-traffickers and landlords while target-ing the usual victims, including community leaders, human rights and health workers, union activists, students, the political opposition, but primarily peasants, in a country where protest has been criminalized. Military support for the killers is rising to 'a record level', HRW reports, up 50 per cent over the 1996 high. AI reports that 'almost every Colombian military unit that Amnesty implicated in murdering civilians two years ago was doing so with US-supplied weapons', which they continue to receive along with training (Chomsky 1996, ch. 1; Giraldo 1996; HRW 1996; AI 1997).

The Universal Declaration calls on all states to promote the rights and freedoms proclaimed and to act 'to secure their universal and effective recognition and observance' by various means, including ratification of treaties and enabling legislation. There are several such international covenants, respected in much the manner of the Declaration. The Convention on the Rights of the Child, adopted by the UN in December 1989, has been ratified 'by all countries except Somalia, and the United States'. After long delay, the US did endorse the International Covenant on Civil and Political Rights (ICCPR), 'the leading treaty for the protection' of the subcategory of rights that the West claims to uphold, Human Rights Watch and the American Civil Liberties Union (ACLU) observe in their report on the continued US non-compliance with its provisions. The Bush Administration ensured that the treaty would be inoperative, first, 'through a series of reservations, declarations and understandings' to eliminate provisions that might expand rights, and second, by declaring the US in full compliance with the remaining provisions. The treaty is 'non self-executing' and accompanied by no enabling legislation, so it cannot be invoked in US courts. Ratification was 'an empty act for Americans', the HRW/ACLU report concludes (HRW 1993).

The exceptions are crucial, because the USA violates the treaty 'in important respects', the report observes. To cite one example, the USA entered a specific reservation to Article 7 of the ICCPR, which states that 'No one shall be subjected to torture or to cruel, inhuman, or degrading treatment or punishment'. The reason is that conditions in US prisons violate these provisions as generally understood, just as they seriously violate those of Article 10 on humane treatment of prisoners and on the right to 'reformation and social rehabilitation' which the USA flatly rejects. Another US reservation concerns the death penalty, which is not only employed far more freely than the norm but also 'applied in a manner that is radically discriminatory', the HRW/ACLU report concludes, as have other studies. Furthermore, 'more juvenile offenders sit on death row in the United States than in any other country in the world', HRW reports (UNICEF 1994; HRW 1995). A UN Human Rights inquiry found the USA to be in violation of the Covenant for execution of juveniles (who committed the crimes before they were eighteen years old): the USA is joined in this practice only by Iran, Pakistan, Saudi Arabia and Yemen. Executions are rare in the industrial democracies, declining around the world, and rising in the USA, even among juveniles, the mentally impaired and women, the UN report observes (*LAT*, 4 April 1998).

The USA accepted the UN Convention Against Torture and Other Forms of Cruel, Inhuman or Degrading Treatment or Punishment, but the Senate imposed restrictions, in part to protect a Supreme Court ruling allowing corporal punishment in schools (Wronka 1992).

HRW also regards 'disproportionate' and 'cruelly excessive' sentencing procedures as a violation of Article 5 of the Declaration, which proscribes 'cruel, inhuman or degrading treatment or punishment'. The specific reference is to laws that treat 'possession of an ounce of cocaine or a $20 "street sale" [as] a more dangerous or serious offence than the rape of a ten-year old, the burning of a building occupied by people or the killing of another human being while intending to cause him serious injury' (quoting a federal judge). From the onset of Reaganite 'neoliberalism', the rate of incarceration, which had been fairly stable through the post-war period, has skyrocketed, almost tripling during the Reagan years and continuing the sharp rise since, long ago leaving other industrial societies far behind. Eighty-four per cent of the increase of admissions is for non-violent offenders, mostly drug related (including possession). Drug offenders constituted 22 per cent of admissions in federal prisons in 1980, 42 per cent in 1990, 58 per cent in 1992. The USA apparently leads the world in imprisoning its population (perhaps sharing the distinction with Russia and China, where data are uncertain). By the end of 1996, the prison population had reached a record 1.2 million, an increase of 5 per cent over the preceding year, with the federal prison system 25 per cent over capacity and state prisons almost the same (HRW 1997a; Donziger 1996; *NYT*, 23 June 1997).

By 1998, close to 1.7 million were in federal and state prisons, or local jails. Average sentences for murder and other violent crimes have decreased markedly, while those for drug offences have shot up, targeting primarily African-Americans and creating what two criminologists call 'the *new American apartheid*' (Sheldon and Brown, forthcoming).

US crime rates, while high, are not out of the range of industrial societies, apart from homicides with guns, a reflection of US gun laws. Fear of crime itself, however, is very high and increasing, in large part a 'product of a variety of factors that have little or nothing to do with crime itself' the National Criminal Justice Commission concludes (as do other studies). The factors include media practices and 'the role of government and private industry in stroking citizen fear'. The focus is very specific: for example, drug users in the ghetto but not criminals in executive suites, though the Justice Department estimates the cost of corporate crime as seven to twenty-five times as high as street crime. Work-related deaths are six times as high as homicides, and pollution also takes a far higher toll than homicide (Donziger 1996).

Expert studies have regularly concluded that 'there is no direct relation between the level of crime and the number of imprisonments' (European Council Commission). Many criminologists have pointed out further that while 'crime control' has limited relation to crime, it has a great deal to do with control of the 'dangerous classes'; today, those cast aside by the socio-economic model designed to globalize the sharply two-tiered structural model of Third World societies. As noted at once the latest 'war on drugs' timed to target mostly black males; trend lines on substance use suffice to demonstrate this. By adopting these measures, Senator Daniel Patrick Moynihan observed, 'we are choosing to have an intense crime problem concentrated among minorities', 'The war's planners knew exactly what they were doing', criminologist Michael Tonry comments, spelling out the details, including the racist procedures that run through the system from arrest to sentencing, in part attributable to the close race–class correlation, but not completely (Tonry 1995; Christie 1993; Bonnie and Whitebread 1974).

As widely recognized, the 'war on drugs' has no significant effect on the use of drugs or street price, and is far less effective than educational and remedial programmes. But it does not follow that it serves no purpose. It is a counterpart to the 'social cleansing' – the removal or elimination of 'disposable people' – conducted by the state terrorist forces in Colombia and other terror states. It also frightens the rest of the population, the standard device to induce obedience. Such policies make good sense as part of a programme that has radically concentrated wealth while for the majority of the population, living conditions and income stagnate or decline. It is, correspondingly, natural for Congress to require that sentencing guidelines and policy reject as 'inappropriate' any consideration of such factors as poverty and deprivation, social ties, etc. These requirements are precisely counter to European crime policy, criminologist Nils Christie observes, but sensible on the assumption that 'under the rhetoric of equality' Congress envisions the criminal process as a vast engine of social control (Christie 1993, quoting former Chief Judge Bazelon).

The vast scale of the expanding 'crime control industry' has attracted the attention of finance and industry, who welcome it as another form of state intervention in the economy, a Keynesian stimulus that may soon approach the Pentagon system in scale, some estimate. 'Businesses cash in', *Wall Street Journal* reports, including the construction industry, law firms, the booming private prison complex, and the 'loftiest manes in finance' such as Goldman Sachs, Prudential and others, 'competing to underwrite prison construction with private, tax-exempt bonds'. Also standing in line is the 'defense estab-lishment ... scenting a new line of business' in high-tech surveillance and control systems of a sort that Big Brother would have admired. The industry also offers new opportunities for corporate use of prison labour, as discussed earlier (Thomas, *WSJ*, 12 May 1994; Donziger 1996; Sheldon 1997).

Other international covenants submitted to Congress have also been restricted as 'non-self-executing', meaning that they are of largely symbolic significance. The fact that covenants, if even ratified, are declared as non-enforceable is US courts has been a 'major concern' of the UN Human Rights Committee, along with human rights organizations. The Committee also expressed concern that 'poverty and lack of access to education adversely affect persons belonging to these groups in their ability to enjoy rights under the ICCPR on the basis of equality', even for that subcategory of the Universal Declaration the US professes to uphold. And while (rightly) praising the US commitment to freedom of speech, the Committee also questioned Washington's announced principle that 'money is a form of speech', as the courts had upheld in recent years, with wide-ranging effects on the electoral system (Wronka 1992).

The USA is a world leader in defence of freedom of speech, perhaps uniquely so since the 1960s (Kalven 1988). With regard to civil–political rights, the US record at home ranks quite well by comparative standards, though a serious evaluation would have to take into account the capacity to uphold such rights, and also the 'accelerated erosion of basic due process and human rights protection in the United States' as 'US authorities at federal and state levels undermined the rights of vulnerable groups, making the year [1996] a disturbing one for human rights', with the President not only failing to 'preserve rights under attack' but sometimes taking 'the lead in eliminating human rights protections' (HRW 1996). The social and economic provisions of the Declaration and other conventions are operative only insofar as popular struggle over many years has given them substance. The earlier record within the national territory is shameful, and the human rights record abroad is a scandal. The charge of relativism levelled against others, while fully accurate, reeks of hypocrisy.

But the realities are for the most part 'kept dark, without any need for any official ban'.

## Notes

### Abbreviations of newspapers, journals and magazines used in chapter 2

| | |
|---|---|
| BG | *Boston Globe* |
| CH | *Current History* |
| CSM | *Christian Science Monitor* |
| CU | *Cuba Update* |
| FEER | *Far Eastern Economic Review* |
| FF | *The Fletcher Forum* |
| FT | *Financial Times* |
| ITT | *In These Times* |
| LAT | *Los Angeles Times* |

MEJN        *Middle East Justice Network*
MEI         *Middle East International*
NY          *New Yorker*
NYT         *New York Times*
TLS         *Times Literary Supplement*
WSJ         *Wall Street Journal*

1  Parts of this article have appeared in *Index on Censorship* July/August 1994.
2  Wronka (1992), citing the judgment in *Filartiga v Peña* (1980). For additional cases
   see his 'Human rights', in Edwards (1995), 1,405–18.
3  The Congressional Research Service (CRS) reported that the USA was responsible
   for 57 per cent of arms sales to the Third World in 1992 (*FT*, 23 July 1993); the
   CRS reports further that among the eleven leading arms suppliers to the 'developing
   countries' from 1989 to 1996, the USA provided over 45 per cent of the arms flow
   and Britain 26 per cent (Grummett 1997; Mann, *NYT* 1997).
4  On British arms sales to Indonesia, which began in 1978 as the slaughter in East
   Timor was peaking, increasing sharply under Thatcher as atrocities continued (in
   Indonesia as well), see Taylor 1991 and Pilger 1992. Thatcherite policy was explained
   by 'defence procurement minister' Alan Clark: 'My responsibility is to my own people.
   I don't really fill my mind much with what one set of foreigners is doing to another'
   (Quoted in Pilger 1992). By 1998, Britain had become the leading supplier of arms
   to Indonesia, not for defence, and over the strong protests of Amnesty International,
   Indonesian dissidents, and Timorese victims. Arms sales are reported to make up a
   least a fifth of Britain's exports to Indonesia (estimated at £1 billion), led by British
   Aerospace (see Gregory (1994)).
5  International Court of Justice 1986, 27 June 1986, General List 70.
6  Panama, *Central America Report (Guatemala)*, 4 February 1994. The US also vetoed
   (with Britain and France) a Security Council resolution (23 December 1989) condemning the invasion and voted against a General Assembly resolution demanding
   the withdrawal of the 'US armed invasion forces from Panama' and calling the
   invasion a 'flagrant violation of international law and of the independence, sovereignty and territorial integrity of states' (see Cronin, *Irish Times*, 11 August 1990).
   The Church estimates that over 650 victims of the intensive bombing of the poor
   El Chorrillo district of Panama City died in hospitals, along with unknown numbers
   of others. US-installed President Endara went on a hunger strike in March 1990 in
   protest against the failure to deliver promised economic aid. Inhabitants of El Chorrillo are suing the US for damages before the Inter-American Human Rights Court.
   *Central America Report*, 19 March 1998.
7  For a review of recently declassified and other evidence, and the interpretive reaction
   throughout, see Chomsky 1993a and 1996b.
8  Resolution of the UN General Assembly condemning 'Terrorism Wherever and by
   Whoever Committed', passed 153 to 2 (US and Israel opposed, Honduras alone
   abstaining); UN Press release GA/7603, 7 December 1987. For a discussion, see
   Chomsky (1989). For more on these matters, see Chomsky 1986 and George 1991.
9  On the bloody Carter/Christopher record in El Salvador, see Chomsky 1992; Herman
   1992; Chomsky 1985.
10  For some scattered exceptions, Riding 1993; Stephens 1993.
11  For discussion, keeping to the special case of protectionism, see Bairoch (1993).
    Among many other sources, see Clairmont (1996 and 1996). On the general picture,
    see Chomsky (1996), ch. 2. On the historic role of the state system (often military)
    in economic development in the USA, see Rosenberg (1982); Tirman (1984); Nelson

(1993). On the growth of the First/Third World gap, see UNDP (1992 and 1994). For discussion Chomsky (1996); Toussaint and Drucker (1995). On the situation internal to the US, see particularly Berstein and Schmitt (1997).

12 Women's International League for Peace and Freedom (Geneva) and International Institute for Human Rights, Environment and Development (Kathmandu) (1994), *Justice Denied!*, Kathmandu, Karnali Offset Press.

13 On Carter policies, see Chomsky and Herman 1979. On subsequent years, see Americas Watch (1993). On Haitian background, see *inter alia*, Wilentz (1989); Chomsky (1993), ch. 8; Farmer (1994); McFadyen and LaRamée (1995).

14 Statement, UN Commission of Human Rights, on Item 8, 'The Right to Development', 11 February 1991.

15 The second-ranking recipient, Egypt, is granted aid to ensure its adherence to the US–Israel alliance, a core part of the system of control of the oil-producing regions. For similar reasons, Turkey has regularly been among the top aid recipients.

16 Commission on Human Rights, Economic and Social Council (1996), *The Realization of Economic, Social, and Cultural Rights*, e/CN. 4 Sub. 2 1996/13.

17 For background, see Alex Carey, *Taking the Risk Out of Democracy*, Urbana: University of Illinois Press, a collection of pioneering essays on this topic.

18 On the dismantling of the Bretton Woods system (primarily at the US/UK initiative from the 1970s), with it principle of regulation of capital flow in order to block attacks on social policies and stimulate trade, see Helleiner (1994). On modalities of contemporary market interference by state/corporation interactions, see Cowhey and Aronson (1993) and van Tulder (1995).

19 A leaked version of the treaty was placed on the internet and distributed by public interests groups, see OECD (1997). See Nova and Sforza-Roderick 1997; Khor 1997; Eggertson 1997; Green 1997; Monbiot, A charter to let loose the multinationals, the *Guardian*, 13 April 1997. See also Chomsky 1998 for updating and further detail.

20 Amnesty International lists twenty-one Lebanese prisoners in Israeli jails, secretly brought to Israel from Lebanon from 1986 to 1994, most held without charge, the others sentenced in Israeli military courts but kept in prison after serving their sentences.

21 Other forms of chicanery were revealed in 1998: Weiner, *NYT*, 17 March 1998. For fuller detail see Nairn, *Nation*, 30 March 1998.

22 National Security Adviser, Anthony Lake, *NYT*, 26 September 1993 and 23 September 1994. On the measures used to impose on the 'restored democracy' and programmes of Washington's defeated candidate, see Chomsky 1994 and 1996a, ch. 5. For extensive details see, McGowan (1997); Richardson (1997).

23 Resolution proposed to the UN Security Council by the USA and other countries.

## References

Americas Watch (1993), *No Port in a Storm*, NY, Washington, National Coalition for Haitian Refugees, Jesuit Refugee Services/USA, vol. 5:7.

Amnesty International (1994), *Lynching in All but Name*, New York, AI.

Amnesty International (1996), *Human Rights and US Security Assistance*, Washington, AI.

Amnesty International (1997), *Amnesty Action: The Colombia Papers*, published on the internet.

Aronson, J. (1993), *Managing the World Economy: The Consequences of Corporate Alliances*, New York, Council of Foreign Relations Press.

Bairoch, P. (1993), *Economics and World History*, Chicago, University of Chicago Press.

Berstein, J. and J. Schmitt (eds) (1997), *The State of Working America*, Armonk, NY, M. E. Sharp (published biennially).

Bonnie, R. and C. Whitebread (1974), *The Marihuana Conviction*, Charlottesville, University Press of Virginia.

Cameron, J. (1996), The Cuban Democracy Act of 1992: the international implications, *The Fletcher Forum*, Winter/Spring.

Chaloupka, F. and A. Laixuthai (1996), *US Trade Policy and Cigarette Smoking in Asia*, Cambridge MA, National Bureau of Economic Research.

Chomsky, N. (1985), *Turning the Tide*, Boston, South End.

Chomsky, N. (1986), *Pirates and Emperors*, New York, Claremont; Montreal, Black Rose.

Chomsky, N. (1989), *Necessary Illusions*, Boston, South End.

Chomsky, N. (1991), *Deterring Democracy*, London, Verso, Vintage.

Chomsky, N. (1992), *Towards a New Cold War*, New York, Pantheon.

Chomsky, N. (1993), *Year 501*, Boston, South End.

Chomsky, N. (1993a), Hamlet without the prince, *Diplomatic History*, 20:3.

Chomsky, N. (1994), Democracy restored, *Z Magazine*, November.

Chomsky, N. (1996), *World Orders, Old and New*, New York, Columbia University Press.

Chomsky, N. (1996a), *Powers and Prospects*, Boston, South End.

Chomsky, N. (1996b), *Rethinking Camelot*, London, Verso.

Chomsky, N. (1998) Domestic Constituencies, *Z Magazine*, May.

Chomsky, N. and E. Herman (1979), *The Political Economy of Human Rights*, Boston, South End.

Chossudovsky, M. (1997), *The Globalisation of Poverty*, Penang, Third World Network.

Christie, N. (1993), *Crime Control as Industry*, London, Routledge.

Christie, N. (1995), *Malign Neglect: Race, Crime and Punishment in America*, Oxford, Oxford University Press.

Clairmont, F. (1996), *The Rise and Fall of Economic Liberalism*, Penang and Goa, Third World Network.

Cowhey, P. and J. Aronson (1993), *Managing the World Economy: The Consequences of Corporate Alliances*, New York, Council of Foreign Relations Press.

Curtis, M. (1995), *The Ambiguities of Power: British Foreign Policy Since 1945*, London, Zed.

Donziger, S. (ed.) (1996), *The Real War on Crime: Report of the National Criminal Justice Commission*, New York, Harper Collins.

Edwards, G. (1995), *Encyclopedia of Social Work*, Washington, NASW.

Eggertson (1997), Treaty to trim Ottawa's power, *Toronto Globe and Mail*, 3 April.

Farmer, P. (1993), *The Uses of Haiti*, Monroe ME, Common Courage.

Fones-Wolf, E. (1994), *Selling Free Enterprise*, Urbana, University of Illinois Press.

Garfield, R., J. Devin and J. Fausey (1995), The health impact of economic sanctions, *Bulletin Of the New York Academy of Medicine*, 72:2.

George, A. (ed.) (1991), *Western State Terrorism*, London, Polity.

Giraldo, J. S. J. (1996), *Columbia: The Genocidal Democracy*, Monroe, ME, Common Courage.

Green, P. (1997), Global giants; fears of the supranational, *Journal of Commerce* (Canada), 23 April.

Gregory, M. (1994), *World in Action*, Granada production for ITV, 2 and 9 June.

Grimmett, R. (1997), *Conventional Arms Transfers to Developing Nations*, Washington, CRS.

Hartung, W. (1994), *And Weapons for All*, New York, HarperCollins.

Helleiner, E. (1994), *States and the Re-emergence of Global Finance*, London, Cornell University Press.

Herman, E. (1982), *Real Terror Network*, Boston, South End.

Hoerr, J. (1992), *American Prospects*, Summer.

Howard, M. (1985), The bewildered American Raj, *Harper's*, March.

Human Rights Watch (1993), *Human Rights Violations in the United States*, New York, Human Rights Watch/American Civil Liberties Union.

Human Rights Watch (1994), *Torture and Ill-Treatment: Israel's Interrogation of Palestinians from the Occupied Territories*, New York: Human Rights Watch.

Human Rights Watch (1996a), *Columbia's Killer Networks: The Military-Paramilitary Partnership and the United States*, New York, Human Rights Watch.

Human Rights Watch (1997), *Human Rights Watch Report 1996*, New York, Human Rights Watch.

Human Rights Watch (1997a), *Cruel and Usual*, New York, Human Rights Watch.

Human Rights Watch Children's Project (1995), *United States: A World Leader in Executing Juveniles*, New York, Human Rights Watch.

Islam, S. (1989–90), America and the world, *Foreign Affairs*, 69:1.

Kagian, J. (1994), *Middle East Justice Network*, February-March.

Kahin, A. R. and G. McT. Kahin (1995), *Subversion as Foreign Policy*, New York, New Press.

Kalven, H. (1988), *A Worthy Tradition: Freedom of Speech in America*, New York, Harper & Row.

Kamm, T. and R. Greenberger (1995), *Wall Street Journal*, 15 November.

Khor, M. (1997), Trade and investment: fighting over investors' rights at WTO, *Third World Economics*, Penang, 15 February.

Kirkpatrick, A. (1996), *Lancet*, 258:9040, 30 November, reprinted in *Cuba Update* (1997), Winter.

Knight, R. (1990), Sanctions, disincentives and US corporations, in R. Edgar (ed.), *Sanctioning Apartheid*, Trenton NJ, Africa World Press.

Kornbluh, P. (1987), *Nicaragua: The Price of Intervention*, Washington, Institute of Policy Studies.

LaFaber, W. (1983), *Inevitable Revolution*, New York, Norton.

Lawyers Committee for Human Rights (1996), *In the National Interest: 1996 Quadrennial Report on Human Rights and US Foreign Policy*, New York and Washington, Lawyers Committee for Human Rights.

Lichtenstein, A. (1994), Through the rugged gates of the penitentiary, in M. Stokes and R. Halpert (eds), *Race and Class in the American South Since 1980*, Providence, Berg.

Low, P. (1993), *Trading Free*, New York, Twentieth Century Fund.

Mallison, T. and S. (1996), *The Palestine Problems in International Law and World Order*, New York, Longman.

McDougall, G. (1990), Implementation of the Anti-Apartheid Act of 1986, in R. Edgar (ed.), *Sanctioning Apartheid*, Trenton, NJ, Africa World Press.

McFadyen, D. and P. La Ramée (eds) (1995), *Haiti: Dangerous Crossroads*, Boston, South End.

McGowan, L. (1997), *Democracy Undermined, Economic Justice Denied*, Washington, Development Gap.

Mishel, L. and J. Bernstein (1994), *The State of Working America: 1994–95*, Armonk, NY, M. E. Sharpe.

Mishel, L., J. Bernstein, and J. Schmitt (1997), *The State of Working America 1996–1997*, Armonk, NY, M. E. Sharpe.

Morici, P. (1997), The United States, world trade and the Helms–Burton Act, *Current History*, February.

Morley, M. and C. McGillion (1997), *Washington Report on the Hemisphere*, Council of Hemispheric Affairs, 3 June.

Nelson, R. (1993), *National Innovation Systems*, Oxford, Oxford University Press.

Nova, S. and M. Sforza-Roderick (1997), M.I.A. culpa, *Nation*, 13 January.

OECD (1997), *Multilateral Agreement on Investment: Consolidated Texts and Community*, OLIS 9 January, DAFFE/MAI/97, confidential.

Pilger, J. (1992), *Distant Voices*, London, Vantage.

Richardson, L. (1997), *Feeding Dependency, Starving Democracy*, Boston, Grassroots International.

Rock, D. (1987), *Argentina*, Berkeley, University of California Press.

Rosenberg, N. (1982), *Inside the Black Box*, Cambridge, Cambridge University Press.

Saville, J. (1993), *The Politics of Continuity*, London, Verso.

Schlesinger, A. (1961–63), *Foreign Relations of the United States*, vol. 12, Washington, Government Publishing Office.

Schoultz, L. (1981), *Comparative Politics*, January 13:2.

Sheldon, R. (1997), The crime control industry and the management, Western Society of Criminologists Annual Conference, February/March.

Sheldon, R. and W. Brown (forthcoming), *Criminal Justice*, Belmont, Wadsworth.

Smith, M. R. (ed.) (1985), *Military Enterprise and Technological Change*, Cambridge MA, Massachusetts Institute of Technology Press.

Smith R. (1997), Creative destruction: capitalist development and China's environment, *New Left Review*, 222, March/April.

Taylor, J. (1991), *Indonesia's Forgotten War: The Hidden History of East Timor*, London, Zed Books.

Tirman, J. (ed.) (1984), *The Militarization of High Technology*, Cambridge MA, Ballinger.

Tonry, M. (1995), *Malign Neglect: Race, Crime and Punishment in America*, Oxford, Oxford University Press.

Toussaint, E. and P. Drucker (eds) (1995), *IMF/World Bank/WTO, Notebooks for Study and Research 24/25*, Amsterdam, International Institute for Research and Education.

van Tulder, R. (1995), *The Logic of International Restructuring*, London, Routledge.

UNDP (1992), *Human Development Report*, New York, Oxford University Press.

UNDP (1994), *Human Development Report*, New York, Oxford University Press.

UNICEF (1993), *The State of the World's Children*, New York, UN.

UNICEF (1994), *The State of the World's Children*, New York, UN.

UNICEF (1996), *The Progress of Nations 1996*, New York, UNICEF House.

UNICEF (1997), *The State of the World's Children*, Oxford, Oxford University Press.

Wachtel, H. (1990), *The Money Mandarins*, New York, Armonk.

Washington Association for World Health (1997), *Denial of Food and Medicine: The Impact of the US Embargo on Health and Nutrition in Cuba*, Washington, American Association for World Health, Executive Summary.

Weeks, W. E. (1992), *John Quincy Adams and American Global Empire*, Kentucky, Lexington.

Wilentz, A. (1989), *Rainy Season*, New York, Simon and Schuster.

*World Labour Report 1994*, Geneva, ILO Publications.

Wright, P. (1997), Making slave labor fly, *Covert Action Quarterly*, Spring.

Wronka, J. (1995), Human rights postscript, *American Society of International Law: Human Rights Interest Group News Letter*, Fall.

Wronka, J. (1997), Towards building peace/human rights cultures: why is the United States so resistant?, *American Society of International Law: Interest Group of the UN Decade of International Law*, 13.

Wronka, J. (1992), *Human Rights and Social Policy in the 21st Century*, Lanham MD, University Press of America.

# Problems of theory and practice

# 3

# The limits of a rights-based approach to international ethics

*Fiona Robinson*

## Introduction

The influence of the idea of human rights in the twentieth century can hardly be overstated. While its potential use as a political tool for ensuring reasonable and uniform standards of human dignity for all may have been frustrated by obstacles of implementation and enforcement, its imaginative, rhetorical and ideological appeal has grown steadily since 1948. Moreover, in the current climate of globalization, the idea of human rights is gaining more attention than ever before. Today, the idea that we are human beings first, and citizens second – an idea upon which the concept of human rights depends – resonates with increasing strength around the world. Indeed, where globalization is viewed as the triumph of liberal and cosmopolitan values, most evident in the spread of capitalism and of liberal democratic institutions, human rights embodies the 'moral wing' of this world view, valorizing individualism, autonomy and liberty, and comfortably occupying the global moral high ground. Just as John Dunn has observed, 'we are all democrats today', likewise, we are all supporters of international human rights (Dunn 1979, 2). To be otherwise, it seems, would be unthinkable.

From the perspective of moral and political philosophy, the proliferation of 'rights talk' is hardly surprising. Since Grotius and Hobbes, the main question in debates on ethics – outside the Kantian tradition – has become not what responsibilities or duties we have but what rights we have.[1] Duties in the rights tradition are seen to be founded on others' rights to their performance (Baier 1995, 231).

Furthermore, international debates since the Second World War have relied heavily on the discourse of rights, claiming as their authority the grand eighteenth-century claims about the rights of man, including the French *Declaration of the Rights of Man and of Citizen* and Thomas Paine's *The Rights of Man* (O'Neill 1986, 103–4).

However, in spite of the influence of the idea of human rights in philosophy, political rhetoric and everyday language, the role of human rights in international relations has always been rather ambiguous. On the one hand, the philosophy and issues surrounding human rights have been explicitly excluded from the study of international relations. Given that the universalism of human rights is apparently at odds with the most basic principles of international relations – sovereignty, statism, non-intervention – it is not surprising that they have traditionally been viewed as marginal, if not irrelevant, to this field. Moreover, the explicitly normative nature of the idea of human rights has meant that there has been little room for such a 'soft' subject in a discipline dominated by positivist epistemology, and empirical and techno-scientific methodologies.

On the other hand, however, the idea of rights has been, and continues to be, intimately connected with international relations. The dominant 'traditions' of international ethics (Nardin and Mapel 1992), and indeed of international relations theory in general, have, paradoxically, been heavily influenced by precisely those traditions of philosophy and political theory which have given rise to the modern notion of human rights. The values promoted by classical political liberalism and contractarianism – rationality, autonomy, non-interference – are now regarded as defining normative principles of the international system of states. Moreover, through their efforts to reconcile the rights of states with the rights of individuals, it has become possible for theorists to embrace the moral reasoning of rights without forfeiting norms regarding sovereignty and non-intervention, and thus to offer essentially conservative accounts of international ethics which seek to legitimate the *status quo*.[2]

The language of human rights, then, has become the acceptable voice – indeed, virtually the *only* voice – of morality in international relations. This is so much the case that we find it in no way unnatural that, while realists claim to eschew the notion that states are the *locus* of responsible moral action, the output of states and of international organizations are replete with moral claims often expressed in terms of universal rights (Vincent 1992, 257). Thus, in spite of the obvious tension between the universal, cosmopolitan idea of human rights and the particularist idea of sovereign states, we must recognize that the international system of states rests upon a contractual model of weak reciprocity, based on negative rights and correlative obligations, which ensures, for each state, its autonomy, liberty and right to non-interference – a liberal model which looks very much like that upon which the idea of individual rights is constructed. As Vincent explains,

> If states have rights in international law, the bearers of the correlative duties are, in the standard formulation, other states. This reciprocal relationship is taken to provide the sanction in international law, as well as a description of the system ... In general I observe your territorial integrity because in doing so I reinforce a system in which you are expected to observe mine. (Vincent 1992, 258)

In this chapter, I will argue that, in spite of the fact that human rights 'have become a kind of *lingua franca* of ethics talk', to understand the ethics of international relations solely in terms of rights is to overestimate the scope of 'right' as a moral concept (Vincent 1992, 267; Neufield 1996, 48).[3] Indeed, our current usage of the terms 'the right' and 'rights' – in popular discourse and in international law and theorizing about international relations – demonstrates a gross disregard for origins of the idea and the limited normative ideals which it can support. The result is that the idea of 'right' simply cannot do the ethical and political work which we seem now to expect of it.

Rights-based ethical theory is based on untenable assumptions about human rationality and the universality of human nature; it is an abstract, impersonal, rule-oriented morality which obfuscates the social and political dimension of global moral problems, and which can tell us remarkably little about who or what is responsible for ensuring that the claims of rights-holders are met. It is not surprising that, in the light of this, both policy-makers and philosophers are united in their constant lamenting of the gulf between the so-called 'theory' and 'practice' of universal human rights. In spite of their recognition that starvation, torture and genocide remain constant features of global politics despite the existence of the Declaration, philosophers (and even some policy-makers) continue to tell and re-tell the same story of universal human rights using the same impersonal, apolitical, principled moral language. The irony, of course, is that this has always been the point of the articulation of rights: to uphold some universal standards of human dignity, precisely because they are not universally observed, recognized and exercised.

But today, we demand more of the concept of human rights, and we must ask serious questions about whether tidy philosophical arguments about rights can deliver any real social and political change in the decidedly untidy world of global politics. This is not an argument against philosophical inquiry; on the contrary, it is a plea to both philosophers and policy-makers to be aware of, and to make explicit, the importance of grounding ethical problems in the context of social and political relations, as well as recognizing that there is a distinctly ethical dimension to virtually all social and political problems.

I will challenge the assumption that this abstract, impersonal discourse of rights is the only feasible way of attending to the moral claims of actors in the international context, arguing that what is required, instead, is an approach to ethics which takes social relations as its starting point, and which is committed to direct responsiveness to others through a real understanding of their needs. Thinking seriously about ethics in the current era, demands some exploration of the capacities involved in moral agency and responsiveness – perception, imagination, the ability to listen and to focus attention.

An adequate approach to global ethics, I will argue, must not be limited to the application of rational principles, universal codes and impartiality in moral judgment; rather, it must be, at least in part, a morality of attachment and connection, which can help us to learn to respond adequately to particular others, rather than the universal, 'all others' of human rights theory.

## Two concepts of liberty, two kinds of rights

> It would be no exaggeration to say that this assumption – that the only coherent idea of liberty is the negative one of being unconstrained – has underpinned the entire development of modern contractarian thought. (Skinner 1984, 194)

To understand the limits, and also the strengths, of rights, we must understand the history of 'the right' as a moral and political idea. The idea of right cannot be separated from the normative principles of liberalism, including a view of the moral agent as essentially autonomous and possessing authority of his or her own will, the negative libertarian view of the substance of rights, the view of individual consent as the legitimate basis for rights, and a pluralist conception of the purposes of rights. All of this is combined, today, to express a view of politics that is required by and legitimates capitalist market practices (Shapiro 1986, 302). Perhaps the most important of these principles is the negative view of liberty, which resonates strongly in libertarian political theory, human rights theory, and much of the theory of international relations.

For liberal theorists in the contractarian tradition, liberty is understood solely as 'negative liberty'. On this view, being free means not being interfered with by others. The wider the area of non-interference, the wider my freedom. This, Berlin argues, is what the classical English political philosophers meant when they used this word; simply, that there ought to exist a certain minimum area of personal freedom which must on no account be violated; 'for if it is overstepped, the individual will find himself [sic] in an area too narrow for even that minimum development possible to pursue, and even to conceive, the various ends which men [sic] hold good or right or sacred' (Berlin 1969, 123–4).

The idea of negative liberty, and the concept of right to which it is tied, are central to Western thought, and are not without value. The idea that all human beings have some fundamental rights is one which was articulated by the early liberals for a specific purpose. It gave voice to a completely revolutionary and utterly radical notion of formal political and legal equality, grounded in a belief in the natural equality of human beings. Inextricably linked to that was the notion of freedom it put forward, which posited that individuals should have a 'space' around them, free from the interference of others and the sovereign, in which to pursue their own vision of the good.

Both of these ideas – natural/political equality, and 'negative' liberty – were, moreover, tied to the ideas of contract and consent; because human beings were 'equal', hierarchy and arbitrary rule were argued to be illegitimate. The new model of authority was based on consent, where individuals contracted with one another and with the sovereign both to protect their freedom and to gain the security provided by 'civil' society. Clearly, the value of this idea for the de-legitimation of patriarchal rule, the birth of liberalism and the idea of the legal equality of persons cannot be underestimated.

Liberals advocate a society in which citizens should be able to exercise their human and civil rights without the threat of undue state intervention. This is based on a strong belief that the individual is the best and only judge of his or her own 'good' on the grounds that 'he has privileged access to the contents of his own mind', and that society should be governed by a set of minimal rules, the purpose of which is not to dictate, but to facilitate the seeking of these individual ends (Shapiro 1986, 275). Thus, Brian Barry has described liberalism as 'the vision of society as made up of independent, autonomous units who cooperate only when the terms of cooperation are such as to make it further the ends of each of the parties' (Barry 1973, 166). The individualism inherent in liberalism – the belief that the ideal human condition is one in which each individual is surrounded by an 'invisible fence' separating and protecting each individual from the interference of others – emphasizes autonomy over attachment, and non-interference over responsiveness.

It is not a coincidence that this description of liberalism resonates in the theory of international relations. The liberal idea of 'sovereign' man – rational and therefore prepared to enter into contractual relations with other self-interested, rational parties – has been transposed onto the sovereign state in the international system. Indeed, the non-intervention principle has often been explained with reference to an analogy with personal liberty. As Wolff argues, '[n]ations are regarded as individual free persons living in a state of nature.' He claims that nations, like persons, are moral equals: 'Since by nature all nations are equal, since moreover all men are equal in a moral sense whose rights and obligations are the same; the rights and obligations of all nations are also by nature the same' (quoted in Beitz 1979, 75). On this understanding, the notion of freedom is not problematized; it is unquestioningly assumed that the negative liberty to pursue one's own ends without interference is an important good, and that it is better to have more of it than less (Beitz 1979, 75–6).

This contractualist model fits comfortably with the 'negative' view of liberty described above. Following this contractualist logic, the most vital human rights are rights that are linked to the negative view of liberty, including rights to engage in activities such as thought, worship, speech, publication and association, and in economic activities such as buying, selling and contracting, without state or other interference (O'Neill 1986, 107).

Moreover, when we talk of 'the morality of states', in which states are the subjects of rights, we focus on those rights which defend the territorial integrity, that is, right to non-intervention, of those states. The reciprocal relationship between 'mutually-disinterested' sovereign states means that 'I observe your territorial integrity (negative liberty) because in doing so I reinforce a system in which you are expected to observe mine'. In this way, the claims of states are the international equivalent of those basic rights of individuals familiar in the domestic arena, including the right to security (of the territory) and the right to liberty (of the independent polity) (Vincent 1992, 256–7). Clearly, these rights represent a powerful and important normative ideal; but does the ontological foundation on which these rights to non-interference are based represent a useful, or indeed accurate, picture of the relations between individuals in society, or between states in the international system? The emphasis on equality and formal equality in international relations theory had contributed to a general account of both personhood and statehood.

The emphasis on autonomy and formal equality (in international relations theory) has contributed to a gendered account of both personhood and statehood. As Peterson and Runyan argue, 'sovereign man and sovereign states are defined not by connection or relationships but by autonomy in decision-making and freedom from the power of others. Security is understood not in terms of celebrating and sustaining life but as the capacity to be indifferent to "others" and, if necessary, to harm them' (Peterson and Runyan 1993, 34). By interpreting as 'indifference' what is normally understood as prudent non-intervention, we begin to highlight a serious moral deficiency of both political liberalism and the so-called 'morality of states'.

Annette Baier argues that to focus on freedom rights at the expense of other, more fundamental moral concepts is to overlook the fact that these other moral categories are necessary for the creation of a morally decent society. For example, rather than capturing the social nature of public life, the language of rights pushes us, she argues, to see the participants in a moral community as 'single, clamorous living human beings, not as families, clans, tribes, groups, classes, churches, congregations, nations or peoples' (Baier 1995, 237). She also stresses the incompleteness of a morality based on a kind of reciprocity of negative liberty. For example, she argues that if the right to life simply means that no one kills me and I kill no one, it overlooks those individuals whose ability to exercise a right to life depends on more than simply being allowed a certain amount of personal freedom. Again, Baier's example is instructive:

> In a sense it is correct that, in order for it [my right to life] to be respected, all that must be done by others is that they not kill me. But although what that means may seem clear enough when I am a reasonably tough adult, it

was less clear when I was a helpless newborn, and will be less clear when I
am a helpless incapacitated old person. (Baier 1995, 242)

While the idea of negative liberty may be an important and valuable notion,
its usefulness is, nonetheless, radically incomplete as a basis for morality,
insofar as it is limited to the articulation of a single moral idea – that an
individual should be entitled to make certain claims to non-interference.

One may object, however, that this describes only one view of freedom,
and that many advocates of rights, including many liberals, would view the
idea of negative liberty as a 'straw man' – too narrow a foundation on which
to base the contemporary idea of universal human rights. On this view,
human rights must include 'economic, social and cultural' ('second generation') rights – rights which ensure that certain fundamental needs are met
– rather than simply 'liberty' rights to act without outside interference.
Indeed, most serious commentators on human rights, including Henry Shue,
and R. J. Vincent, have argued that provision for subsistence rights has a
strong claim, either to priority over, or at least equal standing with, other
human rights (Shue 1980; Vincent 1986). This belief tends to be driven by
the recognition that 'economic rights' must not be neglected because 'basic
human needs must be provided so that people can stay alive and so that
people can live in dignity', or, more strongly, that the suffering of the
starving and malnourished is 'the worst offence to human rights in contemporary society' (Howard 1995, 7; Vincent 1986, 2).

Certainly, it is undeniable that, today, the idea of international human
rights embodies not only civil and political, but also 'economic and social'
rights, which seek to uphold our claims to vital goods such as economic
security, welfare and cultural autonomy. But in spite of the formal recognition
of both kinds of rights, it is often still suggested that civil and political rights
are the only real rights, and that economic and social rights are not rights
at all. Such a claim is based on the idea that civil and political rights are
rights because they are about the individual's entitlement to freedom from
interference by the state. Economic and social rights, by contrast, are 'positive
rights' which usually require positive action, or 'interference' on the part of
states. Thus, the very idea of positive rights serves to undermine the whole
point of talking about rights in the first place. Hence, these positive rights
cannot be classified as rights at all.[4]

While this argument is patently flawed, it does allude to what is, in fact,
a serious confusion about rights. It is flawed because it suggests that the
ability to exercise civil and political rights requires no positive action on
the part of states; moreover, it seems not to recognize that there is room
within most versions of liberalism for the restriction of liberty in order to
maximize some other good – equality, welfare, etc. But where the argument
above is important is where it alludes to the fact that the idea of right is, in

itself, unrelated to any such claims about such positive goods. In order to make sense of this, it is necessary to understand the liberal idea of the separation of 'the right' and 'the good'. While we might define 'the good' as a substantive moral goal, or a moral end in itself, 'the right', by contrast, is that which is decided simply by its instrumental significance for achieving that good. The right is a negative, procedural, rule-like notion; the 'good', by contrast, is that which gives the point of the rules which define the right (Taylor 1989, 89).

The concept of 'right', then, can tell us nothing about *why people ought to have* food and shelter provided for them if they cannot provide for themselves, and it is a grave mistake to use such a concept in the effort to give force to such vital normative claims.'The right to food' and 'the right to housing' are not statements of right, which are statements about the rules and procedures which allow the space to pursue a plurality of goods; rather, they articulate substantive conceptions of the good, which require much more than a statement of right to give them moral legitimacy. This confusion between rights and goods, I would argue, can contribute nothing to the achievement of moral and political change.

It is a profound historical irony that the proponents of so-called 'economic and social' rights today come from the left of the political spectrum. According to Marx, what was wrong with the concept of right was that it posited a particular view of 'natural' man, and in so doing, put forward a normative vision for the organization of society based on that idea of human nature. Interestingly, Marx recognized the relative value of political liberty embodied within the notion of rights; what he did not do, however, was suggest that the language and logic of liberal rights could be used to put forward his own normative vision for human society.[5] Contrary to the illusion of 'neutrality' surrounding the notion of right, Marx argued that the concept of right was, in fact, ideological, and hence incompatible with many value claims about human flourishing.[6]

The problem with economic and social rights, then, is not, as has been suggested, that they are so often unattainable. They are often unattainable for the same sort of reasons as civil and political rights are often unattainable. While it is certainly the case that civil and political rights fit most comfortably with the ideology of liberalism and rights, I am not suggesting that we must focus on 'rights' in order to solve problems surrounding individuals' political liberty, while using some different strategy to address basic needs and welfare rights. Quite simply, I am arguing that although the idea of civil and political rights at least follows the normative reasoning of rights (whereas the idea of economic and social rights does not even do that), ultimately, to concentrate on individual *rights* is to constrain severely what can actually be achieved in the effort to improve people's quality of life. It makes no difference whether we want to ensure that people can speak freely in public or ensure that they have enough food to eat. To work towards the achievement of these goals, we must understand why we believe that it is a good thing that people speak freely, and why certain people *cannot* speak freely, or why they do not have food to eat. And to do that, we must recognize the fact that these are problems, and goods, which exist, and must be realized, not at the level of the individual, but at the level of social relations.

I would suggest that the fact that 'economic and social rights' have been invented demonstrates that what is required is not more rights, but rather the recognition that rights alone cannot answer all the moral crises facing the world today. If we are interested in finding the appropriate starting point for ethical deliberation, we have to ask whether 'securing the largest possible human liberty' can provide an adequate starting point where moral goods are seen to include more than simply 'negative' rights (O'Neill 1986, 115). Moreover, even if it is political liberty (as opposed to, say, food) that we are trying to achieve, we have to ask whether focusing solely on people's rights will actually help us to uncover the social and even structural reasons which render individuals unable to claim and exercise their political freedoms.

Currently, we are faced with a situation where virtually all global moral values, including economic and social security, and the cultural survival of social groups, have been twisted and pummelled in order that they can be expressed in liberal rights language. As Roger Rigterink has argued, the notion that rights can be defeated only by other rights led to the profusion of alleged rights. He suggests that it is the recognition of the moral poverty of rights as non-interference that has led to the creation of positive rights; what these positive rights so feebly attempt to address, he argues, are what he calls concerns of 'care'.

> Philosophers had recognized long before Gilligan that concerns of care could not be addressed as long as rights were conceived of in the traditional Lockean fashion as freedoms. In order to address matters of care, they invented (and 'invented' is the right word) positive rights. They claimed that in addition to the traditional basic freedoms, people also have a right to adequate food, shelter and medical care and, according to the Universal Declaration of Human Rights of the UN, a paid vacation. (Rigterink 1992, 42)[7]

Rigterink is not suggesting that these are not valid human needs and important moral concerns; rather, he is arguing that the preoccupation with rights has obscured the fact that other moral categories and concepts – such as responsibility and care – may be used more effectively to define and secure that which we value for human beings. It is this claim which I will address in the next section.

## Alternatives to rights-based ethics: relationships, responsibilities and care

Recently, a number of feminist philosophers have been asking serious questions about the value of a moral system in which the idea of rights occupies the dominant position, often to the exclusion of other moral concepts. I refer specifically to the relatively recent developments in feminist ethics which have posited the need for alternative moral concepts – such as care, responsibility and trust – which may complement, or in some cases replace, notions of rights and obligations, reciprocity, justice and fairness.

The idea of 'care ethics' has gained notoriety in the context of a debate over the question of gender and morality generated by the work of Carol Gilligan. Disturbed by the theories of moral development articulated by mainstream Kantian moral philosophers, and specifically by her one-time associate Lawrence Kohlberg, Gilligan carried out empirical studies in which a series of moral dilemmas were presented to boys and girls, young men and young women. Gilligan claimed that in conducting this research, she heard a 'different voice' of morality coming from women, one which sees life as 'dependent on connection, as sustained by activities of care, and as based on a bond of attachment rather than a contract of agreement' (Gilligan 1993, 57).

Since the publication of Gilligan's influential work, a number of moral and political philosophers have developed this notion of care (Noddings 1984; Card 1991; Browning Cole and Coultrap-McQuin 1992; Larrabee 1993; Tronto 1993; Friedman 1993; Held 1993 and 1995; Baier 1995; Hekman 1995; Clement 1996). Joan Tronto, for example, has constructed a political argument for an ethic of care which isolates four ethical elements: attentiveness, responsibility, competence and responsiveness. These elements, she claims, must be integrated into an appropriate whole, producing neither moral objectivity nor moral relativism – the familiar dichotomous categories of moral theory – but rather a morality in which judgements about needs, conflicting needs, and strategies for achieving ends are required. Importantly, Tronto makes explicit in her writings her conviction that care must inform not only a private, but a truly public ethics; despite the fact that many writers about care concern themselves with relationships that are now considered personal or private, she argues, the kinds of judgements that care involves require an assessment of needs in a social and political, as well as a personal, context (Tronto 1993, 137).

Clearly, this feminist view of ethics as 'care' contrasts sharply with rights-based ethics. According to the advocates of care, morality is founded in a sense of concrete connection and direct response between persons, a direct sense of connection which exists prior to moral beliefs about what is right or wrong or which principles to accept. Moral action is meant to express and sustain those connections to particular other people (Blum 1993, 51–2).

This view is informed by the strong belief that achieving knowledge of the particular other person towards whom one acts is an often complex and difficult moral task, and one which draws on specifically moral capacities (Blum 1993, 51). Whereas rights-based ethics encourages us to abstract both from the self and from the other, and to understand the plights of others through a simple projection of what one would feel if one were in their situation, care ethics involves the ability to see the other as different in important ways from oneself, such that understanding the needs, interests and welfare of that person requires the use of care, love, empathy, compassion and emotional sensitivity (Blum 1993).

Not surprisingly, advocates of rights-based ethics, and liberal theories of justice more generally, tend to be hostile to the idea of a morality of care. Caring about particular persons, it is argued, may indeed be a fact of life, but it is an inappropriate way to define morality, especially our moral relations to strangers. Indeed, a common response to the notion of care as a moral category is to make what Margaret Walker calls the 'separate spheres' move of endorsing particularism for personal or intimate relations, and universalism for the large-scale or genuinely administrative context, or for dealings with unknown or little-known persons (Walker 1995, 147). Impartialist critics of care argue that while care for others in the context of relationships may constitute a genuinely distinct set of concerns or mode of thought and motivation from that found in impartialist morality, and while these can be deeply important to individuals' lives, nevertheless such concerns are not moral but only personal ones. Caring may be important, but actions which flow directly from it are in that respect without moral significance (Blum 1993, 53).

The apparent personal and private relevance of care has meant that even the advocates of care ethics have often found it difficult to imagine how caring could be translated into a world in which many of the most pressing problems are distinctly global problems. Marilyn Friedman suggests that the 'relational' vision of the self is unable to ground the widest sort of concern for others; Alison Jaggar, moreover, argues that the global context of morality is 'incompatible with the characteristically interactive and personal relation that defines care thinking' (Jaggar 1995, 197). Care does not, at first sight, seem to respond well to distance. This, of course, contrasts starkly with justice ethics, or rights-based moral reasoning, where 'distance' ensures impartiality and is therefore fundamental to sound moral judgement. Given that it is a morality of 'closeness' rather than distance, how useful could an ethics of care be, when applied to the global context? 'How difficult is it to translate care and moral responsibility from family and intimates, to public and especially to international levels?' (Pettman 1996, 119).

I would argue that, rather than trying to translate the moral feelings that we have for our family and intimates to distant strangers, the particularities of whose lives are unknown to us, we can use the philosophy of care as a starting point for rethinking the nature of relationships between individuals and groups in a global context. To say that we can have feelings of care towards strangers, in the same way that we care for those close to us, is to stretch the reasoning of care beyond recognition. The dangers of this move are either that care loses its main strength – namely, its belief that moral motivation and moral responses emerge out of sustained relationships with particular others; or that we end up articulating care as a universal imperative: 'We all have a duty to care about all others'. This is surely undesirable in that it distorts the essence of what a caring ethics is about.

By pointing out these dangers I do not wish to suggest, however, that care ethics is irrelevant to the global context. On the contrary, I would argue that we can use the ethics of care as the basis for rethinking the normative priorities of our societies and our world. Care must be seen not simply as a moral orientation, but as a basis for the political achievement of a good society or, I would add, a morally decent world. By using the ethics of care as a starting point, we can fundamentally revise our understandings of the nature of our moral relations with others in the global context.

As I argued in the first section, rights define some criterion or procedure which will allow us to derive all and only the things we are obliged to do (Taylor 1989, 79). Many moral problems, however, including problems of political liberty, but especially those concerning the provision of basic needs, require more from an ethics than a procedural/legal framework for the application of rules designed to adjudicate, fairly, among competing claims. Most of what passes for 'ethics' in international relations is about the resolution of moral disagreements through the use of moral concepts like rights and obligations, reciprocity and fairness. But it is a mistake to limit morality to conflict resolution. Ethics may also be about the creation of a society in which certain types of conflicts no longer occur. The ethic of care focuses on preventing conflicts, and, specifically, on the importance of human connection in helping to avoid injustice (Clement 1996, 82).

Understood as the basis for the achievement of a good society, caring need not be limited to those with whom we have a relationship of either intimacy or propinquity. As Tronto argues, if caring is used as an excuse to narrow the scope of our moral activity to be concerned only with those immediately around us, then it has little to recommend it as a moral theory. Rather, she argues, we must interrogate the ways in which we, and others, are responsible for our narrow sphere and hence, for who receives our care. Thus, to say that we will care for a stranger at our door, but not for starving children in Africa is to ignore the ways in which the contemporary world is intertwined and the ways in which hundreds of prior public and private decisions affect where we find ourselves and which strangers show up at our doors. An approach to ethics based on caring will need to begin by broadening our understanding of what caring for others means, both in terms of the moral questions it raises and in terms of the need to restructure broader social and political institutions if caring for others is to be made a more central part of the everyday lives of everyone in society (Tronto 1993, 111–12).

Conceiving of care both as a moral orientation and as a practice that informs our daily lives removes the focus from the individual (that is, the rights-holder) and recognizes that human well-being relies on the giving and receiving of care. Because care forces us to think concretely about people's real needs, and about evaluating how these needs will be met, it introduces questions about what we value into the public, and indeed, the international sphere. Interrogating who is and who is not cared for in the world will force us to explore the role of social relations and structural constraints in determining who can and cannot lead a dignified and fulfilled life. Care is not an abstract ethics about the application of rules, but one which recognizes that addressing moral problems involves first an understanding of personal and social relationships, and second, a degree of social coordination and cooperation in order to try to answer questions and disputes about who cares for whom, and about how responsibilities will be discharged. Bringing care into international relations will involve the shaping of existing distancing and depersonalizing institutions to embody expressive and communicative possibilities between distanced groups, as well as a critical examination of the structural conditions in which relationships are situated (Walker 1995, 147). By focusing on the interpersonal and social contexts in which all human relations occur, we have a better starting point for thinking about the claims, entitlements, needs, interests and dignity of persons.

The logic of claiming 'my rights' is one which is necessarily based on putting oneself first. An ethics of care undermines the individualistic ideology that leads us to believe that 'my rights' – that to which I am entitled – are somehow disconnected from the networks of social relations in which my life is situated. Care ethics involves coming to an understanding that we, as moral agents, and potential carers, are not isolated from the moral situations which surround us in our societies and our world. Caring identifies the potential moral value located in relationships, and values a focusing of attention and sustained effort on the promotion of good relations. Whether it is in the context of the family, the community, the nation, or the globe, a recognition of the importance of caring helps us to preserve 'a lively sense of the moral incompleteness or inadequacy' of principled, generalized treatment of individual human beings (Walker 1995, 147).

Rights-based ethics rely on moral impartiality, and on the maintenance of a distanced, impersonal stance towards others. A discourse of universal human rights appears to be appropriate to the international context, in which individuals are both physically and emotionally distanced from one another, and in which relations must, it seems, be mediated through institutions. While this appears reasonable, it is clear that ethics of this kind tells us nothing about certain aspects of morality which are important to real people: about individuals' constructions of their identities and their 'selves'; about why people identify with or value certain others, why or how they build relationships and recognize their responsibilities and others' needs, or about how categories of inclusiveness and exclusiveness are constructed. Because rights-based ethics focuses on our individuality and shared humanity, it takes no account of relevant differences in people's needs and interests which are dependent on our social location. Moreover, because it is insensitive to connections between interests, social location and power, the focus on our common humanity deters questions about the possible malformation of our interests as a result of their development within an inegalitarian social structure (Calhoun 1988, 455).

It is not surprising that most people find it difficult to conceive of how an ethics of care would actually manifest itself in the 'real world' of international relations. The language and logic of international relations, and indeed of what we might call 'public' life in the West, are imbued with notions which are antithetical to care: impartiality, rationality, due process, an emphasis on procedure, rule-making, universality, reciprocity, fairness, contracts, etc. The language of care, by contrast, is regarded as belonging to the private sphere. I am arguing that this dichotomy must be overcome. We need to recognize the role that caring and caring values play in public life, and think about how the very basis of the social order could be transformed in order to put caring at the centre of social and political life. As Tronto suggests, perhaps the impoverishment of our vocabulary for discussing caring is a result of the way caring is 'privatized', thus beneath our social vision for societies. The need to rethink appropriate forms of caring raises broad questions about the shape of social and political institutions in both domestic and international society (Tronto 1995, 113). That is not to say, however, that the answer to the question 'who cares for whom' is either transparent or unproblematic; indeed, it is not only a moral but *a social and political question*, which requires an analysis of the social construction of roles, relationships, communities and institutions in domestic and international life.

## Conclusion

My critique of the moral and political philosophy of rights is intended to show how and why a tradition of moral reasoning that depends on a shared human nature defined in terms of reason and the ability to enter into rational contracts, the existence of universal or, at least, universalizable moral principles, and a conception of moral agents – individuals or states – as independent, autonomous and primarily concerned with protecting their own 'negative liberty', may be untenable in the contemporary world. In an era of increasing globalization, an international system which is built on a set of minimal principles surrounding the negative rights and correlative duties of states may, ultimately, prove inadequate to deal with the moral demands of contemporary life. As Virginia Held argues, 'the mutually disinterested rational individualists of the liberal tradition would seem unlikely to care enough to take the actions needed to achieve moral decency at a global level' (Held 1993, 53).

The notion of rights, and the liberal values it embodies, fit comfortably with both the norms of the international system and with the dominant theorizing in international relations as it has developed over several decades. Indeed, I have suggested that although the 'cosmopolitan' notion of universal rights is often contrasted with the 'communitarian' ideal of the sovereign nation-state as a morally constitutive community, the moral and political philosophy which underwrites the rights tradition supports, rather than contradicts, many of the assumptions of traditional international relations theory.

I have also argued, however, that this reliance on the language of human rights as a means of articulating the ethical dimensions of international life is woefully inadequate. Rights-based ethics are individualistic – in the sense that they isolate the individual from those relationships and responsibilities which define the individual as a moral agent and a social being; but also in the sense that they are prone to a kind of methodological individualism, which ignores the complex structural constraints and social relations which often prevent individuals from acting as truly free, rational individuals, and from being able to claim, and exercise their rights. Moreover, in spite of the contemporary understanding of rights as 'positive' as well 'negative', it remains evident that the language of rights and the ideology of liberalism simply cannot give moral substance to the claim that people ought to be, for example, properly fed and housed. In order to do this, we must employ other concepts and categories, especially those which highlight the interdependent nature of human life. Finally, a thorough analysis of the idea of right demonstrates that simply to state that human beings have 'rights' to food, shelter, medical care, and even 'development', says very little about who or what must act to ensure that this occurs. Moving some of our thoughts towards notions of caring and responsibility, rather than simply rights, may help to redress this balance.

None of this, however, is meant to suggest that the notion of 'right' in liberal political philosophy is of no value; indeed, it has tremendous value. As Benjamin Barber has argued, that we are 'born free' is a useful fiction in opposing the empirical realities of natural (physical, genetic) inequality and was a crucial weapon in the war against absolute authority. That, he suggests, was its great power as a premise of dissent ideology in the seventeenth century, when it first manifested its modern revolutionary potential (Barber

1996, 357). I have argued that we must place the idea of right in this historical context in order to understand both its meaning and its influence on contemporary political thought. However, I have also suggested that the contemporary focus on rights masks the degree to which moral and political progress is a product of the coordination of socially divided responsibilities and of social struggle. 'Rights', continues Barber 'are paper parapets, and are defensible when manned by citizens willing to pay for them with their civic engagement, their social responsibilities and often their lives' (Barber 1996).

I have argued that a moral orientation based on care overcomes many of these problems associated with rights; an ethic of care takes attentiveness to the needs of others as a primary moral virtue, and explores both our responsiveness, our motivation and our responsibilities to others. A moral orientation which is built around the application of rules, by contrast, opposes morality to egoism, and is blind to the inherently interdependent and social nature of all moral situations. The Western culture of individualism and 'self-sufficiency' has elevated rights to such a lofty status that other moral concepts such as care, attentiveness, trust and respect have been reduced to, at best, sentimental banalities and, at worst, potentially sinister breeders of emotional and material dependence of the weak on the strong. While sentimentality and dependence are certainly dangers of care ethics, they are dangers which are not insurmountable. What is required is the development of a method of understanding morality as emerging out of patterns of relationships which does not lose sight of the patterns of power which characterize those relations. Care ethics must not allow its concern with particular relationships and its concentration on attentiveness and responsiveness to obscure the structural causes of people's suffering. As Alison Jaggar has argued, moral thinking must focus not only on meeting immediate needs but on problematizing the structures that create those needs or keep them unfulfilled (Jaggar 1995). By removing the focus from our 'common humanity' towards the recognition of important differences, care ethics recognizes that a sensitivity to how our identities are shaped by our social structure is a crucial part of what attentiveness and responsiveness to others really means.

The contemporary world is a world of difference and inequality. It is also a world which appears not to have been adequately moved by the repeated verbal bludgeoning of human rights declarations which refer to 'human dignity' and the shared nature of all 'humanity'. I have argued that the concept of right can only support our claims to 'negative' freedom – to liberty as non-interference. But if leading a dignified and fulfilled life is seen to require more than this, then right is no longer an adequate moral category. If the attainment of a morally decent world means that we must do more than leave one another alone, then it is likely that we will require new and different moral concepts – such as care and responsibility – in order to work towards achieving such a world.

## Notes

1  Kant's approach to ethics may be described as 'duty-based', rather than rights-based. For Kant, a human action is morally good, not because it is done from immediate inclination, or with self-interest or consequences or results in mind, but because it is done for the sake of duty itself. Moreover, duty is seen as the necessity to act out of reverence for the moral law, which is valid for all rational beings as such independently of their particular desires. See Paton (1991, 19–21).

2  While the view that there is a contradiction between sovereignty and rights is certainly the dominant one, it has been argued that this contradiction can be overcome. Michael Walzer (1977) uses the device of the contract to argue that the rights of states derive ultimately from the rights of individuals. Mervyn Frost, by contrast, uses Hegelian 'constitutive' theory to argue that the contradiction can be best overcome not through the device of the contract, but rather through the recognition that genuine rights can only emerge in sovereign states. Frost (1986, 1996) argues that the intellectual origins of the idea of rights – which see rights as 'natural' in the state of nature, and thus see the state as putting limits on those natural freedoms – provides us with a mistaken view of the nature of rights. Frost argues, instead, that rights are compatible with the notion of sovereignty, because it is only in the context of autonomous, sovereign states that individuals can have any rights at all. See Walzer (1977, 53); Frost (1986, 163); Frost (1996, 141–2).

3  Mark Neufeld has also criticized the overwhelming reliance on the idea of 'the right' in international relations theory. He argues, 'in a context in which it appears self-evident that normative theorizing about international politics must be conceived as a theory of the right – when it becomes difficult even to think of an alternative – the liabilities of a right-oriented approach can go unrecognized, and the normative content (and liabilities) of a theory of the right can be left unexamined' (Neufeld 1996).

4  Rhoda Howard discusses this argument, which she describes as the 'continued unwillingness of some liberals to accept the idea of economic rights', citing Maurice Cranston (1983) and Carnes Lord (1984) as being among those liberal theorists who regard 'positive' rights as 'irrelevant or idealistic' (Howard 1996, 2).

5  This is the case in spite of the fact that socialists, past and present, have used the language of rights in the struggle for, for example, better conditions and benefits for workers.

6  This is an important point. Although many liberals argue for the separation of the right and the good, and the primacy of the right, many critics of this position argue that those liberals, in fact, have to draw on a particular sense of the good to develop principles of right action – principles which are ostensibly compatible with the coexistence of a plurality of goods (Taylor 1989, 89).

7  Rigterink refers here to Carol Gilligan, whose work on moral psychology was the catalyst to the rapidly proliferating literature surrounding the idea of 'care' ethics.

## References

Baier, A. (1995), *Moral Prejudices: Essays on Ethics*, Cambridge MA, Harvard University Press.

Barber, B. R. (1996), Foundationalism and democracy, in S. Benhabib (ed.), *Democracy and Difference: Contesting the Boundaries of the Political*, Princeton, Princeton University Press.

Barry, B. (1973), *The Liberal Theory of Justice*, Oxford, Clarendon.

Beitz, C. (1979), *Political Theory and International Relations*, Princeton, Princeton University Press.

Berlin, I. (1969), Two concepts of liberty, in *Four Essays on Liberty*, Oxford, Oxford University Press.

Blum, L. (1993), Gilligan and Kohlberg: implications for moral theory, in M. J. Larrabee (ed.), *An Ethic of Care*, London, Routledge.

Browning Cole, E. and S. Coultrap-McQuin (eds) (1992), *Explorations in Feminist Ethics: Theory and Practice*, Bloomington, Indiana University Press.

Calhoun, C. (1988), Justice, care and gender bias, *The Journal of Philosophy*, 85:9, 451–63.

Card, C. (ed.) (1991), *Feminist Ethics*, Lawrence, University of Kansas Press.

Clement, G. (1996), *Care, Autonomy and Justice, Feminism and the Ethic of Care*, Boulder, Westview.

Cranston, M. (1983), Are there any human rights?, *Daedalus*, 112:4, 1–18.

Dunn, J. (1979), *Western Political Theory in the Face of the Future*, Cambridge, Cambridge University Press.

Friedman, M. (1993), *What are Friends For: Feminist Perspectives on Personal Relationships and Moral Theory*, Ithaca, Cornell University Press.

Frost, M. (1986), *Towards a Normative Theory of International Relations*, Cambridge, Cambridge University Press.

Frost, M. (1996), *Ethics in International Relations: A Constitutive Theory*, Cambridge, Cambridge University Press.

Gilligan, C. (1993), *In a Different Voice: Psychological Theory and Women's Development*, Cambridge MA, Harvard University Press.

Hekman, S. (1995), *Moral Voices, Moral Selves: Carol Gilligan and Feminist Moral Theory*, Cambridge, Polity Press.

Held, V. (1993), *Feminist Morality: Transforming Culture, Society and Politics*, Chicago, University of Chicago Press.

Held, V. (ed.) (1995), *Justice and Care: Essential Readings in Feminist Ethics*, Boulder, Westview Press.

Howard, R. (1996), *Human Rights and the Search for Community*, Boulder, Westview Press.

Jaggar, A. (1995), Caring as a feminist practice of moral reason, in V. Held (ed.), *Justice and Care: Essential Readings in Feminist Ethics*, Boulder, Westview.

Kant, I. (1991), *The Moral Laws: Groundwork of the Metaphysic of Morals*, translated and analysed by H. J. Paton, London, Routledge.

Larrabee, M. J. (ed.), *An Ethic of Care: Feminist and Interdisciplinary Perspectives*, London, Routledge.

Nardin, T. and D. R. Mapel (eds) (1992), *Traditions of International Ethics*, Cambridge, Cambridge University Press.

Neufeld, M. (1996), Identity and the good in international relations theory, *Global Society*, 10:1, 43–56.

Noddings, N. (1984), *Caring: A Feminine Approach to Ethics and Moral Education*, Berkeley, University of California Press.

O'Neill, O. (1986), *Faces of Hunger: An Essay on Poverty, Development and Justice*, London, Allen & Unwin.

Paton, H. J. (ed.) (1991), *Groundwork of the Metaphysic of Morals*, London, Routledge.

Peterson, V. S. and A. Sisson Runyan (1993), *Global Gender Issues*, Boulder, Westview Press.

Pettman, J. J. (1996), *Worlding Women: A Feminist International Politics*, London, Routledge.

Rigterink, R. J. (1992), 'Warning: the surgeon moralist has determined that claims of rights can be detrimental to everyone's health, in E. Browning Cole and S. Coultrap-McQuin (eds), *Explorations in Feminist Ethics: Theory and Practice*, Bloomington, Indiana University Press.

Shapiro, I. (1986), *The Evolution of Rights in Liberal Theory*, Cambridge, Cambridge University Press.

Shue, H. (1980), *Basic Rights: Subsistence, Affluence and U.S. Foreign Policy*, Princeton, Princeton University Press.

Skinner, Q. (1984), The idea of negative liberty: philosophical and historical perspectives, in R. Rorty, J. B. Schneewind and Q. Skinner (eds), *Philosophy in History*, Cambridge, Cambridge University Press.

Taylor, C. (1989), *Sources of the Self: The Making of Modern Identity*, Cambridge, Cambridge University Press.

Tronto, J. (1993), *Moral Boundaries: A Political Argument for an Ethic of Care*, London, Routledge.

Tronto, J. (1995), Women and caring: what can feminists learn about morality from caring?, in V. Held (ed.), *Justice and Care: Essential Readings in Feminist Ethics*, Boulder, Westview.

Vincent, R. J. (1986), *Human Rights and International Relations*, Cambridge, Cambridge University Press.

Vincent, R. J. (1992), The idea of rights in international ethics, in T. Nardin and D. R. Mapel (eds), *Traditions of International Ethics*, Cambridge, Cambridge University Press.

Walker, M. U. (1995), Moral understandings: alternative 'epistemology' for a feminist ethics, in V. Held (ed.), *Justice and Care: Essential Readings in Feminist Ethics*, Boulder, Westview Press.

Walzer, M. (1977), *Just and Unjust Wars*, New York, Basic Books.

# 4

# Human rights, law and democracy in an unfree world

*Norman Lewis*

## Introduction[1]

Many people believed that the end of the cold war would lead to a more peaceful world. It has not turned out so. The ideological conflict between capitalism and communism has been replaced by a myriad of far more intractable ethnic and national conflicts. Civil society has broken down in numerous areas of the former Third World to the extent that the writ of law barely runs in large areas of the world. Even in the North there is a widespread sense that society is disintegrating, as are traditional moral and social codes. The result is a more dispirited and fragmented world, and one in which routine abuses of human beings and their rights seem more common-place than before.

Against this background, the concept of human rights has acquired new importance and resonance. The idea that people possess certain basic human rights, and that these should be safe from violation by the state or by other groups or individuals, seems today an important bulwark against the break-down of law and order and the degradation of moral norms. From debates about the Iraqi treatment of Kurds to the worldwide scandal of child prostit-ution, from the issue of language rights for American Hispanics to the horrors of female circumcision, human rights has become a major theme of politics and international relations.

One example illustrates this new status clearly. A few years ago, the idea of the world's leading statesmen sitting at a conference table to discuss the welfare and human rights of children rather than the state of the world economy would have been greeted with incredulity. However, for twenty-four hours, starting on the evening of Saturday 29 September through to Sunday 30 September 1990, this is precisely what took place: the human rights of children claimed the exclusive attention of seventy-one of the world's assembled leaders attending the World Summit for Children in New York. At the time, this was the largest such gathering of heads of states and government ever to have been convened. Altogether, representatives of over 150 countries were involved. The conference ended with the seventy-one heads of state and government signing the World Declaration on the Survival, Development and Protection of Children and a Plan of Action for its implementation by the year 2000. This World Summit for Children took place less than a year after the United Nations adopted the Convention on the Rights of the Child (20 November 1989) – thirty years after the adoption of its precursor, the Declaration of the Rights of the Child. When it was opened for signature at UN headquarters on 26 January 1990, an unprecedented sixty-one countries signed on that day. No human rights treaty ever gathered so much support so early in its career. By the time of the World Summit, some twenty countries had ratified the Convention, enough for it to enter into international law (Black 1996).

In many respects, the increased focus upon human rights followed on in the wake of numerous humanitarian crises which followed the end of the cold war. These post-cold war crises – the question of safe havens for the Kurds in Iraq, famine in Somalia, and civil war in Rwanda and the former Yugoslavia – revitalized the international discourse on the role of human rights in global politics (Freedman and Boren 1992; Dacyl 1996). It is in this context that both the former UN Secretary General, Perez Javier de Cuéllar (1991) and the UN High Commissioner for refugees, Sadako Ogata (1995) called for the elevation of human rights to a level where it would be of equal status to the principle of sovereignty in international relations. A significant discussion followed focusing on what rights and responsibilities the international community had with regard to protecting human rights (Chopra and Weiss 1992). What seems to have emerged is a new international discourse which now fundamentally questions the centrality of sovereignty in the future of the global order (Lapidoth 1992; Rosenau 1992; Jackson 1992; Deng 1993; Mayall 1991a; Herbst 1992; Camilleri and Falk 1992; Halperin *et al.* 1992). The new consensus now suggests that new rules for intervention should displace the traditional norms of non-intervention (Carothers 1994; Furedi 1994; Médecins sans Frontières 1993; Mayall 1996).

This questioning of sovereignty and the quest to discover new principles which will guarantee international order and human dignity, has elevated human rights discourse to an unprecedented position in international relations. The proliferation of new human rights legislation, like the UN Convention on the Rights of the Child, has been generally welcomed as a positive development. Yet the more central human rights become to our times, the more confused and contradictory our understanding of them seems to be. The perennial contested debates about what human rights are, whether these are universal or culturally specific, who should enforce them, whether they should take precedence over national sovereignty and why have these become so much more important in the post-cold war era than they were during the cold war, remain as unresolved as they have always been. Yet, despite this, the consensus appears to be one that accepts these developments as positive.

The aim of this chapter is to question this positive view of the contemporary elevation of human rights in international relations. The chapter attempts to re-examine the question of human rights and their relationship to human freedom and international relations. By investigating how the legal subject, or the rights-bearing subject of modern society (the individual at the domestic level and the state at the international level), comes into being and is altered through historical practice, the chapter attempts to grasp what lay behind the elevation of human rights after the end of the Second World War, and what continuities and changes lie behind their elevation today. Paradoxically, the chapter concludes that this new-found popularity represents a greater restriction on freedom: an erosion of democratic rights, from civil and political rights in the domestic sphere, to national rights in the international sphere. In short, the chapter suggests that the ascendancy of the human rights discourse today expresses a social process which is fundamentally eroding democratic rights and threatens to legitimize and institutionalize domestic and global inequalities. The implications this process has for the future of international relations is briefly examined in the conclusion. We begin by examining the concept of the rights-bearing subject.

## The concept of the rights-bearing subject[2]

The central component of all modern law and its starting point is the legal subject or person. The person is assumed to be a moral agent or a self-willing actor. As a rights-bearing subject, the person of modern law is not simply coerced by a legal system that is outside of his or her influence. Rather the law is said to derive from his or her own will. All doctrines of the enforcement of contract, the punishment of crime and the elections of legislatures rest on this core assumption. The ability to distinguish between arbitrary and oppressive authority and justice depends on the doctrine of moral agency, and its implied corollary of responsibility for one's own actions.

To understand what this means for the human rights discourse, it is necessary to first examine the foundations of the concept of the legal subject in the language of rights and then to logically reconstruct the derivation of the law from the legal subject.

The foundation of the legal subject is logically prior to its expression in law. As moral agents, or rights-bearing subject, the subject is the substantial basis of the legal doctrine. But moral agency is something that is found outside of the law and is logically prior to legal reasoning. Much contemporary sociology, moral philosophy and political theory places a premium upon the historical character of the individual subject – a view which defies the outlook of the founders of the concept of the subject, for whom individuality was a natural condition. The rights-bearing subject is not a natural or trans-historical actor. On the contrary, the appearance of the individual as the basic unit of social intercourse, is more or less a datable event: the political transformations of seventeenth and eighteenth-century Europe which ushered in the era of the modern individual – the birth of the social foundation of the legal subject.

Humans have not always been persons, individuals free to make their own decisions. A date can be placed upon the end of servitude in Russia (1860s); the emancipation of slaves in the United States (1860s); the guaranteeing of voting rights and then civil rights to American blacks (1960s); and in Britain the abolition of the slave trade (1840s), the recognition of the rights of married women to own and dispose of property other than their husband's (1832) and the extension of voting rights to artisan's and non-property owners (1860s), and so on. In all these cases the extension of rights is an expansion of the citizenry of responsible persons, capable of entering freely into contracts and other obligations. The individual's own capacity for self-government, the inalienable right to freedom in his or her own person, and in the disposal of his or her property forms the basis of all other rights. Freedom of belief, speech, movement, association, trade and so on, are all logical extensions of the freedom of the historically specific individual in his or her own person and the disposal of his or her property.

These historically specific extensions of rights cannot be seen as a purely legal question. Rather, a more accurate expression is that the extension of rights is ratified in law. But before the constitutional ruling, law or ordinance setting out such a change, it has generally been the case that some political or social struggle has forced the question onto the agenda. When looking at the legal ratification of such claims, the historical question has to be: why then and not at some other point in time? Raising such a question does not mean to fault the legal reasoning that preceded the recognition of rights at a given point in time because the question of legal personality is not in and of itself legal, but historical.

The question of sovereignty and its juridical expression substantiates this proposition quite clearly. The modern doctrine of sovereignty can be dated to approximately the end of the medieval period (De Lupis 1974). The notion that within each nation-state, there must be located a supreme power, the decisive feature of which was its virtually unlimited capacity to make new law, was based upon the already prior existence of the sovereign himself (Lloyd and Freeman 1984). The test of government effectiveness as an expression of sovereignty was based solely upon the existence of a sovereign: as James Crawford argues, sovereignty was 'merely the location of supreme power within a particular territorial unit (which) necessarily came from within and did not require the recognition of other States or princes' (Crawford 1978). Robert Jackson sums this up neatly by suggesting that 'sovereigns preceded sovereignty'; these players 'are logically and in many cases historically prior to the game. They are rulers of substantial political systems who are endowed with domestic authority and power and are therefore credible internationally.' What Jackson correctly suggests is that they were able to demonstrate 'empirical statehood' (Jackson 1990, 34–8). As we will see below, in Jackson's words, 'classical international law is therefore the child and not the parent of states' (Jackson 1990, 52–3).

It is, therefore, quite logical and indeed consistent to suggest that in those areas outside Europe which could not demonstrate 'empirical statehood', sovereignty could not apply. Only those states that demonstrated this capacity were to be regarded as legal persons. For Jackson, the fact that European states were able to partition and colonize Africa in the late nineteenth century proved precisely how the latter's rulers were unable to demonstrate statehood (Jackson 1990, 39). Notwithstanding the racist assumptions of superiority that accompanied this conquest (and, indeed, the technological superiority), the point is that there was no question of sovereign statehood being granted to these peoples, precisely because an extension of such rights to societies that had not attained that capacity to exercise them would have represented a legal fiction without real content, and as such, a threat to existing social relations.

This is where the normative discussion always confuses the point. Many critics have pointed to the inconsistencies in the argument and practices of the upholders of these classic notions of juridical equality. Natural rights' theorists, like Thomas Jefferson, for example, a noted proponent of the inalienable rights of the American colonists and friend of the French Revolution, was a slave owner. These would appear to be profound inconsistencies. But while they do confirm the social character of rights as opposed to their claim to be natural, it would be wrong to simply conclude that their upholders were hypocrites. On the contrary, there were good reasons for circumscribing the extension of rights.

The salient point which flows from this is that the historical subject is the real basis of the subject in law. The subject has a historical and social existence that is logically prior to its legal character. It is, therefore, true to suggest that the subject is a historical creation, but not that it is simply a legal fiction. In this context, the claim of universal 'human' rights serves to confuse this reality because not only is the historically specific process through which the legal subject comes into being obscured, but the content is fundamentally altered. The legal claim is now based upon an abstract and ahistorical subject. This, as we will discuss below, remains the central difficulty with the human rights discourse.

For the purposes of this chapter the relationship between right and the law could be put in the following way: right is negative; law is positive. The essence of right is independence from the state or in the case of negative sovereignty, independence from external coercion and intervention. Right implies nothing about what you do with that freedom. It is a wholly negative, or open-ended proposition. The origins of the modern right concept is the assertion of independence from the state on the part of subjects. As such it is the basis of modern law. But the law itself is positive. Its form is an act, of parliament, congress, constituent assembly or international treaty, or a ruling or adjudication by a court of law. The act or ruling delineates the right but is not the right. This can be realized in different ways. In the British legal system, what is not proscribed is allowed. Rights are the negative image of the positive acts of law. It is a legal fetishism to take the law in and of itself, without understanding that it rests on the anterior question of right.

## The logical derivation of the law from the legal subject

Having established the historical character of the subject, we need to derive, logically, the main elements of the law from the legal subject. If one examines civil, criminal, constitutional and international law it becomes clear how they all express the derivation of the law from the will of the legal subject.

In enforcing contract, the civil law does not impose an alien goal onto individuals. Far from it. Taking the contract to be the will of the parties that make it, the civil law only enforces that will itself. The law, in this sense, is an enforcement of the will of individuals as enshrined in law. The civil law is enacted against a party to a contract who breaks the contract. In principle, what is enforced is a person's willed decision against a later deviation from that decision. Contract has a social, or more precisely, a civil aspect. One person's self-determination is the basis of another's plans and expectations. Self-interests are expressed in, and realized through, contractual obligations. The law is thus justified in enforcing contractual obligations freely entered into. Implicit in civil law is the assumption that we are all equally free. That means we are all equally capable of making responsible decisions for ourselves. That is what it means to be a person, or a legally recognized moral agent. Although the subject is characteristically an individual subject, it is clear that these characteristics are also applied to companies and associations who are also recognized as subjects in civil law, treated as if they were individual persons. Clearly, this forms the basis of states being recognized as legal subjects in international law.

The operation of criminal law, however, is more complex and space precludes a full exposition of this. It suffices to suggest that although the legitimate source of the criminal law has always been contested, the classical explanation of the sources of legislative authority has been the notion of the social contract. The social contract doctrine derives the authority of the law from an implied contract between all citizens and the government. The authority of the law rests on the (notional) consent of the parties. Criminal law is set on the same footing as civil law by this device. As moral agents, offenders are responsible for their decision to break the law, just as they would be responsible if they were to break the terms of a contract. The possibility of punishment, as opposed to mere repression, derives from the recognition of the autonomy of the offender.

The derivation of the law from the will of the offenders as expressed in the social contract is problematic precisely because the contract remains wholly notional. However, in the transition from criminal law to constitutional law, it can be seen how the notional social contract is given content, and indeed, how this becomes the basis for the state to be regarded as a legitimate legal subject in its own right.

The enlarged role of citizens in the election of legislatures gives content to the notional social contract. As electors, the rights of citizens in the drafting of the terms of the social contract through their representatives is recognized. Political rights, the rights to organize political parties, the right to contest elections and the right to representation in the state appear to be a departure from the concept of right in civil and criminal law. The bearer of political rights is not a single individual, but a people, or citizenry. The subject of political rights, then, has a more social appearance than the subject of civil rights.

But despite these appearances there is a crucial continuity between the legal subject of civil law and the collective subject of constitutional law, the people. The subject of civil law was never simply a natural individual. Rather, the formal recognition of the subject in law as a person already implied a social aspect to subjectivity. The subject is a subject not just because of a personal capacity to act (or, crucially for the human rights discourse, for simply being human) but because that capacity is recognized by others as such. As Rousseau wrote: 'Forced to combat nature or the social institutions, one must choose between making a man or a citizen, for one cannot make both at the same time' (cited in Malik 1996, 69). In entering into contracts and other relations with a subject, that subject is recognized as a person in his or her own right. The element of social recognition is as important as the individual capacity. That social recognition is what is formalized in law.

In constitutional law, the social aspect of subjectivity that is implicit in civil and criminal law is made manifest. As a people, the electorate is the subject from whom the authority of the state is derived. Through the election of representatives the general will is distinguished from the will of all. This process is also a process of the transformation of the will of all into the general will. The political process is itself a means for educating the electorate, on a grander scale than the educative role of public justice in the courts. It is also a process of clarification of the general will that abstracts from

special interests and prejudice. In pulling together the general will, the
representative process forges a national outlook among a people. In doing so
it is constrained from departing from the principles of free subjectivity that
are its real basis. The people is represented insofar as it can be reconciled
with the principles of individual liberty that are its foundations. The strict
limitations of this system can be seen in the representation of the interests
of labour in Western democracies.

But for all its limitations, the principle of popular sovereignty is a
profoundly radical conception of the authority of the state. It argues that the
state's authority derives exclusively from the people, without any external
resource for the deployment of power. It is this very process of constituting
the state that allows the state to be regarded as a rights-bearing subject itself,
the legal subject of international law. International law and the international
legal order do not provide a foundation for the state. On the contrary, it
presupposes the state's existence. However, the domestic analogy is limited
because there is no derived authority above the sovereign state (Brierly 1963;
Hoffman 1968). While this is true, international law nevertheless emerges as
the form through which sovereign states relate and interact with each other
as recognized equals. This system of rules and conditions acts in the same
way as all legal relations: it conditions international relations by providing
a regulatory framework which everyone upholds. International law becomes
the means through which the day-to-day existence of international society
can function on the grounds of regulated expectations and reciprocities.
Jackson's analogy is useful in this respect. He argues that

> the state is a legal person or citizen of international society and the rules
> are international law in the broadest sense: the international equivalent of
> the rules of the road. Sovereignty is the right to sail the metaphorical ship
> of state on the open oceans regulated by international law without being
> told where to head but only how to proceed. (Jackson 1990, 39)

So far, a logical reconstruction of the core doctrines of civil, criminal,
constitutional and international law have been set out to show their derivation
from the legal subject. This idealized picture, as has already been alluded to,
is without doubt flawed. But the importance of presenting this argument in
this way is that it reveals the centrality of the legal subject to all aspects of
the law. This is not to suggest that the liberal theory of law has no limitations
or inadequacies. As discussed below, the liberal theory of law is itself a
profound misrepresentation of real freedom. However, the question of the
legal subject and its expression in law holds profound implications for the
human rights discourse because it raises the one question which can unlock
the enigmatic character of the discourse: namely, from which socially constituted legal subject are human rights derived?

## The legal subject and human rights in the aftermath of the Second World War

Asking this question begins to highlight precisely why the human rights discourse is so problematized and indeed incapable of producing a consensus on the very concept of human rights itself (Dacyl 1996, 147). Whether one defines these rights as moral rights of the higher order (Donnelly 1985, 2) or 'claims and demands essential to the protection of human life and the enhancement of human dignity' (Kim 1991, 368–9), the tension between the moral demands of people and the political demands of states, indeed, the tension between the principles of universalism and internationalism which lie at the heart of the discourse remain unresolvable (Evans 1996). At one level, it is relatively easy to see why. Placing the concept 'human' in front of 'rights' may represent a quantum leap up. But this is only in the abstract. No matter how these rights are presented, what they have in common is the fact that they are not derived from socially constituted legal subjects.

The problem is obvious once the question of enforcement is raised: enforcing the conditions of a genuine exercise of human rights necessarily entails the application of an equal standard to the totality of individuals despite the fact that these individuals may not be in a position to exercise such rights (Meszaros 1986). While there is no conceptual difficulty in suggesting that the abstract right expressing the highest interest of humanity overrules the sectional interest, in reality the exercise of human rights remains a mere postulate so long as the sectional interests of a divided world society (be they class or state) prevail and paralyse the realization of the interests of all. The upholding or promotion of human rights represents a denigration of the legal subject precisely because it replaces an enforceable equal standard with an abstract universality which can never be realized within the confines of contemporary society.

This contradiction was clearly recognized by almost every key figure who was concerned to elevate human rights in the emerging new world order and in the formation of the United Nations Organization in the 1940s. Durward Sandifer, a specialist in legal matters assisting the special legal sub-committee set up by the US State Department to prepare a post-war international organization and to draft an international bill of rights, recognized from the outset that the principal problem would be that of 'implementing the guarantees contained in any bill of rights'. He observed that guaranteeing human rights, by their very nature, impinged upon domestic jurisdiction and thus 'immediately brought the tenets of international law into conflict with the prerogatives of national law' (Lauren 1996, 156–7). He cited with approval the opinion of André Mandelstam in *Les Droits internationaux de l'homme*:

> The signature, by all states, of a general convention of the rights of man
> would be at present unattainable, if such a convention should include any
> sanctions ... In fact, it would be falling victim to strange illusions to imagine
> that at the present time, when the Powers have not yet reached an under-
> standing on the subject of the establishment of collective sanctions against
> the state which breaks its solemn obligations to maintain the *external peace*,
> that the same Powers would consent to the institution of a juridical system
> permitting the international community to render judgements followed by
> sanctions in the demand for *interior peace*. (cited in Lauren, 157)

Sandifer's argument is of interest because he highlights how the immediate
priority facing the architects of the post-war order was the maintenance of
the external peace. As a result of this reasoning, he recommended that an
international bill of rights should be promulgated without establishing any
procedures for enforcement, but as a means to this end. In a document
classified as secret, he argued that this would represent the simplest and least
complicated method of putting an international bill of rights into effect. He
continued,

> It is a device used many times in the past. States agree on the adoption of
> new rules of law or a formulation of existing rules and proclaim them to the
> world in a formal international agreement. Reliance is placed primarily upon
> the good faith of the contracting parties ... Such a procedure has the
> advantage of provoking the minimum of opposition, which is important in a
> step as radical in character as giving universal legal recognition to individual
> human rights. (cited in Lauren, 157)

Although Sandifer's somewhat cynical reference to the promulgation of an
international bill of rights as a 'device' to be used by states can be interpreted
as an expression of a hypocritical attitude towards human rights, the substantial point he highlights is that states, not individuals and their rights,
are the 'contracting parties' of any 'formal international agreement'. Sandifer's
recommendation (without the open cynicism expressed in secret) was to
become the guiding principle for US policy for the next few decades and the
model for how this was to be presented to the outside world – a point we
will return to below.

The debate around the formation of the UN and its Charter and later,
the Universal Declaration of Human Rights confirms this reality. The debate
constantly flits between a commitment to the principles of human rights in
the abstract while in effect ensuring that these new principles of universal
human rights did not interfere with a return to 'normal' international politics
(Evans 1996). At the same time as Sandifer made his recommendations in
1942, the Sub-Committee on Political Problems of the US State Department
made it clear that it was the 'vitality of the national state' which was to be
regarded, from the outset, as of 'primary importance in the post-war world'

(Department of State 1950, 113). From the Dumbarton Oaks talks through to the promulgation of the UN Charter itself, what was established was that international disputes would be defined as conflicts of interest between states who alone would be subjects under international law (Evans 1996, 57–65).

One interesting insight into this process can be seen in a statement made in San Francisco by John Foster Dulles, minuted in the proceedings of the Eighth Meeting of Committee 1/1/A – the drafting sub-committee on Chapter II of the UN Charter, the Principles of the UN. Debating as to the scope and applicability of the proposed Economic and Social Council and its concern with the promotion of human rights, Dulles explained the significance of moving the clause relating to domestic jurisdiction and non-intervention from the chapter on pacific settlement of disputes (as discussed at Dumbarton Oaks) to the chapter on Principles.

> United States' Delegation had raised questions ... concerning the problem of domestic jurisdiction. They had always been reassured, however, that the United States need not worry about these points since this amendment to the chapter on *Principles* would apply to all functions of the Organization under the Charter and would provide an adequate safeguard ... if this Article is not retained in Chapter II, *Principles*, his delegation would have to reopen many of these questions in the Assembly, the Economic and Social Council, etc. (Drafting Sub-Committee Reports 1945, 3)

By establishing the non-assailability of the domestic sphere of sovereign states as a principle upon which the UN was to be based, the UN Charter ratified the sovereign state as the legal subject of international relations. For Dulles, establishing the sovereign state as the rights-bearing subject prior to its expression in law, was the overriding consideration for the US Delegation. This is why Dulles refused to support the inclusion of a reference to international law within the UN's principles. Dulles understood that existing international law was 'too narrow a rule on the determination of international versus domestic jurisdiction'. For Dulles it was 'unwise to invoke international law as it exists at present'. Rather, he hoped that 'international law on this subject will tend to become liberalized' (Drafting Sub-Committee Reports 1945, 4). In other words, Dulles confirmed that international law could only be derived from a historically constituted subject which had to exist prior to its expression in law. This was the logical and political priority.

Establishing the sovereign state as the only rights-bearing subject of international relations and law remained at the forefront of all the major powers' considerations in the drafting and promulgation of the UN Charter (Lauren 1996; Evans 1996). This was made explicitly clear during the US Senate's Committee on Foreign Relations hearings on the Charter itself. For example, when asked what the opening statement of the Charter, 'We the Peoples of the United Nations' meant, Leo Pasvolsky, special assistant to the Secretary

of State for International Organization and Security Affairs, and a leading
member of the US delegation to the San Francisco Conference, replied that

> it was clearly understood that the phrase 'We the peoples' meant that the
> peoples of the world were speaking through their governments at the Con-
> ference, and that it was because the peoples of the world are determined that
> those things shall be done which are stated in the preamble that the gov-
> ernments have negotiated the instrument. (Committee on Foreign Relations
> 1945, 227)

And in case there was any misunderstanding, when asked by Senator Austin
to clarify that wherever the word 'Member' appeared in the Charter, this
referred to 'states instead of to individuals', Pasvolsky reassured the Senator
that the word 'Member' was used to refer to a 'state rather than to an
individual. The individuals are referred to as representatives' (Committee on
Foreign Relations 1945, 230).

It was thus inevitable that establishing the sovereign state as the rights-
bearing subject of international law would come into conflict with the notion
of universal human rights, which required the individual as the rights-bearing
subject of law. It should be kept in mind that the San Francisco Conference
took place while the world was still at war. As Edward R. Stettinius, Secretary
of State and head of the US delegation to San Francisco, stated in his report
to the President, the conference was not a 'peace-time conference summoned
to debate the theory of international cooperation, or a post-war conference
convened to agree upon a treaty. It was a war-time conference' (Stettinius
1945, 11). The overriding task was to rebuild the international system on
the basis of socially constituted legal subjects, legally constituted, and ratified
in a new legitimized system of international law.

The contested character of the debate over universal rights (Russell
1958), compared to the consensus upon the domestic jurisdiction of states,
highlights, among other things, the enduring demand of the times and the
reality of this constraint. Thus, whatever Secretary of State Stettinius had in
mind when he stated the following, he nevertheless articulated the juridical
reality of the key points at issue:

> The provisions proposed in the Charter will not, of course, ensure by them-
> selves the realization of human rights and fundamental freedoms for all the
> people. The provisions are not made enforceable by any international machin-
> ery. The responsibility rests with the member governments to carry them
> out ... Whether the opportunity is used effectively or not will depend, as it
> must, upon the governments of the member nations and upon the people
> who elect them to office. (quoted in Evans 1996, 62–3)

In articulating the precise relationship between the legal subject and the
exercise of rights in the domestic and international spheres, Stettinius cap-
tures the inherent contradiction at the heart of the elevation of human rights.

While it is the case that universal human rights was dealt with in the abstract and thus rhetorically, seeing this simply as a ploy or an unwillingness to act boldly misses the fundamental point of why the question arose in the first place. Human rights became an issue at the end of the Second World War because their promotion by the big powers legitimized the new world order in the eyes of domestic and international society. The Second World War threw all the great powers into disarray: the experience of German imperialism under Hitler discredited all forms of imperialism and the long-standing assumptions of racial and cultural superiority these were based upon. As Lauren convincingly illustrates, in many respects the desire to protect the domestic jurisdiction of sovereign states arose by the big powers to limit any attacks upon the absence of these rights within their own societies (Lauren 1996; Furedi 1994).[3]

The debate about human rights and the upholding of human dignity, was in reality a process of re-legitimation of the principles of sovereignty and the non-intervention in the domestic affairs of sovereign states. The most powerful states, through the human rights discourse, made their own priorities the universal concern of others. Human rights in this context came to represent nothing more than an empty abstraction whose function was the legitimation and perpetuation of the given system of power relations, domestically and internationally. And although it is clear that a powerful set of social and economic interests was motivating the process, the reproduction of post-war social relations, could not have taken a different form. The moral concern with human rights and its broad appeal to international society provided much-needed ideological legitimacy to the new world order and international law. While this morality was fundamental in the subsequent evolution of the post-war period, it could not advance human rights in practice, precisely because the barrier to their realization is not a legal but a social one.

In fact, what the elevation of the human rights discourse in the 1940s illustrates is the real limitations of the modern concepts of right and freedom. The problem stems from the fact that rights and freedoms are severely constrained within our society. The shortcomings of freedom in a liberal society are not resolvable in legal terms or by establishing legal regimes. Rather, these shortcomings are discovered in the realm of social organization. Radical critics of liberal law theory argue that the failings of the Declaration arise because of a contradiction in the social structure of modern society, not because of misconceived legal theoretical constructions, which could in principle be remedied through more adequate theoretical solutions. The core failing of liberal societies lies in the progressive alienation of human powers that is the private accumulation of capital. Where society's productive forces, its industry, transportation, media and telecommunications, assume the form of private property, the motive of accumulating profit supplants the goal of human betterment. The ownership of the means of production by a minority is a monopoly that is undisturbed by the formal freedoms of a liberal society (Rosenberg 1994). In reality, these formal freedoms are an essential element to the way domination operates in modern society. Domination is constituted through the structural inequality of the labour contract within the privatized realm of production, where it is reproduced through being put into operation. The free exchange between private property owners – labour and capital – is a legally constituted and recognized relationship. But this formal equality reproduces a society of inequality – a process which goes on in private and which is held in check by economic sanction rather than by the exercise of jurisdiction, and reproduced by the formal separation of economics and politics (Sayer 1991). Thus, a society which enshrines in its laws equality and freedom and proclaims these publicly, masks relations of inequality which are reproduced in the apparent free exchange of commodity owners in the private sphere.

The contradiction between the rhetoric of universal human rights and the particularity of sovereign statehood did not arise because of a lack of foresight or courage on the part of statesmen at the time. It arose, and indeed, continues, because this shortcoming is not a legal postulate, but an insoluble social contradiction at the heart of modern society. As we will see below, it is precisely because these shortcomings are expressed in these juridical forms that attention has always focused upon legal regimes, and has often confused this realm with the philosophical and political (Evans 1996, 3–4).

The question this poses is that, if the elevation of human rights in the 1940s represented a politically expedient means through which to legitimize the sovereign state as the legal subject of international law (and not the individual), what does the ascendancy of the human rights discourse today represent?

In the first instance, the proliferation of human rights today appears to represent a real advance. As noted in the introduction to this chapter, the attempt to elevate human rights to the level of sovereign statehood is regarded as the start of a new, more humane era in world politics. But closer examination reveals that this discourse is based upon a caricatured notion of individual autonomy and its codification in law as the legal subject. One of the clearest examples of this process in the domestic and international sphere is the question of children's rights and the UN Convention of the Rights of the Child.

## The tyranny of children's rights[4]

But when it came to children, a higher law than sovereign rights and territorial imperatives prevailed. Children had a supervening right to protection from the consequences of governmental or anti-governmental forces

struggling to attain and retain power. (Varindra 1993, 12; describing intervention during Biafra in Nigeria between 1967–70.)

[U]sing children as a cutting edge of human rights generally, and of our
many ongoing efforts in diverse fields of development, would contribute more
to international peace and security, and more to democracy, development
and the environment – more to preventing crises and conflicts – in a shorter
period of time and at a far lower cost than any other set of doable actions
aimed at remedying global problems on the threshold of the 21st century.
(Grant 1994/95, 4.)

These quotes aptly express the point made in the introduction, of how
the question of children has come to dominate the international agenda at
the end of the twentieth century. The notion that children somehow invoke
'a higher law than sovereignty and territorial imperatives' or that they
represent 'a cutting edge of human rights' is precisely what needs to be
examined in order to grasp what this recognition really represents.

The UN Convention on the Rights of the Child recognizes childhood
and children's rights as universals applicable to all cultures and societies
across the North–South and the rich–poor divides. The rights dimension
reformulates the cause of the child and the inherent value system associated
with championing the child (Black 1996, 139). Through the Convention,
children's rights assume the status of universal human rights and become
inseparable from the human rights discourse (Lopatka 1992, 48). While the
right to child welfare – adequate nutrition, medical care and so on – has been
regarded as the most fundamental of all human rights (Freeman 1992), the
children's rights framework moves beyond previous welfare discussions. Now
a general principle of 'need' is regarded as a contractual obligation to
guarantee child welfare – the embodiment of a direct claim upon someone
else, which is not just a general statement of good intent or moral entitlement,
but an instrument legally binding on those states that ratify it (Boyden 1990,
193). The UN Convention, thus, provides an apparently universal standard
for children's rights, which contracting state parties must comply with, and
which is implemented through a monitoring and reporting procedure.

The Convention goes further than any previous treaty. In the case of
international humanitarian law, the contractual obligation to uphold children's
rights lies with the state as signatory to international treaties. The rights of
the child in the modern nation are encapsulated in the doctrine *parens patriae*
which grants the child the right to care and protection before the law and
defines the duty of the state to act as the guardian and ultimate guarantor of
child welfare through social planning (Boyden 1990). This protection is the
common thread through all past efforts to provide global standards of childhood – from the Fifth Assembly of the League of Nations in 1924 and its
Declaration of the Rights of the Child in the aftermath of the First World

War to the 1959 Declaration. Material needs and mankind's obligation to protect and nurture children characterized children's rights. Indeed, rather than encourage equality for children with adults, the commitment was to work in the best interests of the child, interests which were defined entirely by adults and which mankind owed to children (Freeman 1992, 4).

The UN Convention, however, extends the notion of right: it recognizes the child's capacity to act independently, bestowing not just *protective*, but also *enabling* rights, such as the right to freedom of expression and association.

Thus, at first sight, the Convention and its conception of universal children's rights appears to be a progressive step. The universal move to recognize children's rights is often compared to the recognition of the rights of women or the emancipation of slaves in America. The further extension of rights to what are perceived to be the most vulnerable sections of humanity, is understood to represent a step forward, indeed, a vast improvement on what existed before: in UNICEF's director, James Grant's words, a step towards the 'first truly universal law of mankind' (Grant 1994). The problem with the Convention, however, is that it is built upon two fundamental fallacies: the fallacy of children's rights, and the fallacy of a universal childhood.

THE FALLACY OF CHILDREN'S RIGHTS

The notion of children's rights contained in the Convention rests upon a basic fallacy which the Convention reproduces within the text of the treaty. This relates to the nature of rights and the competence of children. Children's rights are meaningless unless they are capable of exercising them. The notion of the rights of the child might look good in the Convention, but in reality children are not socially constituted legal subjects since they are not capable of exercising equal rights (Heartfield 1993).

Interestingly, this was recognized at the time when the Declaration was being drafted in 1948. For example, in a letter by the Commissioner of the Federal Security Agency setting down some suggestions for a charter for children's rights, the following point is made:

> In view of the fact that the status of the child before the law varies under different systems of law and in many countries the minor child has no legal entity or rights except through his parents or legal substitute, particular attention should be given to the term 'rights' as applied to the minor child ... (recommends a) careful review of each article of the Declaration of Human Rights to ascertain what special provisions may be needed in view of the minority status of the child to enable him to claim these basic human rights. (US National Archive, 1948)

The distinction between a 'right' and a need to provide special provisions for children, clearly maintained the critical distinction between the child as competent legal subject and as the object of society's concerns. This distinction, upheld in 1948, is precisely what has been scrapped through the development of the children's rights discourse today.

Despite all claims to the contrary, this distinction informs the UN Convention itself: in one of the most significant articles, Article 12, the Convention requires states 'to assure to the child who is capable of forming his or her own views the right to express those views freely in all matters affecting the child, the views of the child being given due weight in accordance with the age and maturity of the child' (UK Committee for UNICEF 1995, 5). Professor Michael Freeman pointedly asks in response to this: 'It is surprising (or is it?) that on the content of the Convention children as such were given no opportunity to input their views?' (Freeman 1992, 5). Freeman points out that despite Article 12, Article 3 – the key provision – directs that the 'best interests of the child' is to be a primary consideration. The Preamble, moreover, undermines not just the child's autonomy but his or her welfare as well, because it acknowledges that 'due account' should be taken of 'the importance of the traditions and cultural values of each people for the protection and harmonious development of the child' (UK Committee for UNICEF, 3). In short, Freeman highlights the conflict within the Convention between the notion of children as competent legal subjects and the fact that their rights have to be exercised on their behalf because, in reality, they are incompetent.

The conflict between Articles 3 and 12 highlights how the UN Convention contains a conflict between those who see children's rights in welfare terms and those who wish to promote a child's self-determination. The inescapable problem this rights discourse throws up through its treatment of children as adults, however, is that, in reality it represents the degradation of the meaning of individual rights (McGillivray 1992, 218). The representation of the 'primary consideration' of the best interests of the child embodied in Article 3 as a right, redefines the meaning of a democratic right – as care and protection exercised by the state. Under the Convention (Article 3), for example, the state acts on behalf of the child to protect it from abuse. The child does not exercise any rights; the state does. Democratic rights are undermined from two directions: first, the idea of democratic rights entailing independence from the state is now redefined as rights through state intervention; and second, the qualifications of competence before the law redefines the meaning of equality before the law. In essence, what the Convention represents is not an extension of rights or the universalization of rights, but its opposite; a shattering of the shell of legal equality – the infantilization of society and the degradation of democratic rights.

In codifying children's rights on the basis of incompetence, the discourse represents a fundamental attack upon the notion of the autonomous individual as a legal subject. It also contains an embedded acceptance of the need for state advocacy on behalf of the child. In reality, the general recognition and prioritization of children as the most vulnerable section of society is confused with a principle of protection. Recognizing this does not (or should not) logically nor automatically lead to the notion that children should be prioritized over adults.[5] In confusing this basic distinction, the Convention universalizes the need for intervention. And precisely because the internationally ratified UN Convention assumes a consensus on the universal application of these rights, the incontrovertibility of the discourse appears to be self-evident. The problem, of course, is that proclaiming the principle of universal children's rights might be fine on paper, but the conditions facing children in the world today are far from universal.

THE FALLACY OF UNIVERSAL CHILDHOOD

The UN Convention is not simply a set of broad principles or general statements. It sets out rights in detail assuming that they apply to a geopolitical area which shares the same attitudes to law, political system and compatible cultural traditions. The UN Convention is thus premised upon the existence of universal childhood – what some of the experts now refer to as the 'globalization of childhood' (Boyden 1992; Burman 1995). However, closer examination reveals that the view of childhood underlying the notion of the 'globalization of childhood' is a western one (Boyden 1992; Burman 1995; Freeman 1992; McGillivray 1992).[6] The dominant definition of childhood is based upon a western model which is fixed and rendered global through the claims of its universal applicability.

A standard of childhood which is specific to the condition of western society is established which becomes a global standard of measurement. Childhood is regarded as a fixed notion, 'determined by biological and psychological facts' (Freeman 1992), rather than historically specific, socioeconomic relations or cultures. The problem, however, is that childhood, within certain biological constraints, is a social construction which appears in a variety of forms and indeed can even result in children acting as autonomous subjects. Different social and economic conditions force southern societies to treat their children quite differently. Boyden contrasts Britain and Peru, for example, where, in the former it is illegal to leave infants and small children in charge of juveniles under the age of 14. In Peru a significant group of 6- to 14-year-olds are heads of households and, as such, are the principal breadwinners in the family (Boyden 1992, 198). The transition to adulthood differs radically in numerous countries. Western conceptions of childhood are, to put it quite bluntly, not a luxury which many countries of the South can afford to enjoy. Realities like the prolonged dependency of western children on their parents, universal education past teen years, high levels of consumption, healthcare and nutritional development, are not available in southern societies. Economic deprivation robs millions of children of a western childhood.

The problem with the globalization of western models of childhood, however, is not a normative but a political one. By setting this standard *southern childhood* is not only effectively erased from international view but the western model of childhood becomes the standard by which to judge *southern societies.* The relationship of the West to the South is represented as the relations governing western domestic childhood itself. The western child model dominates and symbolizes what is natural and good, spontaneous and authentic. The southern child, more often than not, violates this image and by default, becomes the object of western intervention, either in the form of aid as nurture, or as a constraint and moral condemnation of southern society as a whole. The ultimate effect is to call into question the southern state as a legal subject in itself.

## THE INFANTILIZATION OF THE SOUTH

The globalization of childhood establishes a moral framework and hierarchy which Burman perceptively argues 'infantilizes the South' (Burman 1995, 125). The relationship between the North and the South is reworked as the global reproduction of western domestic relations between adults and children. Burman's argument is compelling. In the case of southern aid where children are the beneficiaries, children are presented as innocent victims, who elicit sympathy without being held responsible for their suffering (while by implication their parents and families *are* responsible). Where they are depicted accompanying their parents,

> Southern women are represented as helpless, rendered into a state of childlike dependency not only through their need, but by implication through having transferred their parental responsibilities to the Northern donor ... the iconography of the South ... infantilizes peoples of the South as passive and powerless. It also indicates a process of feminization, determined not only by the overt infantilization of women as helpless victims, but also more implicitly through the gendered assumptions inscribed within definitions of development ... The binary opposition of adult and child is thus played out through colonial relationships of paternalism, so that relations of patronage, of help, of aid, secure a sense of competence and potency of Northern adults. (Burman 1995, 125–6)

Burman highlights the dualism embedded in this discourse: the 'binary opposition of adult and child ... played out through colonial relationships' reproduces the western model of childhood on a global scale which in turn determines the relationship between the West and the South and within the South itself. What Burman also points towards is how the international projection of this model of childhood reproduces the international relations of western domination which are internalized and are represented as natural developmental imperatives within the South. In effect, all humanitarian intervention in the South reproduces this dualism.

The fundamental implications of the UN Convention and its underlying assumptions concerning the universality of childhood should now begin to be apparent. In effect, the Convention openly condemns southern societies for their failure to give an equal share of resources and rights to children in general, and the girl child, in particular.[7] The demand for children's rights, although presented as a positive intervention, in actual fact, represents a fundamental intrusion into the domestic affairs of these states, effectively destroying their sovereign status, because the call carries an agenda which insists that these societies have to alter their social structures and allocate their limited resources according to an externally constructed set of priorities. This standard – a so-called 'universal' one which is externally determined – now represents the measure of the ability of these states to fulfil the criteria of legitimate state behaviour.

Remarkably, very few advocates of this new interventionism feel it necessary to dwell upon some of the glaring inconsistencies embedded in the discourse. It seems that the insistence upon the principle of the paramountcy of the child suffices to justify a level of intrusion into southern societies of which most Victorian colonialists could only have dreamt. While it might sound good, the principle of paramountcy is as fallacious as is the notion of children's rights or global childhood. Indeed, it does more than set an interventionist agenda. It globalizes a double standard which in effect condemns the South while hiding the failings of the West itself. What is never spelled out is how western society does not allow children's interests to determine how our society is organized. Citing the fact that one in four children are raised in poverty-stricken households in Britain or that 32 per cent of children in the UK live in families with less than half of the average income, shows how this principle does not apply in reality (Reece 1996, 299). This is hidden from view through locating the problem at the level of individual parent responsibility. But when it comes to the South, the formula is reversed: the position of children is analysed at the level of individual values but in this case, southern *society* is held responsible.

Once this framework is in place, the positive exercise of rights is inextricably linked to outside agency and thus, outside intervention. Indeed, for many advocates of humanitarian intervention today, the parallels between the shift from inviolable sovereignty to humanitarian intervention has a parallel precedent in the historical evolution of the family and child abuse. George Kent provides the clearest example. He argues that in the nineteenth century, parents could abuse their children without fear of intervention by the state. There was a strict separation of the private and public sphere (Burman 1995). He continues:

> Parents in effect had sovereign control over their families. Now, however, it is widely accepted that when there are gross violations of a child's rights,

outside agencies should intervene to protect that child. The rights of supervising adults are not absolute, but must be balanced by consideration of the best interests of the child; under some special circumstances it may be necessary to intervene on behalf of the child. Now that principle is coming to be acknowledged at the societal level. (Kent 1995, 160)

The assumptions informing this kind of analogous argument are quite clear: intervention rather than sovereignty should be the organizing principle governing children's welfare and rights.

In all essentials, what advocating children's rights means in this context is giving up the right to national self-determination. The UN Convention, from this point of view, represents a codification of a new international moral division in world affairs – between the South as failure and source of problems and the West as provider and solution. Today, it suffices to merely invoke the principle of child paramountcy to demand international armed intervention into southern societies where children are threatened by armed conflicts (Southall and Carballo 1996). Sovereignty, particularly in the South, now represents an enigma, a historical relic held on to by corrupt leaders in defiance of 'universal human rights'. In short, what we see evolving before our eyes, is a new interventionist framework which legalizes international inequality in the guise of a new moral universalism. Some have termed this the 'moral rehabilitation of imperialism' (Furedi 1994; Bienefield 1994).

Whatever one might think about this new interventionist framework, the threat this new discourse represents to democratic equality and freedom cannot be overstated. The solution it posits to society's problems today actually serves to provide a theoretical justification for the legal formalization of social inequality. By denigrating the concept of the legal subject itself, by conferring rights upon legal subjects who are incapable of exercising these rights, they serve to denigrate the equality of free subjects. Social justice is apparently elevated over legal niceties, like the juridical framework of sovereignty and international law. Social justice now stands above legal equality. Protecting children, indeed women or racial minorities, now overrides the considerations of liberty expressed in the classical concept of right and formalized in law. Outcomes are counterpoised to need while ignoring the fact that the notion of a legal subject has disappeared in the process.

The question that needs to be posed is how this approach resolves the fundamental problem of social inequality? If inequality is a condition that is prior to the operation of the law (as it is due to the social and property relations of modern society) what purpose can be served in changing the law? Presumably the argument is that the law can compensate for social inequality by pushing in the opposite direction. The law will act as a counterbalance to the negative effects of social inequality. But the practical effect of changing the law to suspend the formal equality of free subjects would be quite different. All that would happen is that social inequality would be reflected in legal inequality. Indeed, the shell of legal equality would be shattered so that it can be brought into line with social inequality. Social subjugation is not arrested by formalizing the degradation of the legal subject. On the contrary, the less people are reckoned as subjects in their own right, with their own goals and interests, the easier it is to subjugate them. Indeed, the only beneficiaries of the legalization of the degradation of the legal subject would be the *status quo*.

If anything, the children's rights discourse illustrates how far the attack upon democratic freedoms has already gone. Classic notions of right and freedom, for all their flaws, at least represented a realization that to advance these rights and freedoms in this society, equality and freedom from state interference was the bottom line. This is rapidly being replaced by a carica-tured notion of individual autonomy and its codification in law as the legal subject. This is what the elevation of the human rights discourse represents today – a fundamental attack upon democratic freedoms and rights.

## The decline of the legal subject

However, an important rider needs to be inserted in conclusion. The outcome discussed above is not the result of a legal process. As we discussed earlier, the development of the rights-bearing subject was not a legal process, but a social one which was reflected in law. The degradation of the legal subject today has not come about through legal sanction. Rather, the legalization of inequality reflects a broader social process in which subjectivity itself and the very notion of a socially derived legal subject has diminished.

During the 1990s, it is no exaggeration to suggest that the majority of western society has been squeezed out of public life – the diminishing numbers of people participating in political parties, trade unions, churches and all kinds of cultural organizations – demonstrates as much (Brierly 1991; Jenkins 1995; Hutton 1995). People's lives have, as a consequence, become more individuated and privatized. But that does not mean that individuals' sense of themselves has been strengthened. Far from it. Individuals have retreated defensively into private life and have become less assertive about their interests. It would be more accurate to say that today's individualism is a weakened sense of self that is more cautious, vulnerable and self-effacing than before. But this is not the way things are generally seen.

In Britain, as in America, the changed attitude towards individualism is expressed above all in a retrospective criticism of the excesses of the 1980s. The concerns of community are now elevated against the foil of the 'greedy 1980s' when, it is claimed, Thatcherism and Reaganism swung the pendulum too far in the direction of individual avarice. While it is true that the 1980s were characterized by an ideological commitment to setting the individual free from the constraints of collectivism and excessive state expenditure, the practice of the 1980s proved to be quite different from the theory.

The irony of the 1980s is that western societies have become more dependent upon state subsidies and supports. States in the OECD countries are spending more today in real terms for these purposes, than they ever have. After fifteen years of 'rolling back the state', state expenditure is now the equivalent of a higher proportion of national output. The *Economist* (7 October 1995) estimates that in the big economies, the public spending ratio has increased on average from 36 per cent to 40 per cent since 1980. Far from liberating individuals from the constraints of welfare dependency and state regulation, the 1980s produced an entirely opposite effect: a comprehensive undermining of almost every section of society's capacity to organize their own lives and further their own interests.

Space precludes a full discussion of this. But it suffices to say that the ideological and political assault upon society unleashed in the 1980s in the context of economic slump, undermined the most basic solidarities of neighbourhood, workplace and industry in a way that had immense consequences for contemporary society. The defeat of numerous trade union struggles allied to the ideological triumph of liberal democracy, as all alternatives seemed to disappear with the former Soviet Union, created uncertainty, despair and disillusionment, rather than a growth of an entrepreneurial spirit. In short, the 1980s did not give rise to a new individualism but the defeat of individual self-assertion and independent organization.

It is this degradation of subjectivity which is now being reflected in law in general, and within the ascendancy of the human rights discourse, in particular. There can be no clearer example of contemporary societies' tendency to hold free subjectivity in low esteem than the assertion of the existence of new rights unconnected to legal subjects like children or animals. In the international sphere, the turn to the UN and the debate about 'governance' expresses the same diminution of the legal subject, the state. New institutions and new arrangements are posed as alternatives to the perceived inability of the state to function as it has done in the past. The globalization discourse articulates this most clearly, where global 'flows, scapes and interactions' are assumed to be beyond the control of the nation state (Beck 1992; Camilleri and Falk 1992; Bergsten and Graham 1993; Mlinar 1992; Scholte 1995; Saurin 1995; Agnew 1994; Cerny 1995; Archibugi and Held 1995; Macmillan and Linklater 1995; Falk 1995; Williams 1993). However, in this instance, the tendency to hold the state in low esteem expresses a real loss of legitimacy and has produced a quest to find new legal subjects like 'global civil society' or 'new social movements', or indeed, human rights which can replace the state as the legal subject of international relations.

The attempt to create new legal frameworks which codify the denigration of the state as a legal subject can only end up where the human rights debate began in the 1940s – as an ideological legitimation of a new world order. In fact, it is worse than that. In the 1940s, the appeal to universal human rights attempted to re-legitimize the state as the legal subject of the post-war order. As caricatured as this might have been, it at least held out the possibility of struggling for national self-determination with all its shortcomings. Today's discourse holds out nothing but a future return to empires and colonies, to a world where paternalistic great powers exercise democratic rights on the behalf of their dependencies. As we approach the end of the twentieth century we are set to enjoy an array of newly discovered human rights in an increasingly unfree world. It seems the project of elevating human society and the dignity of people is further from being realized than it was when the last new world order was proclaimed in the 1940s.

## Notes

1 Thanks are due to James Heartfield for his valuable insights and generosity. What follows is, of course, my responsibility.
2 The following section has been derived from Heartfield (1996).
3 See also Anderson (1996) for an excellent discussion on the failure of the National Association for the Advancement of Coloured People to raise the question of the denial of human rights to America's black community at the time of the debate about the Human Rights Charter.
4 What follows is a much condensed version of Lewis (1996).
5 See Reece (1996) for an excellent dissection of the 'paramountcy principle' and its place within the Children's Act 1989.
6 Following McGillivray (1992) the term 'western' relates mainly to liberal democracies: Canada, the USA and the UK. In these states, the child abuse/children's rights histories are closely parallel.
7 See Black (1996), ch. 7, for how UNICEF's contribution to the development debate coalesced with the feminist rights discourse to produce a new 'human-centred' notion of southern development.

## References

Agnew, J. (1994), The territorial trap: the geographical assumptions of international relations theory, *Review of International Political Economy*, 1, 131–7.
Anderson, C. (1996), From hope to disillusion: African Americans, the United Nations, and the struggle for human rights, 1944–47, *Diplomatic History*, 20:4, 531–63.
Archibugi, D. and D. Held (1995), *Cosmopolitan Democracy – An Agenda for a New World Order*, Cambridge, Polity Press.
Ashley, R. K. (1988), Untying the sovereign state: a double reading of the anarchy problematique, *Millennium*, 17:2, 227–62.
Beck, U. (1992), *Risk Society: Towards a New Modernity*, London, Sage.
Beitz, C. R., M. Cohen, T. Scanlon and A. J. Simmons (eds) (1985), *International Ethics*, Princeton, Princeton University Press.
Bergsten, C. F. and E. M. Graham (1993), *The Globalization of Industry and National Economic Policies*, Washington DC, Institute for International Economics.

Bienefeld, M. (1994), The new world order: echoes of a new imperialism, *Third World Quarterly*, 15:1, 31–48.

Black, M. (1996), *Children First*, New York, Oxford University Press.

Boyden, J. (1990), Childhood and the policy makers: a comparative perspective on the globalization of childhood, in A. Jones and B. Prout (1990), *Constructing and Reconstructing Childhood*, Basingstoke, Falmer Press.

Boyden, J. (1992), *Families: Celebration and Hope in a World of Change*, London, Gaia/ UNESCO.

Brierly, J. L. (1963), *The Law of Nations*, London, Oxford University Press.

Brierly, P. (1991), *Christian Europe: What the English Church Census Reveals*, MARC, Europe.

Bull, H. (ed.) (1984), *Intervention in World Politics*, Oxford, Clarendon Press.

Burman, E. (1995), Developing differences: gender, childhood and economic development, *Children and Society*, 9:3, 121–42.

Camilleri, J. and J. Falk (1992), *The End of Sovereignty? The Politics of a Shrinking and Fragmented World*, Aldershot, Edward Elgar.

Carothers, T. (1994), Democracy and human rights: policy allies or rivals?, *Washington Quarterly*, 117:3, 109–20.

Cerny, P. G. (1995), Globalization and the changing logic of collective action, *International Organization*, 49:4, 594–628.

Chopra, J. and T. G. Weiss (1992), Sovereignty is no longer sacrosanct: codifying humanitarian intervention, *Ethics and International Affairs*, 16, 95–117.

Committee on Foreign Relations, US Senate (1945), *The Charter of the United Nations: Hearings*, Seventy-Ninth Congress, First Session, 2 July.

Crawford, J. (1978), *British Yearbook of International Law 1976–77*, Oxford, Oxford, University Press.

Dacyl, J. W. (1996), Sovereignty versus human rights: from past discourses to contemporary dilemmas, *Journal of Refugee Studies*, 9:2, 136–65.

De Cuellar, J. P. (1991), *Report on the Work of the Organization*, UN Doc. A46/1, 6 September.

De Lupis, I. D. (1974), *International Law and the Independent State*, Aldershot, Gower Publishing.

Deng, F. M. (1993), Africa and the new world dis-order: rethinking colonial borders, *The Brookings Review*, Spring.

Department of State (1950), *Post-war Foreign Policy Preparation*, Publication 3580, Washington 1949.

Deutsch, K. W. and S. Hoffman (eds) (1968), *The Relevance of International Law*, Cambridge, MA, Harvard University Press.

Donnelly, J. (1985), Human rights and human dignity, *The American Political Science Review*, 76:2, 303–17.

*Economist*, the (1995), The myth of the powerless state, and who's in the driving seat?, 7 October.

Evans, T. (1996), *US Hegemony and the Project of Universal Human Rights*, London, Macmillan.

Falk, R. (1995), The world order between inter-state law and the law of humanity: the role of civil society institutions, in D. Archibugi and D. Held (1995), *Cosmopolitan Democracy – An Agenda for a New World Order*, Cambridge, Polity Press.

Freedman, L. and D. Boren, 'Safe havens' for Kurds in post-war Iraq, in N. Rodley (ed.) (1992), *To Loose the Bounds of Wickedness: International Intervention in Defence of Human Rights*, London, Brassey's.

Freeman, M. (1992), Rights: ideology and children, in M. Freeman, and P. Veerman (eds) (1992), *The Ideologies of Children's Rights*, Dordrecht, Martinus Nijhof Publishers.

Freeman, M. and P. Veerman (eds) (1992), *The Ideologies of Children's Rights*, Dordrecht, Martinus Nijhof Publishers.

Furedi, F. (1994), *The New Ideology of Imperialism*, London, Pluto.

Grant, J. (1994), Child rights: a central moral imperative of our time, Statement to the Third Committee of the 49th General Assembly of the United Nations, New York.

Grant, J. (1994–95), Final speech to the General Assembly of the United Nations, Armistice Day 1994, *UK Annual Review*, UNICEF.

Halperin, M. H., D. J. Scheffer and P. L. Small (eds) (1992), *Self-Determination in the New World Order*, New York, Carnegie Endowment for International Peace.

Heartfield, J. (1993), Children's rights? Wrong, *Living Marxism*, 60, 12–14.

Heartfield, J. (1996) Law and the legal subject, *Freedom and Law Discussion Paper*, London.

Held, D. and A. McGrew (1994), Globalization and the liberal democratic state, in Y. Sakamoto (ed.), *Global Transformation: Challenges to the States System*, New York, United Nations Press.

Herbst, J. (1992), Challenges to Africa's boundaries in the new world order, *Journal of International Affairs*, 46:1, 17–30.

Hoffman, S. (1968), International law and the control of force, in K. W. Deutsch and S. Hoffman (eds), *The Relevance of International Law*, Cambridge, MA, Harvard University Press.

Hutton, W. (1995), *The State We're In*, London, Jonathan Cape.

Jackson, R. H. (1990), *Quasi-States: Sovereignty, International Relations and the Third World*, Cambridge, Cambridge University Press.

Jackson, R. H. (1992), Juridical statehood in Africa, *Journal of International Affairs*, 46:1, 1–16.

James, A. (1986), *Sovereign Statehood*, London, Allen & Unwin.

Jenkins, S. (1995), *Accountable to None*, London, Penguin.

Kent, G. (1995), *Children in the International Political Economy*, Basingstoke, Macmillan.

Kim, S. (1991), Global human rights and world order, in R. Falk, S. Kim and S. Mendlovitz (eds) (1991), *The United Nations and a Just World Order*, Boulder, CO, Westview Press.

Lapidoth, R. (1992), Sovereignty in transition, *Journal of International Affairs*, 45:2, 325–46.

Lauren, P. G. (1996), 2nd edn, *Power and Prejudice: The Politics and Diplomacy of Racial Discrimination*, Oxford, Westview Press.

Lewis, Morman (1996), A new age of intervention: the globalisation of American liberal discourse, paper presented to the British International Studies Association Annual Conference, Durham.

Lloyd, Lord and M. D. A. Freeman (1984), *Lloyd's Introduction to Jurisprudence*, London, Stevens and Sons.

Lopatka, A. (1992), The rights of the child are universal: the perspective of the UN Convention on the Rights of the Child, in M. Freeman and P. Veerman (eds), *The Ideologies of Children's Rights*, Dordrecht, Martinus Nijhof Publishers.

Macmillan, J. and A. Linklater (eds) (1995), *Boundaries in Question*, London, Pinter.

Malik, K. (1996), *The Meaning of Race*, London, Macmillan.

Mayall, J. (1991), *Nationalism and International Society*, Cambridge, Cambridge University Press.

Mayall, J. (1991a), Non-intervention, self-determination and the New World Order, *International Affairs*, 67:3, 422.

Mayall, J. (1996), *The New Interventionism 1991–1994*, Cambridge, Cambridge University Press.

Mayall, J. and A. Payne (eds) (1991), *The Fallacies of Hope: The Post-Colonial Record of the Commonwealth Third World*, Manchester, Manchester University Press.

McGillivray, A. (1992), Reconstructing child abuse: western definition and non-western experience, in M. Freeman and P. Veerman (eds), *The Ideologies of Children's Rights*, Dordrecht, Martinus Nijhof Publishers.

McGrew, A. G. and P. G. Lewis (1992), *Global Politics: Globalization and the Nation State*, Cambridge, Polity Press.

Médecins sans Frontières (1993), *Life, Death and Aid: Report on World Crisis Intervention*, London, Routledge.

Meszaros, I. (1986), *Philosophy, Ideology and Social Science*, Sussex, Wheatsheaf Books.

Mlinar, Z. (ed.) (1992), *Globalization and Territorial Identities*, Aldershot, Avebury.

Ogata, S. (1995), International security and refugee problems after the Cold War, Olof Palme Memorial Lecture, *SIPRI*, Stockholm, 14/6.

Picciotto, S. (1996), *Fragmented States and International Rules of Law*, Inaugural Lecture, Lancaster University.

Reece, H. (1996), The paramountcy principle: consensus or construct?, *Current Legal Problems*, 49, 267–304.

Rodley, N. (ed.) (1992), *To Loose the Bounds of Wickedness: International Intervention in Defence of Human Rights*, London, Brassey's.

Rosenau, J. (ed.) (1992), *Governance without Government*, Cambridge, Cambridge University Press.

Rosenberg, J. (1994), *The Empire of Civil Society – A Critique of the Realist Theory of International Relations*, London, Verso.

Russell, R. (1958), *A History of the United Nations Charter: The Role of the United States 1940–1945*, Washington, DC, Brookings Institute.

Saurin, J. (1995), The end of international relations? The state and international theory in the age of globalisation, in J. Macmillan and A. Linklater (eds), *Boundaries in Question*, London, Pinter.

Sayer, D. (1991), *Capitalism and Modernity*, London and New York, Routledge.

Scholte, J. A. (1995), Governance and democracy in a globalized world, paper for the ACUNS/ASIL Summer Workshop on International Organization Studies, *The Evolving Nature of Sovereignty and the Future of Global Security*, The Hague, 16–28 July.

Southall, D. and M. Carballo (1996), Can children be protected from the effects of war?, *British Medical Journal*, 313.

Stettinius, Jr. E. R. (1945), *Report to the President on the Results of the San Francisco Conference by the Chairman of the United States Delegation, the Secretary of State*, Department of State, Publication 2349, Conference Series 71.

UK Committee for UNICEF (1995), Oxford, Oxford University Press.

UNICEF (1983), The impact of world recession on children, Chapter 4 of *The State of the World's Children 1984*, New York, UNICEF and Oxford University Press.

United Nations Archive, Report of the Eighth Meeting of Committee I/1/A, Continuation of Discussion of Chapter 2, Principles, 24 May 1945. UNCIO, 2.2.3 Box 2, Committee I/1/A (Drafting Sub-Committee Reports).

United States National Archive (1948), Letter to Walter Kotschnig, Chief of International Organization Affairs at the State Department, from Commissioner Federal Security Agency of the Social Security Administration in Washington, RG 59, Box 2168, 501. BD/12–1548.

Varindra Tarzie Vittachi (1993), *Between the Guns: Children as a Zone of Peace*, Sevenoaks, Hodder & Stoughton.

Walker, R. B. J. (1988), State sovereignty, global civilization and the articulation of political space, *World Order Studies Program*, Occasional Paper No. 18, Centre for International Studies, Princeton University.

Walker, R. B. J. and S. Mendovitz (eds) (1990), *Contending Sovereignties: Redefining Political Community*, Boulder, CO, Lynne Reinner.

Waltz, K. (1979), *Theory of International Politics*, Philippines, Addison-Wesley Publishing.

Weber, C. (1995), *Simulating Sovereignty: Intervention, the State and Symbolic Exchange*, Cambridge, Cambridge University Press.

Williams, C. H. (1993), *The Political Geography of the New World Order*, London and New York, Belhaven Press.

Wood, E. M. (1995), *Democracy Against Capitalism*, Cambridge, Cambridge University Press.

Wriston, W. B. (1992), *The Twilight of Sovereignty: How the Information Revolution is Transforming Our World*, New York, Charles Scribner.

# 5

# International law and human rights

## Christine Chinkin

## Introduction

The events of the Second World War brought human rights violations into prominence and since its end there has been an enormous commitment to the legal guarantee of human rights and fundamental freedoms. Articulation of international legal standards preoccupied the human rights bodies of the UN from the drafting of the Universal Declaration on Human Rights and the Genocide Convention for acceptance by the General Assembly in 1948, to the completion of the two UN covenants in 1966 (the International Covenant on Economic, Social and Cultural Rights (ICESCR) and the International Covenant on Civil and Political Rights (ICCPR), 16 December 1966). After the covenants entered into force in 1976, attention turned to mechanisms for the implementation of those standards, although further elaboration continued through refinement of particular prohibitions[1] and assertions of particularly apposite rights for especially vulnerable groups.[2] Dozens of human rights treaties now derive from the UN human rights system,[3] many of them widely ratified by states from all geographic areas and religious and political ideologies.[4] The plethora of implementation mechanisms include the evolving competencies of the Economic and Social Council of the UN (ECOSOC),[5] its human rights commissions, sub-commission, and working groups,[6] the committees of independent experts formed under the human rights treaties,[7] the growing number of thematic and special rapporteurs and the post of UN Commissioner for Human Rights established after the Second World Conference on Human Rights held in Vienna in 1993.

Lawyers have been 'in the front line of the battle' in transforming human rights from 'the exclusive realm of philosophy and moral reflection into the domain of law' (Alston 1988, 8). The formal elaboration of norms and procedures generated by the Declaration make it appropriate to celebrate the legal achievement on its fiftieth anniversary in 1998. However, the reality is more sobering. Despite the legal and bureaucratic energy invested in human rights guarantees, these standards are regularly and routinely infringed throughout the world.[8] The greater number of international commitments, coupled with increasingly sophisticated procedures and monitoring mechanisms, have not reduced the scale or intensity of violations to which the world has inexcusably become accustomed in the first half century of the legal regime engendered by the UN Charter.

The reasons for the failure by states to observe the human rights obligations they have undertaken are complex. Although many are outside the realm of law,[9] this chapter demonstrates that tensions surrounding the place of human rights law within the substantive principles and structures of the international legal system limit its capability to protect individuals from governmental abuse. Human rights law is too often seen as a distinct discipline from international law with its own principles and methodologies (Alston 1988, 11).[10] This separation impedes the application of basic international legal doctrine to human rights law, impedes its conceptual and academic development and obscures conflicts between the two. Alston comments that maintaining human rights law distinct from general international law is favoured by human rights lawyers who may apply 'less rigorous standards of legal analysis in order to support their desired policy positions' (Alston 1988, 12). This chapter examines especially the friction between the doctrines of state sovereignty and human rights, internal inadequacies within human rights law, institutional barriers and the enforcement deficiencies of international law. These tensions lead to the query of whether law, and in particular international law as currently defined, is a worthwhile instrument for the attainment of respect for the dignity and worth of the human person (UN Charter, Preamble).

## State sovereignty versus individual rights

### RECOGNITION OF STATEHOOD

The foundational doctrine of international law, the sovereign equality of states (UN Charter, Article 2 (1)), assures states the prerogatives of territorial integrity and political independence. In legal terms, these are upheld by the principle of non-intervention into matters of domestic jurisdiction, either by other states (Declaration on Principles of International Law) or by the institutions of the legal order, including the UN (UN Charter, Article 2). The fundamental challenge to the doctrine of sovereign equality of states presented by the human rights canon lies at the heart of the dilemma of international regulation which is played out in a number of key areas.

First is the concept of statehood upon which the entire legal edifice is constructed. The traditional legal criteria for the attainment of statehood are that an entity must possess territory, a permanent population, have an effective government and the capacity to enter into international relations (Montevideo Convention). These objective criteria for statehood are neutral and value free, while human rights are predicated upon a value system, predominantly that of western liberal democracy rooted in the moral standards of Judaeo-Christianity (Cassese 1986, 288).[11] However, it is through political acts of recognition by other states, made on the basis of subjective evaluation rather than reliance upon the objective criteria listed above, that claimants to statehood, or government, come to enjoy the benefits of that status (Brownlie 1990, 87–106; Shaw 1997, ch. 7; Reisman and Suzuki 1976, 403). Recognition of states whose internal mechanisms do not conform with the liberal democratic model betrays the articulated commitment to human rights based upon that model, is likely to cause conflict with individuals within the state who demand adherence to those rights, and to provoke internal repression in response to those demands.[12]

There has been some indication that states do require some guarantee of respect for human rights before bestowing recognition. For example, the long-denied recognition of an independent Southern Rhodesia was based, at least in part, upon the regime's denial of majority representation [13] and South Africa's apartheid policy was denied recognition in the Bantustan and Namibia.[14] More recently, the guidelines formulated by the European Community (EC) for the recognition of new states formed out of the break-up of the former USSR and Yugoslavia made recognition dependent upon a commitment to the rule of law, democracy and a guarantee of minority rights (Warbrick 1992).[15] In the former Republic of Yugoslavia, Serbia-Montenegro (the 'rump' state after the disintegration of Yugoslavia) was somewhat equivocally denied automatic succession to the seat within the UN formerly occupied by Yugoslavia (*Bosnia and Hercegovina* v. *Serbia-Montenegro*), although continued adherence to the human rights treaties accepted by the former Yugoslav state was assumed. However, members of the EC were ambivalent in the execution of these prerequisites to recognition, as was seen in the failure to insert guarantees of minority rights in binding treaties and in the inconsistent application of the guidelines, despite formal arbitration of claims to statehood.[16] The lack of political will to give credence to the importance of human rights criteria may have been due to an unwillingness to subject recognition to regional collective will and, perhaps, to an uneasiness about imposing higher standards upon claimants to statehood than are required of existing states.

In the closely connected issue of recognition of governments, a number of states have expressly renounced passing judgment upon claimants that have seized power through unconstitutional means.[17] By so doing states maximize their options for commercial dealings with new regimes, but fail to offer support to individuals whose constitutional guarantees have been disregarded.

SELF-DETERMINATION AND HUMAN RIGHTS

Claims to statehood in contemporary international law invariably use the rhetoric of the right to self-determination, the right of all peoples freely to determine their political status and pursue their economic, social and cultural development (ICCPR, Article 1; ICESCR, Article 1). Through its association with the process of European decolonization, the right to self-determination has become the cornerstone principle of claims to statehood and to observance of human rights in the UN Charter era. However the group right to self-determination confronts those very concepts of contemporary international law that it upholds: those of the political independence and territorial integrity of sovereign states on the one hand, and the guarantees of fundamental rights and freedoms to individuals encapsulated in human rights law on the other.

The challenge to individual rights presented by claims to self-determination arises out of the assumption of a community of interests within the self-determining unit. This is not inevitably the case and individual rights may be subordinated to the demand of the group to political or cultural identity. Such a clash was present in *Lovelace* v. *Canada*, a claim brought before the Human Rights Committee under the First Optional Protocol to the ICCPR. The complainant was a female member of the Maliseet Indian tribe who, in accordance with the Canadian Indian Act, had lost her right to live on the Tobique Indian reservation upon her marriage to a non-Indian. After her divorce she wished to return to the reserve where she had been raised. The Canadian government argued that the legislation protected the continuation of the Indian tribe and that change could not occur without consultation with members of the tribe. The Human Rights Committee held that denying Lovelace the right to reside on the reserve violated her rights as 'persons who are brought up on a reserve who have kept ties with their community and wish to maintain these ties must normally be considered as belonging to that minority ...' (ICCPR, Article 27). This opinion discounts the possibility of the group determining the conditions for membership in accordance with its own values, in favour of Lovelace's individual right to assert her continuing identity as a member of the group.

The right to self-determination has been most readily accepted in its assertion of free political choice for those entities previously colonized by European powers. It does not however accord a right to secession or to the break-up of the territorial integrity of a state.[18] The doctrine of *uti possidetis* maintains the colonial boundaries of newly independent states and all states retain the inherent right to self-defence and survival (*Burkina Faso* v. *Mali*). This has legitimated states' rejection of limitations upon their sovereign right to resist a threat to their territorial integrity, including human rights limitations.[19] Thus the prohibition on the use of force applies to inter-state, not intra-state relations (UN Charter, Article 2 (4)), the legal regime for humanitarian protection is stronger with respect to international armed conflict than internal conflict,[20] and human rights treaties allow for derogation in times of national emergency, of which challenge to the fabric of the state is paramount (ICCPR, Art. 4; European Convention, Art. 15; American Convention, Art. 27). The events surrounding the break-up of the former Yugoslavia provide only too vivid an illustration of the vulnerability of human rights when the continuation of the state itself is threatened from within (Franck 1996, 359).

At the same time, the ideology of human rights, notably the collective right of self-determination, has been the motivating factor for wars of nationalism and liberation against forms of domination – apartheid, racism, colonialism and foreign occupation. Some groups reject constraints upon pursuit of their right to self-determination and resort to terrorist attacks and human rights abuses against civilian populations. The escalation of violence and state repression of those challenging the authority of those holding power within the state again illustrate the frailty of human rights guarantees in these situations (*Ireland* v. *UK*; Morgan 1989). Another aspect is the protection of the human rights of refugees who flee from such situations. It is legitimately asked whether the law is for the protection of states against the incursions of peoples across their borders, or for the protection of those peoples against further violations (Convention Relating to the Status of Refugees; Protocol Relating to the Status of Refugees).

## HUMAN RIGHTS AND NON-INTERVENTION

A further tension is that between the right to self-determination and the duty of non-intervention into the affairs of another state. Those legitimately seeking self-determination can expect:

> In their actions against and resistance to such forcible action in pursuit of the exercise of their right to self-determination, such peoples are entitled to seek and to receive support in accordance with the purposes and principles of the Charter of the United Nations. (Declaration on Principles of International Law 1970)

The distinction between legitimate support for those denied their acknowledged right to self-determination and wrongful intervention in the affairs of other states is imprecise and open to cynical manipulation. During the cold war years covert support for governmental opposition became a regular tactic of both the USA and the USSR and fomented further human rights abuses by all sides in conflict. In the action brought by Nicaragua against the USA, the International Court of Justice (ICJ) affirmed the illegality of any such intervention, but denied the right to collective self-defence against wrongful intervention not amounting to an armed attack under the terms of UN Charter, Article 51 (*Nicaragua* v. *USA*). This ruling, made against the backdrop of cold war covert operations across Central America, was asserted neutrally in terms of political ideology, but disallowed a weaker state from seeking assistance against attempted violent overthrow of its government and consequent further denials of human rights. It contributed little to the prospects of peace in the region, that was achieved through political, not legal negotiation.

The articulation of international human rights norms has eroded the domestic jurisdiction exclusion for violations of civil and political rights.[21] Nevertheless states continue to restrict the corresponding erosion of sovereignty by limiting the applicability of treaties through reservations,[22] claw-back provisions and derogations.

Arguments of domestic jurisdiction remain potent to inhibit the use of force to prevent gross human rights abuses in another state. The legality of unilateral intervention for purported humanitarian ends has been controversial since the prohibition of the use of force by Article 2 (4) of the UN Charter. Although the protection of human rights is a stipulated purpose of the UN, state practice remained on balance against justifying coercive action for humanitarian ends, even in such extreme cases as the Vietnam invasion of Kampuchea in 1979, which resulted in the overthrow of the Pol Pot regime, and the Tanzanian invasion of Idi Amin's Uganda (Fonteyne 1973–74; Lillich 1973; Simon 1996; Murphy 1996). The preference was to justify forcible intervention in traditional terms of self-defence, rather than on humanitarian grounds.

The Charter prohibition of the use of force has led to what has been called the 'classic/realist schism' between legal scholars as to the legality of intervention on humanitarian grounds (Lillich 1993). Classicists (or positivists) rely upon the formal sources of international law, that is the written text of express agreements interpreted in light of the intention of the drafters and customary international law as evidenced by unambiguous state practice.[23] They argue that the Charter text is explicit and that the only legitimate exceptions are self-defence and collective action under Chapter VII. Their position is bolstered by reference to the cardinal principles of the UN: the sovereign equality of states and non-interference into the domestic jurisdiction of states (Henkin 1989). Realists reject this conservatism and urge a dynamic interpretation of international law.

> Classicists want to preserve law's contribution to order by protecting its autonomy from ephemeral shifts in power and interest. Realists want to save it from irrelevance. (Farer 1991, 118–19)

Realist arguments can proceed from one of two positions. The first posits that Article 2 (4) does not prohibit all use of force but only that contrary to the 'territorial integrity or political independence' of states 'or in any other manner inconsistent with the purposes of the United Nations'. A limited use of force directed at the removal of human rights abuses does not interfere with a state's political independence and amounts only to a technical interference with territorial integrity. It also upholds the human rights purposes of the Charter. As has been commented, it would be strange if the first international instrument to promote protection of human rights as a major objective of the international community also removed the right to give effect to that protection (Bazlyer 1987).

Underlying these textual debates is a strongly held moral conviction that a stated commitment to the protection of human rights means nothing if gross violations continue without sanction. International lawyers should not be afraid to assert priorities based upon moral convictions and values. Such convictions allow acceptance of the position that the use of force for humanitarian motives technically constitutes a violation of international law, but is morally justified in extreme cases. An alternative approach is to regard humanitarian intervention as a further exception to the Charter. Teson, in perhaps the fullest theoretical analysis of the need for a moral theory of international law (Teson 1988), argues that the ultimate justification of the state is the protection and enforcement of the natural rights of its citizens. A government that violates these rights betrays the very purpose for which it exists and forfeits its domestic and international legitimacy (Teson 1988). This justifies foreign intervention, provided that intervention is proportionate to the evil it is designed to suppress. Teson does not locate sovereignty within the people,[24] but instead balances the rights of the state against those of its citizens.

Since the easing of tensions within the Security Council after the disintegration of the Soviet Union, the doctrine of unilateral humanitarian action has to some extent merged with that of collective security action under Chapter VII of the Charter (Lillich 1993). Unfortunately, Security Council decision making has not resolved the controversy. The explicit purpose of Chapter VII is the restoration of international peace and security,[25] not the preservation of human dignity and human rights. This may lead to conflicting agendas in that the humanitarian option might further disrupt international peace and not conform with the political priorities of members of the Security Council. Nevertheless, since 1990 it has used its powers to intervene in situations demanding a humanitarian response, for example to 'condemn repression of the Iraqi civilian population'[26] to authorize the use of 'all necessary means' to create conditions for humanitarian relief in Somalia (SC Res. 794, 3 December 1992) and to achieve humanitarian objectives in Rwanda.[27] However, the requirements that UN peace-keeping forces maintain impartiality in an internal conflict while delivering humanitarian services and that they operate on the basis of consent have generated a legal and military quagmire. This was demonstrated in Somalia, and in the obscenity of legally asserted safe havens in Bosnia and Hercegovina without the corresponding political or military will to ensure more than a temporary refuge for civilians. Despite the extensive human rights guarantees in the Dayton Peace Accords (Sloan 1996), the constitutional legitimacy accorded to the Republika Spsrska denies the unacceptability of human rights abuses, including ethnic cleansing (*Dayton Peace Accords*, Article III, Annex 4; *Constitution of Bosnia and Herce-govina*, Article I (3)).

The Security Council has other options than the use of military force. Under Article 41 it can impose economic and other measures against states. The use of non-physical force against a target state has evident humanitarian advantages, but studies of the impact of economic sanctions against Iraq make it at least arguable that they violate the ICESCR, Articles 11 and 12.[28] Although extreme hardships have been documented by UN specialized agencies, the Security Council is not accountable for the consequences of its peacemaking or peace-keeping activities under Article 41.[29]

Martii Koskenniemi has described the UN as functionally and ideologically founded upon a separation of activities: competence over 'hard' matters of the primacy of international order is allocated to the Security Council and that over 'soft' matters of justice and human rights to the General Assembly (Koskenniemi 1995). In such situations as Somalia, the Security Council expanded its understanding of international peace by drawing upon its 'hard' policing powers to try to restore internal justice. But, Koskenniemi argues, the Security Council is an ill-equipped forum for dispensing justice in internal conflicts where civilian casualties are high. Restoring justice requires attributes not readily assumed by military peace-keeping forces whose mandate is determined by international political decision-makers. These include nation building, participative decision making, accountability, consistency and monitoring processes. Koskenniemi concludes that the clash between the objectives of order and justice prevent the Security Council from achieving any genuine transformation of international society through the system of collective security.

A further obstacle to relying upon the Security Council to champion human rights is that its political nature makes intervention on humanitarian grounds highly selective. This undermines the notion of universally applicable standards that will be upheld. Thus US interests meant that democracy in Haiti has been restored by Security Council authorized action (SC Res. 940, 31 July 1994), while human rights abuses in East Timor continue without collective response.

## Human rights law: dilemmas of claims, claimants and violators

### CLAIMS OF NEW HUMAN RIGHTS

The discussion thus far has indicated some of the tensions presented by the place of human rights law within the state oriented system of international law. Others are presented by the evolving concept of human rights law. The Declaration provides a 'unitary and universally valid concept of what values should be cherished by all States within their own domestic orders' (Cassese 1986, 299). It includes both civil and political rights and economic, social and cultural rights, although only five of the thirty articles refer to the latter group. This initial unity in the formulation of human rights standards was disrupted by the drafting of separate covenants in 1966. Although neither covenant was accorded priority, the more forceful language of obligation, and the more effective enforcement measures in the ICCPR, have supported western claims of primacy for the so-called first generation civil and political rights.[30] Although the ICESCR has been widely accepted, argument continues as to whether economic and social rights are properly so regarded.[31] Despite post-cold war reaffirmation of the indivisibility of all human rights (Vienna Declaration), there remains an unwillingness to regard such government action as mass evictions or failure to feed its population in terms of human rights abuses because this would entail scrutiny of governmental policies of distributive justice, not of human rights.[32]

A further question is what rights should be recognized. The proliferation of claims of rights has been constant, especially from activists who seek to strengthen their demands with the powerful language of rights.[33] How are claims for new rights to be assessed? Is the category of rights closed? Is the category of claimants closed? If new rights cannot be accommodated, there is a danger of human rights failing to meet changed demands for individual freedom from state intervention. However, assertions of new rights that are not fully defined, are not framed within legal instruments,[34] are not widely accepted and are constantly denied can trivialize the entire human rights venture. Alston has urged a system of UN 'quality control' to maintain the integrity of the human rights system (Steiner and Alston 1996, 374–81).[35] This can be regarded as appropriate caution against excessive extension of the category of rights or, alternatively, as an attempt to privilege certain claims over others.

The concept of group rights, or third generation rights, encapsulates the dilemmas. Group rights were included within the 1966 Covenants through the peoples' right of self-determination. Peoples' rights do not readily fit within the canon of human rights discourse based on the autonomy of the individual person. Nevertheless other peoples' rights have been claimed: the right to equality, to free disposal of wealth and natural resources, to economic, social and cultural development, to peace and security, and to a satisfactory environment.[36]

The right to development is illustrative. It is cast as an 'inalienable human right' in the Declaration on the Right to Development (GA Res. 41/128 1986), although it is aimed at improving the 'well-being of the entire population' (GA Res. 41/128, Preamble). The Declaration was negotiated over many years and is to some extent a compromise between the conflicting views of the North and the South. The former regarded development as predicated upon full respect for human rights, especially participatory civil and political rights, although many states were prepared to concede that greater attention needed to be given to economic and social rights.[37] The latter viewed the Declaration as a means to further their own economic development, while denying any restrictions upon their human rights policies (Alston 1991). The understanding of development as economic growth has led to denials of human rights, for example those of indigenous persons displaced through development projects, despite the assertion that the 'human person is the central subject of development' (*Declaration on the Right to Development*, Article 2). The imprecise linkage between individual human rights and development was further confused by the World Conference on Human Rights which reaffirmed the 'universal and inalienable right to development'. It urged the Working Group on the Right to Development to eliminate obstacles to its implementation and 'the realization of the right to development by all States' (Vienna Declaration, Part II, para. 72).

In some instances (for example, peace and the environment) peoples' rights are not claimed for an identifiable group but at large, and even for subsequent generations.[38] But who has the responsibility to ensure their performance: states, states acting through international institutions, individuals? How is adequate performance to be gauged? Acceptance of such rights requires radical rethinking on the allocation of responsibilities and procedures for implementation, but these claims also embrace some of the most significant global issues. On one view, a system of human rights that cannot accommodate such concepts lacks credibility. On another view their formulation within the constraints of human rights law presents an anthropocentric stance that world peace and preservation of the environment are solely for the benefit of humanity that rejects the 'intrinsic or inherent value of other species and the environment in general' (Boyle 1996, 51). The answers to such questions cannot be found solely within a legal framework, but as Alston asserts, '[T]here is an unwillingness on the part of human rights lawyers to develop a sound theoretical framework from which *inter alia* claims to new rights can be assessed and arguments distinguishing human rights from other claims can be coherently distinguished' (Alston 1996).

CLAIMANTS TO RIGHTS

Further tensions have been caused by new claimants for rights, frequently in the form of demands for the reinterpretation of traditionally accepted rights. Such claimants include women and indigenous persons. Campaigns by both have dominated the human rights scene in the 1990s.[39] The strains generated can be illustrated by the intensive and largely successful campaign in the 1990s to have women's rights formally accepted as human rights.

Women have argued that human rights law is based upon the life experiences of men and that, despite its apparently neutral and objective language, it offers more to men than to women (Bunch 1990; Charlesworth 1994, 58). In particular, the doctrine of attributability asserts state responsibility only for the public acts of state officials, or acts instigated or acquiesced to by state officials. State responsibility has not traditionally been extended to similar acts when committed by private individuals.[40] This limitation to the public sphere has limited the applicability and relevance of human rights to women where many violations are committed by private individuals, typically members of the family or local community.[41] It also allows an environment of abuse to continue unchallenged and weakens the relevance of human rights to those who are economically, structurally and politically without power.

Women have argued accordingly, that the legal understanding of, for example, torture should be expanded to incorporate acts of domestic violence,[42] and rape and other forms of sexual abuse in armed conflict (*Prosecutor* v. *Gagovic and Others*). Such a (re)conceptualization would entail legal consequences in domestic law, including extending universal jurisdiction to such acts (*Torture Convention*, Articles 4 and 5), imposing the 'extradite or prosecute' principle to alleged offenders (*Torture Convention*, Article 7), and facilitating claims by victims for asylum (in accordance with the *Torture* Convention, Article 3). It would also extend the opprobrium expressed towards torture to these acts of violence, that are currently too often tolerated, condoned or ignored. Although the General Assembly has accepted that states have an obligation to eliminate violence against women (*Declaration on Elimination of Violence Against Women*), the inclusion of such claims within the ambit of binding human rights law is resisted.[43] There is apprehension that to transform the vision of human rights to include acts by private individuals would disturb and undermine the entire edifice of human rights. Women in turn argue that the system has excluded harms most frequently inflicted upon them and that the vision has never held out the same promise of fulfilment of human dignity to them as to men. If human rights law is so fragile that it cannot withstand such reconceptualization, then it is barely worth protecting.

VIOLATORS OF HUMAN RIGHTS

Human rights law provides legal protection to individuals against wrongful intervention by states. States however are not the only abusers of individual rights. Other powerful élites, including religious and corporate enterprises, are protected by the restriction of responsibility to the actions of state public officials. Economic globalization and the liberalization of trade through the free flow of capital has weakened states' control over international markets and financial exchanges. The search for maximum profits through investment where there is cheap labour also means that states either ignore, or connive in, for their own economic advantage, violations of international labour standards, participatory rights and other economic and social rights. The activities of transnational corporations are only minimally subject to international regulation. Protests are frequently met by further repression. Large-scale human migration for forms of employment operating outside any national or international protection add to the violations of human rights, for example the abuses suffered by women recruited for domestic service abroad (Pettman 1996).

Powerful religious groups too resist claims of the universality of civil and political rights, such as those relating to freedom of expression and of religious expression.[44] These claims may be directly backed by state agencies, operating through their own international power base, as is the case with the Vatican, or provide a powerful internal force which governments cannot resist.[45] In particular, religious interests are used to justify denying equality to women. An expression of this is in the substantive reservations that have been entered by states to the Convention on the Elimination of All Forms of Discrimination Against Women that in turn have provoked little dissent (Cook 1990; Clark 1991). Added currency is bestowed upon such claims by assertions of domestic jurisdiction, of religious and cultural autonomy, and of the inherent illegitimacy of human rights law because of its foundations in western morality and political philosophy (Teson 1985). The positivist response is that states voluntarily accept the obligations of treaties they have entered into. However, compliance depends upon a conviction of legitimacy that is not necessarily invoked by formal adherence. Some scholars have attempted to discount claims of cultural relativism by arguing that human rights are rooted in all religions and cultures (An-Na'im 1992, 19; Marasinghe 1984, 32). Contrary assertions serve primarily to protect contemporary political and economic power bases. Others have attempted to devise strategies that respect and accommodate local mores while nevertheless asserting rights (Gunning 1992, 189). Dissonance between international human rights norms and those allegedly based in religion or local culture remains one of the greatest obstacles to the effective enforcement of the legal regime.

## Institutional barriers to the guarantee of rights

The institutional structures of the international legal system inhibit development and implementation of human rights. Human rights are within the competence of ECOSOC and its specialist human rights commissions. The body of substantive law and processes that they have evolved remain separate from the mandates of other international institutions, most notably the global financial institutions, such as the World Bank, the International Monetary Fund and the GATT/World Trade Organization, and from the environmental and development agencies (Steiner and Alston 1996, 15). This institutional fragmentation contributes to the duplication of effort and expertise and the lack of awareness of the norms and practices favoured elsewhere in the system. More importantly, an effective human rights law must be fully integrated into the substance and procedures of other branches of international law, both for determining the causes of human rights violations and for ensuring that they are taken into account in decision making of all types. This is not currently the case. For example the adverse consequences of structural adjustment programmes as a contributory factor to poverty is now widely acknowledged, but remains primarily a development concern rather than one of human rights. The World Conference on Human Rights recommended coordination and cooperation between institutions (*Vienna Declaration and Programme of Action*, Part II, para. I) but human rights institutions lack the resources to offer their services or technical expertise to these other bodies.[46]

## Procedural barriers

The international legal system lacks procedural mechanisms for its enforcement. As has been seen, use of the coercive collective measures available under Chapter VII of the UN Charter to address human rights abuses is problematic. Processes for the peaceful settlement of disputes, including adjudication, are based upon consent (UN Charter, Article 33). States have remained especially reluctant to concede legal rights to individuals in the context of claims and mechanisms for enforcement. One of the doctrinal roots of human rights was the principle of diplomatic protection whereby states incurred responsibility for failure to treat aliens in accordance with international minimum standards. These principles were championed by western states for the protection of their nationals engaged primarily in economic or other self-serving ventures abroad and were not infrequently upheld through force. They provided no challenge to state sovereignty in that the claim was that of the state, not of the injured alien, and it was the state's decision guided by its own interests whether to pursue it. Concepts of state responsibility were brought into the new arena of human rights, but the elevation of the individual to procedural capacity to pursue a claim against his or her own state was not. Thus the contentious jurisdiction of the ICJ has not been opened to individuals, or even to international institutions (Statute of the International Court of Justice, Article 34). Hence human rights concerns are only indirectly subject to authoritative interpretation by the court. The court's discouragement of any form of third-party intervention, even in the form of *amicus* briefs, prevents other actors from raising human rights concerns in litigation before it (Chinkin 1993, ch. 10). Even within the regional frameworks, adjudication of individual complaints has evolved slowly, and remains limited.[47]

Within the UN human rights treaty bodies, new techniques to make states accountable for their treatment of their citizens have been devised. The most widely used monitoring mechanism is that of state reporting to the relevant committee on progress made in implementing the applicable convention. The reporting system assumes that states will engage in self-evaluation of their national laws and practices and that exposure of violations will shame recalcitrant states into reform (Bayefsky 1994, 229). However states' reports are inevitably self-serving and omissions and inaccuracies may be difficult to identify by committees that sit for just a few weeks every year. With increased adherence to the human rights treaties, the backlog of reports before all committees constantly increases. There is the dual problem that many states fail to submit timely reports but the committees cannot deal immediately with them. Unless the questions asked of government representatives are searching and responses scrutinized, the reporting system cannot produce the desired effects. Publicity is frequently not forthcoming as governments fail to inform domestic audiences of the procedure. Concluding comments are not binding upon states and are frequently bland.

Widespread abuses that are either directly ordered by governments or connived in by them, as where state forces are used to curtail opposition without questions being asked as to their methods, have been committed with impunity. Impunity may be defined as the impossibility *de jure* or *de facto*, of bringing the perpetrators of human rights violations to account. This situation creates a climate of terror and fosters a cycle of further abuses, silence and lack of accountability. Political change, for example in Eastern Europe, Latin America and South Africa, has posed the dilemma of whether the truth should be revealed and those accused of such actions during previous regimes now be made answerable, or whether reconciliation and rebuilding demand continued impunity. Within national jurisdictions, different solutions have been sought, ranging from legislation according amnesty, the setting up of truth commissions and compensation mechanisms.[48] The Inter-American system of human rights has asserted the duty of the state to investigate, prosecute and punish alleged violations of human rights and has articulated a right to know the truth that is especially compelling in the light of widespread disappearances (*Velasquez Rodriguez* v. *Honduras*; Krsticevic 1996).

Internationally, the most dramatic breakthrough for liability for widespread and systematic abuses has been the establishment of war crimes tribunals with respect to atrocities committed in the former Yugoslavia and Rwanda.[49] Negotiations for the establishment of a Permanent Criminal Court are progressing.[50] Nevertheless these advances reveal further, and familiar, tensions. Establishment of the war crimes tribunals by Security Council decision made them binding upon all members of the UN. However cooperation and effectiveness depend upon individual state consent, especially from those most directly involved. In the former Yugoslavia the opposing demands of peace and justice have distorted the Dayton Peace Accords through their silence on the required arrest of persons indicted by the tribunal, thereby undermining their instrumentality in redressing crimes against humanity. The gap may be partly filled by the US assertion of civil jurisdiction over those accused of crimes against the law of nations, including, *inter alia*, former President Marcos of the Philippines, army generals from Argentina and Indonesia (*Filartiga* v. *Pena-Irala*; *Hilao* v. *Marcos*; *Forti* v. *Suarez-Mason*; *Xuncas* v. *Gramajo*), and Radovan Karadwicz (*Kadic* v. *Karadwicz*). This strategy has been extended to actions against multinational corporations with claims pending against, for example Shell and Unocal, for complicity in such offences as torture, forced relocation of indigenous persons and forced labour of civilians in Nigeria and Burma respectively (*Doe* v. *Unocal*). This assertion of jurisdiction is especially significant in light of the lack of accountability of such corporations under international law.

While no damages have yet been paid in consequence of judgment, litigation before domestic courts is beneficial in that it allows victims to present evidence on events that have occurred to them and to have their claims vindicated. It also inhibits the freedom of action of those subjected to judgment and thus has some punitive effect. On the other hand, such litigation depends upon the accident of jurisdiction and is therefore selective. The extension of extra-territorial jurisdiction that it involves can also be seen as a way of promoting US foreign policy interests, especially in light of its own reticence in ratifying human rights treaties. Where alleged human rights concerns are coupled with restrictions upon trade and sanctions, opposition has been expressed by other states, including US allies and trading partners.[51]

## Conclusions

The capacity of the international legal system to provide an effective framework for the protection of human rights is severely undermined. These tensions however pose more fundamental questions: should attention be directed towards improving the international legal system or should the legal strategy be abandoned? Is the concerted effort for universal ratification of human rights treaties pointless given the ease with which states evade or ignore their obligations? Are the procedural and substantive innovations that have been made over the last few years no more than tinkering around the peripheries, or are they steps that can evolve into a widely adhered to regime? Can law empower those who are disadvantaged within their respective societies and thus especially vulnerable to human rights abuse? Is the international legal guarantee of rights worthwhile for those discriminated against on racial grounds, for women, indigenous persons dispossessed of their tribal lands, migrant workers or refugees? Have NGO campaigns for greater legal implementation of human rights been a waste of energy and time, or worse, positively detrimental in that they have diverted resources from political or other campaigns? Does economic globalization make concentration upon states' obligations worthless? There can be no positive answers to these questions that go to the heart of the contemporary structure of international legal ordering.

Scepticism has been expressed about the appropriateness of rights to achieve social transformation, especially by feminist activists and theorists (Smart 1989; Charlesworth 1994). Many of their anxieties are equally applicable to others who suffer societal disadvantage. A few of these doubts can be listed. First, the individualistic, atomist language of rights does not lend itself readily to claims for advancement of disadvantaged peoples. Second, in human rights discourse, rights are normally presented in terms of equality.[52] The underlying philosophy is that achievement of equality with the dominant group (white, affluent males) will enhance the dignity of all persons. But the yardstick of equality fails to address difference and is effective only where there is such a relevant comparator. The formal bestowal of rights facilitates the illusion of equality without requiring any further consideration of the complexities of structural and economic power imbalance that inhibit its accomplishment.[53] Third, conflicting rights, for example between the right to religious freedom and non-discrimination against women, assume a hierarchy that can only be resolved through subjective value choices by decision-makers. These preferences may not be made explicit, or even acknowledged, but are likely to favour those already advantaged through allocations of power and influence. Fourth, rights can be readily appropriated and are consistently used to benefit those already privileged within society, rather than those for whom the benefits were intended.

These concerns carry a good deal of validity. Nevertheless, while conceding the limited outcomes of rights strategies there are some strengths in legal instrumentality. Experience has shown people who have received legal recognition of rights will challenge their denial.[54] It seems that the usefulness of human rights has only been challenged when previously disempowered claimants have gained some international standing and voice to challenge the state monopoly over the parameters of rights. Claims of rights are subversive and rights discourse provides a familiar and symbolically powerful vocabulary to challenge political and societal wrongs. Internationally accepted human rights provide a yardstick against which to assess government performance or non-performance. The guarantee of rights is most effective at the national level where international rights instruments can provide judges with a basis for finding against governments that reject their own commitments to rights. A growing case law testifies to the filtering down of international standards into domestic courts. Admittedly this outcome depends upon the receptivity of judges to arguments based upon rights and their independence from and willingness to confront the executive. Even when unsuccessful, claims can help foster a human rights culture through their educative function and public articulation of the legal basis of rights. The formal existence of rights is self-evidently insufficient. They must be accompanied by legal literacy programmes, human rights education programmes, training aimed at law enforcement officials, policy and decision-makers at local and national levels in race, gender and other forms of discrimination. Access to the courts must be ensured. This is not unfounded optimism that the legal canon can correct human rights abuses, but rather a conviction that it should not be discarded.

It is not only national decision-makers to whom appeals of rights can be made. Decisions of all international bodies should be informed by the human rights dimensions of situations before them. This requires the collapsing of institutional boundaries and regular use of human rights indicators. For example, the Security Council deliberately sought evidence of abuses in Bosnia and Hercegovina before setting up a war crimes tribunal for former Yugoslavia. This same starting point should have continued throughout all other decision making, including the deployment of UNPROFOR (United Nations Protection Force in the Former Yugoslavia) and its mandate with respect to designated safe areas. If the political will to ensure the optimum response from the human rights perspective does not exist, this should be admitted and accommodated. It can be counter-productive, and disastrous for those concerned, to enunciate humanitarian objectives and subsequently to retreat from their consequences.

Compliance with the horizontal structure of the international legal system rests upon reciprocity of interests between states, not upon a hierarchical system of compulsory enforcement. Human rights treaties formulate legal standards of behaviour applicable to those subject to the state's jurisdiction. There is no notion of reciprocal enforcement and the treaties do not contain the basis for effective self-regulation. Demands for compliance with human rights are demands for fundamental attitudinal changes by states towards the structure of the international legal system itself, and of their supremacy within it. States must perceive the furtherance of human rights as advantageous to their overall objectives. This becomes ever more problematic as globalization decreases states' control over domestic policies and their ability to support effective human rights regimes. Thus the capability of the international legal system to be relevant to human rights requires dislodging legal and conceptual boundaries between, for example, human rights law and international economic law, between state sovereignty and transnational law, between international humanitarian law and military necessity, between law and non-law and between states and non-state actors. The understanding of rights must be made relevant to those whose interests are largely excluded from its scope and to those non-state actors that remain outside its formal constraints. This requires a continual process of redefinition of the traditional scope of human rights law that goes beyond inequality, or even specific issues such as racial, gendered or ethnic violence. It also requires rethinking the primary role of the state in guaranteeing human rights in light of global forces that limit its freedom of internal choice. These phenomena must be analysed in their entirety to reveal the multiplicity of disadvantage and addressed in their wider political, economic and social contexts. Non-compulsory legal regulation cannot achieve such fundamental restructuring of power but it nevertheless has its role in the process.

## Notes

1 For example, Convention Against Torture and Other Cruel, Inhuman or Degrading Treatment, 10 December 1984, GA Res. 39/46 (Torture Convention).

2 For example, Convention on the Elimination of All Forms of Discrimination Against Women, 18 December 1979, 1249 UNTS (United Nations Treaty Series) 14 (the Women's Convention); Convention on the Rights of the Child, 20 November 1989, GA Res. 44/25 (the Children's Convention).

3 There has been considerable human rights activity at the regional level, especially through the European Convention for the Protection of Fundamental Rights and Freedoms, Rome, 4 November 1950, ETS No. 5 and 11 Protocols; the American Convention on Human Rights, San Jose, 22 November 1969, 1144 UNTS 123 and 2 Protocols; and the African Charter on Human Rights and Peoples Rights (Banjul Charter), 27 June 1981, rep. 21 ILM 58 (1982).

4 The UN World Conference on Human Rights: Vienna Declaration and Programme of Action, 25 June 1993, rep. 32 ILM 1661 (1993) Part I para. 26 urged universal ratification of human rights treaties. This target is nearing attainment with the Children's Convention that by 1997 had been adhered to by over 190 states, with the significant exception of the United States of America.

5 Especially the procedures based on ECOSOC Res. 1235 (XLII) 1967 and ECOSOC Res. 1503 (XLVIII) 1970. See also Steiner and Alston (1996).

6 The Commission on Human Rights, the Commission on the Status of Women, the Commission on Crime Prevention and Criminal Justice and the Sub-Commission on Prevention of Discrimination and Protection of Minorities.

7 ICCPR, Article 28 (Human Rights Committee); ICESCR (Committee on Economic, Social and Cultural Rights); International Convention on the Elimination of All Forms of Racial Discrimination, 21 December 1965, 660 UNTS 195, Article 8 (Committee on the Elimination of Racial Discrimination); Women's Convention, Article 18 (Committee on the Elimination of All Forms of Discrimination Against Women); Torture Convention, Article 17 (Committee Against Torture); Children's Convention, Article 43 (Committee on the Rights of the Child).

8 Reports of the violations of human rights are well documented, for example in the Annual Reports of Amnesty International and reports of the International Human Rights Watch bodies.

9 Alston suggests that formulation of legal norms has contributed to the isolation of human rights law from other disciplines (Alston 1988, 8).

10 This trend has been strongly attacked, by leading international lawyers, for example Brownlie who considers that the 'specialized' has attracted the unskilled (Brownlie 1982, 109, cited in Alston 1988).

11 For an overview of the history of human rights law see S. Davidson (1993), ch. 1.

12 'Even a very traditional view of states, and of human rights, points towards basic tensions within international law that surface repeatedly in arguments about internal interference and external demands for compliance with basic international standards' (Wright undated).

13 A collective decision of illegitimacy and non-recognition was made; SC Res. 216, 12 November 1965; SC Res. 277, 18 March 1970.

14 SC Res. 2775E (XXVI) 29 November 1971; GA Res. 3411D (XXX) 28 November 1975; GA Res. 31/6A, 27 October 1976 recommend non-recognition of the South African Bantustans of Transkei, Bophuthatswana and Venda. On the SC requirement of non-recognition of South Africa's presence in Namibia see *Legal Consequences for States of the Continued Presence of South Africa in Namibia* (South West Africa). Notwithstanding Security Council 276 (1970), 1971 ICJ Rep. 16 (Adv. Op. 21 June).

15 European Community Guidelines for the Recognition of New States in Europe and the former Soviet Union, 16 December 1991.

16 The Badinter Commission was established by the European Community to determine claims to statehood by the Republics of the Former Yugoslavia in accordance with the Guidelines (Weller 1992).

17 For example, the UK changed its recognition policy to cease recognition of foreign governments, Statement by Foreign Secretary, Lord Carrington, Hansard, HL, vol. 408, cols 1121–22, 28 April 1980; cf., News Release, Commonwealth Minister of Foreign Affairs and Trade, 19 January 1988, rep. 11 *Australian Yearbook of International Law* 205 (1991).

18 The General Assembly Declaration on the Granting of Independence to Colonial Territories and Peoples, GA Res. 1514 (XV), para. 6 states that 'Any attempt aimed at the partial or total disruption of the national unity and territorial integrity of a country is incompatible with the Purposes and Principles of the Charter of the United Nations.' Cf., UN World Conference on Human Rights: Vienna Declaration and Programme of Action, Part I, para. 2.

19 The ultimate rights of the state to survival was epitomized by the ICJ in the Legality of the Threat or Use of Nuclear Weapons, 1996 ICJ Rep. (Adv. Op. 8 July) rep. 35 ILM 809 (1996). Despite the human right to life, 'in view of the current state of international law, ... the Court cannot conclude definitively whether the threat or use of nuclear weapons would be lawful or unlawful in an extreme circumstance of self-defence in which the very survival of a State would be at stake'.

20 In the four Geneva Conventions of 12 August 1949 for the Protection of War Victims only common Article 3 is applicable to internal armed conflict. Protocol Additional to the Geneva Conventions of 12 August 1949 and Relating to the Protection of Victims of International Armed Conflicts (Protocol I) has 102 Articles compared to 28 in Protocol Additional to the Geneva Conventions of 12 August 1949 and Relating to the Protection of Victims of Non-International Armed Conflicts (Protocol II).

21 This view was mainly developed with respect to apartheid in South Africa and has received further impetus from the end of the cold war (Steiner and Alston 1996, 364–74). It is not accepted by all states, for example the Peoples Republic of China.

22 On the problem of substantive reservations to the ICCPR, see Human Rights Committee, General Comment 24, General Comment on issues relating to reservations made upon ratification or accession to the Covenant or the Optional Protocols thereto, or in relation to declarations under Article 41 of the Covenant (52 session 1994) HRI/Gen/1/Rev. 2. (More generally, see Lijnzaad 1995.).

23 The traditional statement of the sources of international law is found in the Statute of the ICJ, 1945, Article 38 (1).

24 Reisman, for example, views human rights abuses as violations of peoples' sovereignty

that other states can legitimately protect. He links this to democratic principles to justify intervention to restore democratic governance (Reisman 1984; 1990). For a reply to Reisman, see Schachter (1984).

25 UN Charter, Article 39 authorizes the Security Council 'to determine the existence of any threat to the peace, breach of the peace, or act of aggression' in order to decide upon appropriate measures.

26 SC Res. 688, 3 April 1991. The Resolution insisted that 'Iraq allow immediate access by international humanitarian organizations to all those in need of assistance'.

27 SC Res. 929, 22 June 1994. The humanitarian objectives of UNAMIR (UN Assistance Mission for Rwanda) were specified in SC Res. 925, 8 June 1994, para. 4 (a) as being to 'Contribute to the security and protection of displaced persons, refugees and civilians at risk in Rwanda, including through the establishment and maintenance, where feasible, of secure humanitarian areas; and (b) Provide security and support for the distribution of relief supplies and humanitarian relief operations.'

28 The rights to an adequate standard of living, food, clothing and housing (Article 11); to the highest attainable standard of physical and mental health (Article 12). See Bhatia, Kawar and Shahin (1991); Orford (1996).

29 This was to some extent acknowledged by the *Fourth UN Conference on Women, Beijing, Platform for Action,* 15 September 1995, para. 14 (i) requires governments, international and regional organizations to take measures 'with a view to alleviating the negative impact of economic sanctions on women and children'.

30 For example, the obligation to 'take steps ... with a view to achieving progressively the full realization of the rights' (ICESCR, Article 2 (1)) contrasts with the immediate obligation 'to respect and ensure' the rights within the ICCPR (Article 2 (1)). The Human Rights Committee was established by the ICCPR, Article 28(1) while the Economic, Social and Cultural Committee was not formed until 1986, by ECOSOC.

31 This is especially associated with the USA which has not become a party to the ICESCR.

32 See, however, Committee on Economic, Social and Cultural Rights, General Comment No. 4, UN Doc. E/1992/23, Annex III, The right to adequate housing, rep. (Steiner and Alston 1996, 318).

33 Alston describes the tension between activist demands for immediate results and the creation of an enduring conceptual framework based on 'coherent intellectual foundations' (Alston 1988, 9).

34 It is unarguable that states incur obligations through treaties. However the 'soft law' effect of GA resolutions is more controversial and the binding nature of rights articulated in such instruments are open to challenge. An example is the Declaration on the Right to Development, discussed below.

35 The GA has adopted guidelines 'to maintain consistency with the high quality of existing international standards', GA Res. 41/120, 4 December 1986.

36 The African Charter includes more peoples' rights than other human rights treaties: Article 19 (equality), Article 20 (self-determination), Article 21 (free disposal of natural resources), Article 22 (economic, social and cultural development), Article 23 (peace and security), Article 24 (satisfactory environment).

37 The United States rejects the right to development as well as the status of economic and social rights.

38 For example, Stockholm Declaration, Principle I asserts the 'solemn responsibility to protect and improve the environment for present and future generations'. Rio Declaration, Principle 3 states 'The right to development must be fulfilled so as to equitably meet developmental and environmental needs of present and future generations'.

39 The Draft Declaration on Discrimination Against Indigenous Peoples was adopted by the Working Group on Indigenous Populations of the Sub-Commission on Prevention of Discrimination and Protection of Minorities of the Human Rights Commission in August 1994. It was submitted to the Human Rights Commission in March 1995, which is now working on the subject.

40 International Law Commission, Draft Articles on State Responsibility, adopted on First Reading, A/CN.4/L.528/Add. 2, 16 July 1996, Article 11.

41 Preliminary Report of the Special Rapporteur on Violence against Women, The Elimination of Violence against Women, E/CN.4/1995/42.

42 Report of the Special Rapporteur on Violence against Women, its Causes and Consequences, 5 February 1996, E/CN.4/1996/53, para. 47.

43 Violence against women as a violation of human rights has not been included in any binding instrument, with the exception of the *Inter-American Convention on the Prevention, Punishment and Eradication of Violence against Women.*

44 The fatwa imposed upon Salman Rushdie is one example of this.

45 Coomaraswamy describes how Muslim street protests persuaded the Indian government to reverse the decision in *Md Ahmed Khan* v. *Shah Bano Begum* to apply the Indian Criminal Code to a Muslim woman, to make her subject to the less advantageous Muslim personal law (Coomaraswamy 1994, 39).

46 *Vienna Declaration and Programme of Action*, Part II, para. 9 notes with concern 'the growing disparity' between human rights activities and the financial resources available, and requested the Secretary-General and GA to examine the human rights budget. In light of the financial crisis of the UN increased resources are not forthcoming.

47 American Convention on Human Rights, Articles 44 and 61; European Convention on Human Rights, Articles 25 and 45. The jurisdiction and procedures of the European Court of Human Rights will be extended by Protocol 11, when it comes into force.

48 This functional division is taken from 10 *Interights Bulletin*, 1996, 10:3, 96–7. This issue contains steps taken by twenty-seven states.

49 The former Yugoslav Tribunal was established pursuant to SC Res. 827, 25 May 1993; that for Rwanda by SC Res. 955, 8 November 1994.

50 On 17 December 1996 the GA resolved that a diplomatic conference will be held in 1998 with the objective of adopting a convention establishing a permanent international criminal court.

51 For example, the Cuban Liberty and Democratic Solidarity (Libertad) Act, 1996 (the 'Helms–Burton' Act) by which the USA asserted the protection of the commercial interests of American nationals against the expropriation of their property by the Castro regime in Cuba, in the name of Cuban democracy. Opposition has been expressed, *inter alia*, by the EU, Canada and Mexico.

52 The exception is the Convention on the Rights of the Child.

53 Nicola Lacey argues that the liberal guarantee of equality assumes a world of autonomous individuals starting a race, or making free choices, that has no cutting edge against the fact that men and women are simply running different races (Lacey 1987).

54 The Fourth World Conference on Women expressed confidence in the legal strategy: 'While women are increasingly using the legal system to exercise their rights, in many countries lack of awareness of the existence of these rights is an obstacle that prevents women from fully enjoying their human rights and attaining equality.' (Platform for Action, para. 227.).

# References

Alston, P. (1988), Making space for new human rights: the case of the right to development, *Human Rights Yearbook*, Cambridge, MA, Harvard University Press, 8.

Alston, P. (1991), Revitalising United Nations work on human rights and development, *Melb. Uniform Law Review*, 18, 218.

An-Na'im, A. (1992), Towards a cross-cultural approach to defining international standards of human rights: the meaning of cruel, inhuman or degrading treatment, in A. An-Na'im (ed.) *Human Rights in Cross-Cultural Perspectives*, Syracuse, Syracuse University Press.

Bayefsky, A. (1994), Making the human rights treaties work, in L. Henkin and J. Hargrove (eds), *Human Rights: An Agenda for the Next Century*, Washington, American Society of International Law.

Bazlyer, M. (1987), Re-examining the doctrine of humanitarian intervention in light of the atrocities in Kampuchea and Ethiopia, *Stanford Journal of International Law*, 23, 54.

Bhatia, B., M. Kawar and M. Shahin (1991), *Unheard Voices: Iraqi Women on War and Sanctions*, London, Change Thinkbook No. 8.

Boyle, A. (1996), The role of international human rights law in the protection of the environment, in A. Boyle and M. Anderson (eds), *Human Rights Approaches to Environmental Protection*, Oxford, Clarendon Press.

Brownlie, I. (1982), Problems of specialization, in B. Cheng (ed.), *International Law Teaching and Practice*, London, Stevens.

Brownlie, I. (1990), *Principles of Public International Law*, 4th edn, Oxford, Oxford University Press.

Bunch, C. (1990), Women's rights as human rights: towards a revision of human rights, *Human Rights Quarterly*, 12, 486.

Cassese, A. (1986), *International Law in a Divided World*, Oxford, Oxford University Press.

Charlesworth, H. (1994), What are 'women's international human rights'?, in R. Cook, *Human Rights of Women National and International Perspectives*, Oxford, Oxford University Press.

Chinkin, C. (1993), *Third Parties in International Law*, Oxford, Oxford University Press.

Clark, B. (1991), The Vienna Convention reservations regime and the Convention On Discrimination against Women, *American Journal of International Law*, 85, 281.

Cook, R. (1990), Reservations to the convention on the elimination of all forms of discrimination against women, *Virginia Journal of International Law*, 30, 643.

Coomaraswamy, R. (1994), To bellow like a cow, in R. Cook (ed.), *Human Rights of Women National and International Perspectives*, Philadelphia, University of Pennsylvania Press.

Davidson, S. (1993), *Human Rights*, Oxford, Oxford University Press.

Farer, T. (1991), Human rights in law's empire: the jurisprudence war, *American Journal of International Law*, 85, 117.

Fonteyne, J. P. (1973–74), Customary international law doctrine of humanitarian intervention: its current validity under the United Nations Charter, *Cal. WILJ*, 203.

Franck, T. (1996), Clan and superclan: loyalty, identity and community in law and practice, *American Journal of International Law*, 90, 359.

Gunning, I. (1992), Arrogant perception, world travelling and multicultural feminism: the case of female genital surgeries, *Col. Hum. R. LR*, 23, 189.

Henkin, L. (1989), The use of force: law and US policy, in Council on Foreign Relations, *Right v. Might, International Law and the Use of Force*, New York, Council on Foreign Relations Press.

Koskenniemi, M. (1995), The police in the temple, order, justice and the United Nations: a dialectical view, *EJIL*, 6, 325.

Krsticevic, V. (1996), The development and implementation of legal standards relating to impunity in the inter-American system of human rights protection, *Interights Bulletin*, 10:3, 91–5.

Lacey, N. (1987), Legislation against sex discrimination: questions from a feminist perspective, *Journal Law and Society*, 14, 411.

Lijnzaad, L. (1995), *Reservations to UN Human Rights Treaties: Ratify and Ruin?*, Dordrecht, Martinus Nijhoff Publishers.

Lillich, R. (1973), *Intervention and the United Nations*, Charlottesville, University Press of Virginia.

Lillich, R. (1993), Humanitarian intervention through the United Nations: towards the development of criteria, *ZAORV*, 53, 557.

Marasinghe, C. Welch *et al.* (eds) (1984), Traditional conceptions of human rights in Africa, in C. Welch *et al.* (eds), *Human Rights and Development in Africa*, Albany, State University of New York Press.

Morgan, R. (1989), *The Demon Lover: On the Sexuality of Terrorism*, London, Methuen.

Murphy, S. (1996), *Humanitarian Intervention – The United Nations in an Evolving World Order*, University of Pennsylvania.

Orford, A. (1996), The politics of collective security, *Mich. JIL*, 17, 373.

Pettman, J. (1996), *Worlding Women*, London, Routledge.

Reisman, W. M. (1984), Coercion and self-determination: construing Charter Article 2 (4), *American Journal of International Law*, 78, 642.

Reisman, W. M. (1990). Sovereignty and human rights in contemporary international law, *American Journal of International Law*, 84, 966.

Reisman, W. M. and E. Suzuki (1976), Recognition and social change in international law, in W. M. Reisman and B. Weston (eds), *Toward World Order and Human Dignity*, London, Free Press.

Schachter, O. (1984), The legality of pro-democratic invasion, *American Journal of International Law*, 78, 645.

Shaw, M. (1997), *International Law*, 4th edn, Cambridge, Grotius.

Simon, S. (1996), Contemporary legality of unilateral humanitarian intervention, *Cal. WILJ*, 24, 117.

Sloan, J. (1996), The Dayton Peace Agreement: human rights guarantees and their implementation, *EJIL*, 7, 207.

Smart, C. (1989), *Feminism and the Power of Law*, London, Routledge.

Steiner H. and P. Alston (1996), *International Human Rights in Context Law, Politics, Morals*, Oxford, Clarendon.

Teson, F. (1985), International human rights and cultural relativism, *Virginia Journal of International Law*, 25, 869.

Teson, F. (1988), *Humanitarian Intervention: An Inquiry into Law and Morality*, Dobbs Ferry, Transnational Publishers.

Warbrick, C. (1992), Recognition of states, *International Comparative Law Quarterly*, 41, 473.

Weller, M. (1992). The international response to the dissolution of the socialist federal republic of Yugoslavia, *American Journal of International Law*, 86, 569.

Wright, S. (undated), Redefining international legal norms for the 21st century: the incorporation of different voices, paper in possession of author.

## Treaties and declarations

*African Charter on Human Rights and Peoples Rights* (Banjul Charter), 27 June 1981, rep. 21 ILM 58 (1982).

*American Convention on Human Rights*, San Jose, 22 November 1969, 1144 UNTS 123 and
  2 Protocols (American Convention).
*Convention on the Prevention and Punishment of the Crime of Genocide*, 9 December 1948, 78
  UNTS 277 (Genocide Convention).
*Convention Relating to the Status of Refugees*, 28 July 1951, 189 UNTS 150.
*Convention on the Elimination of All Forms of Discrimination Against Women*, 18 December
  1979, 1249 UNTS 14 (the Women's Convention).
*Convention Against Torture and Other Cruel, Inhuman or Degrading Treatment*, 10 December
  1984, GA Res. 39/46 (Torture Convention).
*Convention on the Rights of the Child*, 20 November 1989, GA Res. 44/25 (the Children's
  Convention).
*Declaration on Principles of International Law Concerning Friendly Relations and Cooperation
  among States in Accordance with the Charter of the United Nations*, GA Res. 2625, 24
  October 1970.
*Declaration on Environment and Development*, Rio de Janeiro, 14 June 1992, rep. 31 ILM
  876
*Declaration on the Elimination of Violence against Women*, GA Res. 48/103, adopted 20
  December 1993.
*European Convention for the Protection of Fundamental Rights and Freedoms*, Rome, 4 No-
  vember 1950, ETS No. 5 and 11 Protocols (European Convention).
*General Framework Agreement for Peace in Bosnia and Hercegovina* (Dayton Peace Agree-
  ment), initialled Dayton, Ohio, 21 November 1995, signed Paris, 14 December 1995,
  rep. 35 ILM 75 (1996).
*Inter-American Convention on the Prevention, Punishment and Eradication of Violence against
  Women*, adopted by the General Assembly of the Organization of American States,
  Belem do Para, 9 June 1994.
*International Convention on the Elimination of All Forms of Racial Discrimination*, 21 December
  1965, 660 UNTS 195.
*International Covenant on Economic, Social and Cultural Rights* (ICESCR), 16 December 1966,
  993 UNTS 3.
*International Covenant on Civil and Political Rights* (ICCPR), 16 December 1966, 999 UNTS
  171.
*Montevideo Convention on the Rights and Duties of States*, 1933, 165 LNTS 19.
*Protocol Relating to the Status of Refugees*, 31 January 1967, 606 UNTS 267.
*Stockholm Declaration on the Human Environment*, adopted by the UN Conference on the
  Human Environment (1972), rep. 11 ILM 1416.
*Universal Declaration of Human Rights*, 10 December 1948, GA Res. 217 A (III).
*Vienna Declaration and Programme of Action*, 25 June 1993, rep. 32 ILM 1661.


## Cases

*Bosnia and Hercegovina* v. *Serbia–Montenegro* (1993), ICJ Rep. 3 April.
*Burkina Faso* v. *Mali* (The Frontier Dispute Case) (1986), ICJ Rep. 554.
*Doe* v. *Unocal* (CD Cal.) (Burma).
*Filartiga* v. *Pena-Irala*, 630 F. 2nd 876 (2nd Cir. 1980), Rep. 19 ILM.
*Forti* v. *Suarez-Mason*, 672 F. Supp. 1531 (ND Cal. 1987).
*Hilao* v. *Marcos*, 25 F. 3rd 1467 (9th Cir. 1994).
*Ireland* v. *UK*, ECHR, Ser. A, vol. 3 (Judgment of 18 January 1978).
*Kadic* v. *Karadwicz*, 70 F. 3rd 232 (2nd Cir. 1995).
*Lovelace* v. *Canada*, 2 Selected Decisions Human Rights Committee 28 (1981).

*Nicaragua* v. *USA* (1986) (Case concerning military and paramilitary activities in and against Nicaragua), ICJ Rep. 14.

*Prosecutor* v. *Gagovic and Others* ('foca'), Case IT–96–23–1, 26 June 1996, International Tribunal for the Prosecution of Persons Responsible for Serious Violations of International Humanitarian Law in the Territories of Former Yugoslavia Since 1991.

*Velasquez Rodriguez* v. *Honduras* (Inter-American Court of Human Rights, Judgment of 29 July 1989) rep. 28 ILM 294 (1989)

*Wiwa* v. *Shell Oil* (SDNY) (Nigeria).

*Xuncas* v. *Gramajo* 886 F. Supp. 162 (D. Mass. 1995).

# Human rights as social exclusion

# 6

# Are women human? It's not an academic question[1]

## V. Spike Peterson and Laura Parisi

[Amnesty International] concluded that women suffer more violations of human rights than any other group in the world, both in times of war and through traditional practices excused by culture (Bahar 1996, 107).

The exclusion of any group – whether on the basis of gender, class, sexual orientation, religion, or race – involves cultural definitions of the members of that group as less than fully human (Bunch 1995, 12).

## Introduction

This chapter considers the question: 'are women human?', by examining the constitution and meaning of the category 'human' in relation to the binary codification of 'men' and 'women'. A vast feminist scholarship demonstrates that modernist references to an ostensibly universal (non-gender-differentiated) 'human' are in fact androcentric. That is, they are implicitly references to men: their bodies, experiences and stereotypical attributes (e.g., reason, agency, independence). Assuming men as the norm, and generalizing their concerns as universal, precludes symmetry between the subcategories of male and female. On the contrary, women and women's bodies, experiences and stereotypical attributes (e.g., affect, non-agency, and dependence) are excluded from the 'universal' category and cast instead as particular and partial. Viewed through this lens, only men occupy the unmarked universal category 'human'; women are not human but the 'other', that is, the marked – and denigrated – subcategory.

Most feminist critiques of human rights focus on this androcentrism and argue that, ostensibly, human rights are in actuality men's rights. As a consequence, exclusions, constraints and abuses more typical of women's lives are neither recognized nor protected by human rights instruments. In this chapter, we take a deeper look at how 'human' rights are gendered by interrogating the binary of male-female and the normalization of heterosexism. We first define heterosexism and its relationship to sex difference (male and female bodies) and oppositional gender identities (masculine and feminine subjectivities). We then consider sex difference in the context of heterosexist group reproduction and the constitution of masculinist relations.[2] This is followed by a discussion of the role of states in normalizing heterosexism and its attendant, gendered binaries. Having developed our theoretical articulation of gender, heterosexism, and states, we shift to its implications for a feminist critique of human rights. We organize the latter by examining the three familiar 'generations' of human rights from the perspective of women's lives and experiences under conditions of heterosexism.

It is in the spirit of this volume that our focus in this paper is consistently critical.[3] We intend this neither as a simplistic indictment of human rights, nor as condemnation of activities in pursuit of rights. Rather, we present our critique as necessary ground clearing: a radically disruptive analysis that enables us to see more clearly just what is at stake – and how far we have to go – to take gender seriously in pursuit of justice.

## Heterosexism and gendering subjects

> What has not been generally recognized is the bias that often underlies studies of both sex roles and male dominance – an assumption that we know what 'men' and 'women' are, an assumption that male and female are pre-dominantly natural objects rather than predominantly cultural constructions. (Ortner and Whitehead 1981, 1)

What are the political effects of coding the human body as two mutually exclusive and oppositional 'types' cast as male and female? How was this coding institutionalized such that we take few things more for granted than the presumption of dichotomized sex difference, codified in the binary form of male and female bodies, masculine and feminine identities, and heterosexual practice? And what does the normalization of heterosexuality entail for the meaning of 'human', and therefore our understanding of human rights?

In this section, we consider how the dichotomy of sexual difference is integral to, and mutually constitutive of, heterosexism. Whereas hetero-sexuality refers to sex/affective relations between people of the so-called opposite sex, heterosexism refers to the institutionalization of heterosexuality as the only 'normal' mode of sexual identity, sexual practice and social relations. That is, heterosexism presupposes a binary coding of polarized and hier-archical male/masculine and female/feminine identities – ostensibly based on a dichotomy of bio-physical features – and denies all but heterosexual coupling as the basis of family life and group reproduction. In Judith Butler's words:

> The heterosexualization of desire requires and institutes the production of discrete and asymmetrical oppositions between 'feminine' and 'masculine', where these are understood as expressive attributes of 'male' and 'female'.

> The cultural matrix through which gender identity has become intelligible
> requires that certain kinds of 'identities' cannot 'exist', that is, those in which
> gender does not follow from sex and those in which the practices of desire
> do not 'follow' from either sex or gender. (Butler 1990, 17)

Heterosexism is rendered natural and normal by reifying 'the family' (in
practice, a historically specifiedealized western/liberal definition of the family)
as 'prepolitical' – as 'sentiment-based' and non-contractual (Rao 1996, 245).
Liberal commitments are crucial to this depoliticization of the family insofar
as they naturalize a categorical distinction between public and private spheres
that privileges the former only as political, and relegates sex/affective relations to the latter. Human rights discourse and practice reproduce this
naturalization of heterosexism and the family, including gender inequalities
within the family, by upholding the distinction between public/state and
private/family spheres and focusing exclusively on states as both protectors
and violators of individual rights.

   If the gender binary and heterosexism are socially constructed (the effects
of contingent, historically specific conditions), how was heterosexism (and its
effects, suggested above) institutionalized? Until recently, the 'origins' of
sexual difference were addressed almost exclusively from two vantage points.
Freud and his followers probed the psychological dimensions of sexual
differentiation and its corollary subjectivities and sexualities, while Marx and
his followers analysed social structures as determining divisions of labour
and their corollary social relations and inequalities. Both approaches take the
transition to 'civilization' as key – marking for Freudians the need to control
instinctual desires [4] and for Marxists the institutionalization of social hierarchies.[5] More recently we have witnessed an explosion of scholarship on both
the meaning and production of sexuality, subjectivity and gender (e.g.,
Foucault 1978; Ortner and Whitehead 1981; Caplan 1987; Butler 1989;
Sedgwick 1990; Lacquer 1990; Stanton 1992). Given space limitations, we
focus here on feminist analyses within these literatures that illuminate the
construction of 'human' and its marginalization of 'woman'.

   From the psychoanalytic tradition, feminists draw upon Freud's and
Lacan's attention to the unconscious, desire and sexualities, while criticizing
masculinist bias in these accounts (e.g., Braidotti 1991; Brennan 1989; Flax
1989; Butler 1990; Irigaray 1985). The psychoanalytic tradition, and especially Lacan's theory of the symbolic, enables feminists to explicitly
interrogate phallocentric thinking, patriarchal structures of language, and the
move from 'symbolic to sexual difference' (Brennan 1989, 2). The arguments
are complex and resist brief summarization.[6] We make two points here.

   First, psychoanalytic perspectives are unique in analysing the unconscious – with its affective, 'irrational' and libidinal features – and the role of
linguistic systems in constituting sexuated subjects, gender identities and
sexual practices. They are therefore crucial for analysing relationships among

the unconscious, social meaning systems, and the development of sexually differentiated persons who exhibit 'appropriate' heterosexist gender identities. In brief, Lacan argues that the infant's maturation, as a separate and 'social-ized' being, is effectuated by entry into the symbolic order, which places human beings in relation to others, and gives them a sense of their place in their world, and the ability to speak and be understood by others' (Brennan 1989, 2). Moreover, the symbolic order is phallocentric: the binary coding of masculine-feminine and privileging of that which is masculine is inscribed in language itself. The key point here is that language becomes a key dimension in analysing the construction of subjects (humans).

Second, through their emphasis on language, psychoanalytic and, esp-ecially, Lacanian theories afford illumination of social structures as well. Lacan's symbolic is not independent of cultural context. It refers not only to language but also to the incest taboo structuring kinship and to patriarchal social relations assumed operative in the transition to 'culture', to 'civiliz-ation', and to recorded history. In social science terms, this is the transition that marks early state formation and the development of hierarchical social relations theorized by Marx and Engels. Stated differently, the symbolic refers as well to what Teresa de Lauretis calls 'the oedipal contract', by which she brings into view

> the semiotic homology of several conceptual frameworks: Sausseure's notion of language as social contract; Rousseau's 'social contract', with its gender distinction; Freud's 'Oedipus complex' as the structuring psychic mechanism responsible for the orientation of human desire and the psychosocial con-struction of gender; ... and finally, Wittig's 'heterosexual contract' as the agreement between modern theoretical systems and epistemologies not to question the *a priori* of gender, and hence to presume the sociosexual oppos-ition of 'man' and 'woman' as the *necessary* and founding moment of culture. (de Lauretis 1987, 277, citing Wittig 1980)

What we observe here are recent attempts to bring diverse literatures and disciplinary vantage points into relation through feminist interrogations of sexed bodies, gender identities, phallocentric language and patriarchal social orders. In particular, feminists are exposing the unexamined assumptions about binary gender/sexuality that pervade psychoanalytic, Marxist and liberal treatments of civilization, early states, the social contract, and human entry into cultural systems. Bringing psychoanalytic and social structural explanations into relation, feminists 'flesh out' our understanding of the historical – and interactive – constitution of individual subjectivities (the binary of masculine-feminine gender identities), sexuated bodies (the binary of sex difference embodied in 'man' and 'woman'), and heterosexual relations (normalized by patriarchal state making that prohibits alternative sex/gender identifications and/or forms of social reproduction).

These studies have not, however, been integrated with conventional frameworks of political science and international relations. We argue that such integration enhances not only our understanding of gender, subjectivities and sexualities, but contributes significantly to contemporary theorizations of politics, states and sovereignty. Of particular relevance to the present chapter, such integration informs our understanding of human rights as theory *and* practice. Before sketching the arguments underlying these claims, we first recapitulate the larger framing of these arguments to clarify how various components are linked.

Stated most succinctly, we argue that the heterosexual contract (naturalizing binary gender identities and heterosexism), the social contract (naturalizing centralized political authority, hierarchical social relations, and the transition from pre-contractual relations associated with the state of nature to contractual relations associated with culture) and language codification (the invention of writing attendant on early state formation) are mutually constituted – historically interdependent – processes (e.g., Peterson 1996b, 1997). Moreover, this mutuality is not simply a conceptual linkage (e.g., between symbolic constructions of masculinity, heterosexuality and stateness) but a historical, empirical and structural linkage that is visible through a feminist lens on early state making and its ideological productions. Stated differently, we understand these linkages as structural in two *interactive* senses: both as historical-empirical material practices and institutions – the more conventional sense of social structures – and as meaning systems, knowledge claims and ideologies that produce, even as they are produced by, material structures.

What we are linking within an overarching framework are the following:[7] the normalization of a gender binary of bodies and subjectivities/identities (introduced above; involving the unconscious as well as conscious thought, the making of gender-differentiated individuals through immersion in and deployment of culturally shared meaning systems/language); the constitution of sexualities in a binary gender form that normalizes heterosexuality (involving oppositional gender identities and socialization in support of heterosexist identities and practices); heterosexism as a regulatory regime in service to group reproduction in a temporal and spatial sense (involving the primacy of particular *group*/collective identifications and heterosexist 'family forms' structuring biological reproduction); the conceptual and material constitution of separate spheres of social activity – in western state making, the public and private – that structure divisions of authority, power, labour and resources (involving group reproduction through a particular heterosexual family/household form of sex/affective relations separated from ostensibly asexual, contractual relations in the public sphere of formal power); and state orders institutionalizing centralized authority/power/accumulation and dependent upon social reproduction that accommodates state-led objectives (involving regulation of biological and social reproduction, attempted through state-led ideological productions of culture, education, etc. – including normalization of dichotomized thought in language, philosophy, religion, political theory – as well as the more formal disciplining practices of police and military activities; and involving the context of an interstate system within which particular states are constituted and act).

In short: the normalization and reproduction of binary gender identities (sex difference embodied and internalized as male-female) is inextricable from the normalization of heterosexism (denying all but heterosexual forms of identity/subjectivity, family forms and group reproduction), which is inextricable from western state making (with centralized authority and hierarchical divisions of labour) and its concomitant ideological productions (the social contract, public–private dichotomy, and in the modern era, androcentric human rights, etc.). For Teresa de Lauretis, coming to terms with these linkages means

> that one begins the process of critical thinking and scholarly writing with the firm, general assumption that official culture and its forms of representation are male-centered, as well as man-made; and, in particular, that the cultural construction of sex into gender, and the asymmetry that characterizes each gender system as the primary semiotic apparatus through which the female (or the male) body is represented, are 'systematically linked to the organization of social inequality'. (de Lauretis 1987, 260, quoting Collier and Rosaldo 1981, 275)

Having earlier provided some sense of contemporary feminist theorization of the gender binary of bodies and subjectivities/identities, we turn now to situating those analyses in relation to the normalization of heterosexism, analyses of group reproduction and state making.

## Group reproduction in relation to normalizing heterosexism

How is the reproduction of a social group ensured? That is, in the absence of any biological connection beyond some females bearing and breast-feeding infants, how are social relations institutionalized, become marked by group coherence, identified with the group itself, and sustain continuity through time? Jill Vickers argues that patriarchal social relations can be interpreted as *one* way of 'constructing enduring forms of social organization, group cohesion and identity' (Vickers 1990, 483).[8] Men, who lack any immediate biological connection, appropriate an abstract concept of the blood-tie and employ it to promote bonding among males and loyalties to a male-defined group extending beyond the mother-infant bond.

To the extent that women are denied agency in the definition of group interests, and compelled to comply with male-defined needs, their freedom and autonomy are limited. Historically, this pattern of domination has been marked by denying women the authoritative status of 'personhood' accorded to those who are empowered as group decision-makers (e.g., Lerner 1986).[9] In short, group continuity – and the gender hierarchy it imposes – is 'secured only by limiting the autonomy, freedom of choice and social adulthood of the group's physical and social reproducers' (Vickers 1990, 482).

What Vickers calls the 'battle of the cradle' is about regulating under what conditions, when, how many and whose children women will bear. The forms it takes are historically specific, shaped by socio-religious norms, technological developments, economic pressures and political priorities. The common feature is promoting reproduction of one's 'own' group on the assumption of competition with 'other' groups. Depending on the type of group (e.g., based on national, ethnic or religious identification) this implicates women of different classes, ethnicities and races in complex and context-specific ways. The common feature is a tendency to preclude women's primary identification with 'women' as a group in favour of their identification with the (territorial, class, religious, ethnic, race) group of which they are a member and which is based on male-defined needs (and heterosexual norms).

Heterosexism affords several advantages for masculinist group reproduction: it promotes binary gender identities and the naturalization, therefore 'acceptance', of women's subordination to male-defined interests; it promotes heterosexual relations which promote women's investments in group projects (through emotional identification with male partners and children, etc.), and, as a corollary, heterosexism precludes such bonding and/or group identification and organization among women *qua* women, thus foreclosing alternative group forms and interests at odds with heterosexist male-defined groups. At the same time, heterosexism is oppressive: it privileges males/masculinity and male-defined interests over females/femininity and interests of women *qua* women, and it denies/represses all other sexual orientations and gender identifications.

The 'battle of the nursery' is about ensuring that children born are bred in culturally – and sexually – appropriate ways. This involves the socio-cultural, legal and coercive regulation of sexual liaisons so that membership boundaries are maintained. It also involves ideological reproduction through socialization of group members and cultivation of particular identities. Under patriarchal relations, women are the primary socializers of children and the family/household is the primary site of socialization and cultural transmission. Cultural transmission includes learning the 'mother tongue', as well as the group's symbols, rituals, divisions of labour and world views – including the normalization of heterosexism and, where appropriate, the meaning and subjects of human rights. This socialization extends beyond the household to structure how we understand – and relate to – sexual stereotypes, work expectations, exchange relations, social hierarchies and authoritative power more generally. At the same time, family/household relations are shaped by state policies and sub-national and transnational dynamics (Peterson 1996a).

What emerges here is the centrality of gender hierarchy and hetero-sexism in processes of identification and group reproduction. Specifically, the reproduction of groups under patriarchal conditions involves a gendered – also class and often ethnic/race – division of power and labour that institutionalizes inequality(ies) within the group. This divides women from men *and from each other* insofar as any primary identification with 'women as a group' is disrupted in favour of identification with the male-defined group. Hence, women within particular groups may oppress or be oppressed by women invested in other heterosexist groups.

What also emerges is the political significance of reproductive processes. Conventionally ignored as a dimension of the ostensibly apolitical private sphere, the power relations of reproduction/families fundamentally condition who 'we' are – as sexuated individuals, gender identities and collective identities – how group cultures are propagated, and how groups/nations align/identify themselves in cooperative, competing and complementary ways. Insofar as these reproductive processes occur within the family/household, the latter is a crucial site of power and politics.

As with any organizing principle or institutional strategy, heterosexist group reproduction involves multiple and complex trade-offs. While hetero-sexist practices afford a number of identifiable advantages for the coherence, commitments and continuity of groups, they do so at the expense of alternative gender and inter-group relations. This is especially the case because the gender binary is deployed not only to organize hierarchical sexual relations but as an ideological given as well. In the latter capacity, gender hierarchy not only subordinates the interests of women *qua* women within particular groups, but naturalizes the subordination of all that is associated with the feminine and which is thereby objectified as an appropriate target of domination: females, nature and 'others' (read: barbarians, the uncivilized, natives, and all who are deemed outside of the group's circle of cultural acceptance). Hence, and this is key, gender hierarchy naturalizes not only intra- but also inter-group asymmetries.

## Group reproduction in the context of state making

International relations scholars tend to focus exclusively on the modern state system. And while political theorists at least acknowledge the canonical importance of Athenian texts, international relations theorists tend to ignore how these texts established binary constructions of identity, politics and public–private spheres that continue to discipline the theory/practice of world politics – including, and in particular, the theory/practice of human rights.

What particularly drops out of sight in a historical picture of states is the institutionalization (read: normalization) of gendered and hierarchical relations associated with early state making. Early state making is, after all, what we celebrate as the transition to western civilization: the settlement of peoples, a new scale of societal organization, specialization of labour, and hence, through the development of writing, the beginning of history. What this transition also marks is the effective centralization of political authority and accumulation processes, military consolidation, centralized regulation through formal laws, a hierarchical division of labour by gender, age and 'class', the reconfiguration of individual and collective identities appropriate to that division of labour, and ideological legitimization of these transformations. Subsequent naturalization – that is, depoliticization – of these arrangements effectively obscures how they were *made* (not found) and their dependence on particular, historically contingent relations of power. In early state making, key sources of power include the enhanced control afforded by centralized authority and the latter's domination of symbol systems/writing. As Athenian texts reveal, the regulation of sexual activities and institutionalization of masculinist law, philosophy and politics were absolutely central features of early states. It is in this sense that group reproduction (as sketched above) and heterosexism are embedded in state-making projects.

Feminists analyse the state from diverse perspectives.[10] In anthropological and historical studies, feminists theorize the institutionalization and ideological normalization of the patriarchal heterosexual family/household, dichotomized gender identities, and gendered divisions of labour, power and authority, masculinist language systems, and the separation of public and private spheres. For example, they argue that the masculinism of the state begins not in modernity but with early states and is explicit in Greek political theorizing. For it is in this earlier context that the state institutionalizes heterosexual families/households and justifies hierarchical power by reference to the hierarchical dichotomies of public–private, reason–affect, mind–body, culture–nature, civilized–other and masculine–feminine. Moreover, the continued patriarchal commitments of states are exposed by feminist research: the state intervenes in private sphere dynamics in part to impose centralized authority over birth rate patterns, property transmission and reproduction of appropriately socialized family members, workers and citizens. The means include laws circumscribing sexual behaviour, control of women's reproductive rights and the promotion – through state policies, public media and educational systems – of gendered ethnic and race identifications, heterosexism and particular family forms.

In sum, to apprehend the larger picture of linkages outlined above, we must take a longer view. Early state formation marks an important turning point in human history. This involved normalizing foundational dichotomies (public–private, reason–affect, mind–body, culture–nature, civilized–barbarian, masculine–feminine) both materially (in divisions of authority, power, labour and resources) as well as conceptually (in western metaphysics, language, philosophy, political theory). Not least because early state making also marked the invention of writing, these systemic transformations were codified and that codification in western philosophy, political theory and particular texts has profoundly shaped subsequent theory/practice. In particular, early western texts resurfaced to influence and shape political theory in the context of modern European state making. The effects of earlier codification and its modern counterparts continue to discipline our theory/practice, as exemplified in the theory/practice of human rights. Because we take modern state making as our starting point and fail to investigate this earlier transition, we 'forget' how *political* the *making* of sexuality and subjectivities – of 'men' and 'women' – has always been, and remains so today.

This necessarily brief and vastly oversimplified sketch of linkages and developments suggests the following in regard to 'women' and 'human' rights. First, and of particular relevance to first generation rights, women are not included in the western, liberal, public sphere definition of individuals that underpins the discourse of human rights. This has several implications (treated in greater detail below). In brief, existing human rights are in fact men's rights; it is 'citizens' (implicitly male/masculine) who enjoy civil and political rights. As a consequence, women may enjoy these rights *only* to the extent they become like men. In addition, the state's complicity in perpetuating the alleged separation of public and private spheres, combined with the human rights emphasis on state violations only, means that inequalities, expressions of violence and infringements of freedom within the putatively private sphere – where women are most vulnerable – are not deemed violations of human rights and states are not held accountable for their complicity in instituting, legitimating and sustaining gender hierarchy. As a consequence, gender inequalities within the 'family' are depoliticized and women are not free to enjoy bodily security or reproductive freedoms. Finally, men and women who do not conform to normalized gender identities and sexualities are 'outside' of human rights protections and are at risk in two related senses: first, by being outside of naturalized norms (therefore vulnerable to discriminatory and violent acts), and second, by having gender/sexual oppression treated as private sphere phenomena and therefore not protected by human rights laws.

Second, and of particular relevance to second generation rights, unlike men (especially, élite men), women are not constructed as agents/subjects/persons in their own right or as full adults/decision-makers in groups seeking intergenerational continuity. Heterosexist principles of group reproduction both relegate women to reproductive roles and denigrate that which is associated with the feminine. Women are marginalized – not treated as 'human' *agents* – in relation to economic, social and cultural practices, which are, in addition, construed as exclusively public sphere manifestations. Rights to work, for example, presume a public sphere understanding of work that is gender differentiated and exacerbates the invisibility of reproductive labour typically performed by women. Moreover, and in literally deadly ways, second generation rights often worsen women's vulnerability and subordination by endorsing cultural and religious beliefs that devalue women and deny gender equality.

Third, and of particular relevance to third generation rights, women's structural location within heterosexist collectivities means that women *qua* women are not 'free' to constitute groups in their own right. However much women may benefit from membership in particular heterosexual groups – and they *do* so benefit – under conditions of heterosexism/masculinism, they enjoy these benefits as secondary members, not as full-status agents or women participating in woman-identified groups. And historically there is no exception to the practice of women's interests *qua* women being subordinated to (male-defined) group interests: self-determination has meant the expression of men's (again, especially élite men's) selves, desires and dreams. Women's interests are repeatedly put on hold, ostensibly until the 'priority' battles are won. Here women are triply marginalized: because they are not members of women-identified groups, they do not benefit *qua* women from group rights; because they are subordinated within heterosexist groups, they do not enjoy the rights to self-determination that men in such groups may achieve through group rights; and because they are members of particular groups, they may suffer from oppression by (and/or oppress) women in other heterosexist groups.

## Women's marginalization in three generations of rights

To examine these issues more concretely – to explore how women are indeed not 'human' in the context of contemporary international human rights – we consider women's rights in relation to the three generations [11] of human rights. We address the first generation in greater detail because civil and political rights engage all of the issues raised in our theoretical framing and are so privileged in contemporary human rights theory/practice.

FIRST GENERATION RIGHTS: CIVIL AND POLITICAL LIBERTIES
The first generation emphasizes civil and political rights and is codified in the Universal Declaration of Human Rights (UDHR) and the International Covenant on Civil and Political Rights (1966; hereafter ICCPR). Feminists criticize both the definition of rights as androcentric (that is, human rights – based on public sphere/citizenship activities – are men's rights; Hosken 1981; Holmes 1983; Bunch 1990; Peterson 1990; Charlesworth, Chinkin and Wright 1991; Kerr 1993; Cook 1994; Peters and Wolpers 1995) and how international

human rights law sustains and exacerbates the public–private dichotomy (Eisler 1987; Charlesworth 1994; Romany 1994; Sullivan 1995).[12]

The argument regarding androcentrism is both empirical and conceptual. On the one hand, women's lived experiences and particular vulnerabilities (under conditions of patriarchy) are excluded '[b]ecause the law-making institutions of the international legal order have always been, and continue to be, dominated by men' (Charlesworth 1995, 103). Quite simply, it is therefore men's bodies, experiences and perspectives that are reflected in human rights law. On the other hand, women's conceptual exclusion from the definition of agent and human (wrought by heterosexist practice and ideology and the universalizing move that renders men as humans, women as others) precludes their experience being included in how human rights are conceptualized – and hence practised. In regard to the public–private dichotomy, feminists are nowhere more united than in criticizing how this dichotomy obscures systemic power relations and, specifically, gender inequalities in intimate, family and household relations. In general, the public–private split 'refers to the (artificial) distinction between the private sphere of the home, to which women are assigned, and the public sphere of the workplace and government, to which men are assigned' (Peterson and Runyan 1993, 192). This division of activities rests on a gender-differentiated conception of citizenship that dates back to the Greek polis, yet continues to structure western liberal thought (Grant 1991, 12–13; Elshtain 1981). In the Athenian context, citizenship was linked to owning property and participating in military defence of the city-state. In the European context of bourgeois revolutions, citizenship was additionally linked to the 'human' capacity for reason. These are all gender-differentiated criteria: women have been denied property rights – and treated as property themselves; women have until recently been excluded from military activities, and their continued exclusion from combat duties exposes military retention of gender stereotypes and inequalities; and stereotypes of feminine irrationality have everywhere served to justify women's *de facto* exclusion from public sphere power. In short, existing models of citizenship rest on a gendered construction of the public–private in which only the public sphere is associated with power, politics and privileged masculinity.

These masculinist assumptions similarly underpin international human rights laws, as the latter apply only to the public sphere of society, in the form of protecting citizens from state abuse, thus denying state responsibility in private sphere activities. This emphasis on the state and public sphere is problematic for women because it does not recognize the masculinist state's complicity in naturalizing – depoliticizing – the public–private dichotomy, masculinist citizenship, patriarchal families and heterosexism. By upholding the *status quo*, states uphold women's oppression and the stigmatization of non-heterosexist identities and social relations. In particular, the public sphere focus of human rights discourse denies the private sphere/family, where women are particularly vulnerable, as a site of human rights violations.

The masculinist state institutionalizes and sustains gender hierarchy – which denies women equal 'human' rights – both directly and indirectly. Direct intervention takes the form of laws and policies – regulating marriage, divorce, parenting, custody, sexuality, property, taxes and welfare – that normalize and *institutionally* reproduce women's subordination through, for example, heterosexist families and masculinist labour markets that assume male breadwinners. The state's regulation of women's lives is especially visible in denying women the right to control their own bodies. State abuse may take the form of reproductive coercion and control, exemplified in forced pregnancies, sterilization and limited or no access to abortion. Heterosexism favours men's initiation of and control over sexual liaisons and contraceptive practices.[13] State-sanctioned barriers to women's control of their bodies condone male control. For example, many countries require spousal permission before women can acquire contraception or have abortions. The effects on women's lives are disastrous: marital rape, sexually transmitted diseases, unwanted pregnancies, ill-health from excessive childbearing and violence against women who resist men's control.

Masculinist cultural norms favour males. The preference for sons has translated into the abortion of female foetuses as well as female infanticide on a harrowing scale. It has also translated into malnourishment and other indicators of poor health and diminished quality of life among females who are not favoured in the distribution of food and other subsistence goods. And worldwide, male privilege translates into higher proportions of men in élite decision-making positions, ensuring that in spite of long-lasting and widespread resistance, the cycle of masculine dominance and women's subordination is repeated.

The state also acts indirectly to ensure gender hierarchy and its denial of women's rights. Here the state is complicit in several senses: by failing to acknowledge and punish abuses that occur in the private sphere, by reproducing masculinism through public forums, and by obscuring the state's role through ideologies that naturalize the public–private dichotomy and gender inequalities.

An example of this complicity is the state's treatment of the heterosexual family as both pre-political and non-contractual: pre-political in the sense that it is viewed normatively as an arena for something other than rights, and non-contractual in that the family functions according to (non-contractual) sentiments – love, affection, emotion, passion – that are distinct from rationalist and rights-based characteristics of the public sphere/state (Rao 1996, 245). The heterosexual nuclear family unit becomes the primary social unit to be preserved and protected by the state, even as the state denies intervention in the private sphere. Yet, as Frances Olsen notes, 'the state constantly defines and redefines the family and adjusts and readjusts family roles' (Olsen 1985, 842–3, quoted in Rao 1996, 244). It does so in part by establishing the criteria by which 'the family' is recognized; the hegemonic definition being a nuclear, co-residential heterosexual unit of close-kin members. This heterosexist model excludes other possible family forms and bases of social reproduction, especially same-sex marriages.

International human rights documents reproduce and similarly privilege this narrow construction of the family. The UDHR defines the family as a heterosexual union, as evidenced by Article 16, Section 1: 'Men and women of full age, without any limitation due to race, nationality, or religion, have the right to marry and to found a family'. And Article 16, Section 3 declares that the 'family is the natural and fundamental group unit of society and is entitled to protection by society and the State'. As Arati Rao notes, the UDHR 'not only defines the family in profoundly orthodox terms but places its institutional integrity under the purview of the state' (Rao 1996, 246). The identification of the family as a heterosexual union that constitutes the basis of society serves to further naturalize heterosexist practice and gendered division of identity, authority and power.

It is important to note that the state uses its power not only to interfere in the private sphere to suit male-dominated state interests but also to obscure that intervention by espousing the public–private as protecting the private from state interference (Eisenstein 1981). One of the most destructive effects of this contradictory situation is that the state opts *not* to intervene when domestic violence is at issue. Ultimately, this amounts to a loss of security for women's bodies in the family/household, which is inextricably linked to state-sanctioned mystification of the family/home as the site of harmony/ love/safety.

Understood not as agents in their own right – full 'humans' – but as reproductive members of the group or even as property, women are subject to objectification and abuse. This is related to a 'war against women' in the global context of traffic in women (Barry 1995) and in the home as domestic violence. This abuse is both physical and psychological and it is *not* covered by the UDHR (Schuler 1992; Thomas and Beasley 1993; Copelan 1994; Bahar 1996; Rao 1996). Manifestations of this violence include, but are not limited to, rape, battering, murder (such as bride burning, honour killings and dowry murder), mutilation, deprivation of food and confinement (Schuler 1992, 14; Bahar 1996, 103). While the argument cannot be developed here, rape is inextricable from heterosexist practice.[14] As such, it is implicated in the heterosexist project of state making and its naturalization of male dominance (e.g., MacKinnon 1989). In some countries 'national laws generally mis-characterize rape as a crime against honor or custom, not as a crime against the physical integrity of the victim', and thus minimize its seriousness

(Human Rights Watch 1995, 5). Many countries condone marital rape by implicitly or explicitly assuming that a wife cannot refuse to have intercourse if her husband demands it. Rape is a worldwide phenomenon and affects women of all classes and ethnic/racial groups. Most rapes are committed by men that are known to the victim – often by associates, relatives and partners. And females of all ages are vulnerable. The state is complicit in reproducing heterosexist social relations that promote the social control of women through the threat/actuality of sexual violence both by failing to intervene when such violence takes place in the private sphere and by defining rape from a male point of view in both spheres (MacKinnon 1989).

Finally, the state's heterosexism in general, and the heterosexual family that is embodied in the public–private split and privileged in human rights documents, render all other sex/affective relations 'deviant'. In the terms of this paper, homosexuality is threatening because it exposes the fragility of the state's normalization project; it suggests instead that the binary of heterosexism is not exhaustive: other identities and meaningful social relations are possible. Even more disturbing to guardians of the *status quo*, non-heterosexist identities and social relations are politically *desirable* insofar as they are less tainted by the inequalities and violence attending institutionalized heterosexism.

States promote homophobic oppression in two senses (Amnesty International 1994; LaViolette and Whitworth 1994; Dorf and Perez 1995; Sanders 1996). By normalizing heterosexism, non-heterosexual identities and practices are stigmatized as abnormal, thus fuelling persecution of those who do not conform. And by creating the category of deviants while refusing to take responsibility for their protection, the state denies the violence it colludes in producing. States promote heterosexism and punish homosexuality by various means. Most common is the criminalization of consensual same-sex relations. This is true of countries as diverse as Romania, Nicaragua, Australia, Russia, and the United States (Amnesty International 1994). Even when homosexuality is not specifically criminalized, sexual minorities are subject to harassment, cultural and physical 'bashing', and sometimes arbitrary detention. And even when individuals avoid persecution by state actors, the homophobic climate of hostility and threat deeply affects the freedom of sexual minorities to express identities and activities that diverge from heterosexist norms. Here it is important to note that 'many laws effectively criminalize not only the sexual behavior of gay men and lesbians but also their association, speech and use of the press', thus denying civil and political freedoms extended to other groups (Dorf and Perez 1995, 327).

In regard to 'family law', states normalize heterosexism by preventing same-sex marriages and limiting the rights of gay men or lesbians to have or adopt children (LaViolette and Whitworth 1994; Dorf and Perez 1995). As another example, when states sanction early marriage, they impose heterosexual norms without allowing adolescents time to explore their sexual identity (Tambiah 1995). And in an effort to sustain heterosexuality as the dominant sexual identity in society, states have often tortured gays and lesbians (Amnesty International 1994). In Iran, this may translate into executions; in Columbia it has meant the murder of gay men by paramilitary groups; and similar murders have been reported in Argentina, Brazil and Mexico (LaViolette and Whitworth 1994, 565). More generally, many states identify homosexuality as a disease that must be treated by drug therapy, electroshock, 'punitive psychiatry' or incarceration (LaViolette and Whitworth 1994). This is a dramatic instance of denying agency to lesbians and gay men.

Article 2 of the UDHR states that: 'Everyone is entitled to all the rights and freedoms set forth in this Declaration, without distinction of any kind, such as race, colour, sex, language, religion, political or other opinion, national or social origin, property, birth or other status.' It is clear from our discussion, however, that rights as defined by the UDHR and other covenants are selectively intended and applied. The UDHR does not affirm the right of women to freedom from masculine dominance and the structural violence it constitutes against women and others stigmatized by association with the feminine. Rather, the masculinist state typically protects the private *and* public interests of men. The consequences are that women are systematically denied due process under international human rights law (Thomas and Beasley 1993) and the right to privacy becomes 'interpreted as protecting from scrutiny major sites for the oppression of women: home and family' (Charlesworth 1994, 73).

SECOND GENERATION RIGHTS: ECONOMIC, SOCIAL AND CULTURAL

Identified with the International Covenant on Economic, Social and Cultural Rights (1966; hereafter ICESCR), the second generation emphasizes socio-economic rights and to a limited degree cultural rights. It is often thought that second generation rights transcend the public–private split and might therefore be more relevant to women. But how these rights are codified in the ICESCR 'indicates the tenacity of a gendered public–private distinction in human rights law' (Charlesworth 1994, 74). By continuing to focus on activities in the public sphere, second generation rights fail to address economic, social and cultural issues of particular relevance to women's lives. By reference to our theoretical framing, insofar as women are secondary and not fully adult members of heterosexist groups, what they do – economically, socially, culturally – is not taken as seriously as what men do.

Hence, the definition of work and rights to work in the UDHR and ICESCR is informed by androcentric discourse that equates what is valued with masculine public sphere activities. Consequently, only paid labour in the public sector is valued economically. The work that women do – defined as reproductive rather than productive – is devalued and considered secondary to men's work, interests and needs. Inequalities in compensation for work done are documented by the fact that although women perform two-thirds of the world's labour, they receive only 10 per cent of the income and barely hold 1 per cent of the property (Binion 1995, 511). The global significance of women's work is suggested by UNDP (United Nations Development Programme) estimates that 'the non-monetized invisible contribution of women is $11 trillion a year' (UNDP 1995, 6; also Waring 1988).

Making women's contribution invisible obscures how dependent the public sphere is on private sphere activities. As Mies notes, 'the productivity of the housewife is a precondition for the productivity of the (male) wage labourer. The nuclear family, organized and protected by the state, is a social factory where this commodity 'labour power' is produced' (Mies 1986, 31). Defining the housewife as an unpaid reproducer of future workers rather than a paid producer of commodities provides an 'indirect subsidy to the employers of wage laborers' (Wallerstein 1988, 8). Women provide this subsidy by 'manag[ing] the household resources [so] as to feed, clothe, house, and educate the rest of the household' – whether or not women also work in the formal sector (Elson 1992, 35). The economic disenfranchisement of women serves to normalize the family/household/private realm where women are subordinate to the patriarchal family and masculinist state. Since human rights law generally applies to the public sphere, the identification of women as reproducers and housewives limits their claims to socio-economic rights: because male breadwinners are expected to provide basic needs, women are less able to claim them as rights. In this process, the public realm of male power is protected, while the private realm of women's reproductive work is obscured, and this contributes to the cycle of women's marginalization and exploitation.

The gendered division of labour in the home tends to be replicated in the formal sector of the marketplace. Since women's identities are tied to their socially constructed roles as feminine (read: housewife, reproducer, mother, emotional care-giver), their identities in the labour market are devalued as well. This devaluation translates into systemic discrimination against and exploitation of women in the formal sector. Coupled with discriminatory and exploitative practices is the stereotypical assumption that women's paid labour is secondary and supplemental to men's, who are identified as the primary breadwinners in the family (Rao 1996). This stereotype is fuelled by masculinist ideologies, even as global data indicate that approximately one third of today's households are headed by women (United Nations 1991).

That we obscure women's economic responsibilities and deny them the status of agents in their own right is suggested empirically by recurring salary inequities. The UNDP documents that 'the average wage for women is only about three fourths of the male wage outside agriculture. The ratio varies from 92% of male wage in Tanzania to 75% in the United States to 42% in Bangladesh' (1995, 36–7). This systemic disparity constitutes nothing less than structural violence against women, the dominant manifestation of which is the increasing feminization of poverty.[15]

The state's role in perpetuating gendered economic inequality takes a variety of forms. First, states may either not legislate equal pay rights, or not enforce existing equal pay rights legislation. Second, states may promote welfare policies that (as in the United States) actually discourage women from working in the public sphere, through lack of training, jobs, child-care provision and/or inadequate wages. Third, states may not create or enforce non-discriminatory hiring and promotion practices, thereby sustaining and condoning the glass ceiling which ensures male dominance in the economic arena. As noted earlier, discrimination against women is fuelled by stereotypes that identify women exclusively as mothers and reproducers and deny women's productive roles and rights. Fourth, when states comply with structural adjustment programs of the IMF and World Bank, women suffer disproportionately. This is due in part to treating 'the household as a unit. Here [a] male bias lies in not disaggregating the household to examine the different positions of women and men in the household, thus ignoring the implications of the household as a site for the subordination of women' (Elson 1992, 35).[16]

Structural adjustment affects women in multiple ways. First, privatization and austerity measures encourage the reduction of state social spending, which is unprofitable monetarily. This exacerbates the situation of the poorest and most vulnerable, who are disproportionately female. Second, if structural adjustment policies fail or falter when global economic competition increases and the drive for competition and efficiency is accelerated, women are typically the first to be laid off, due to stereotypes of their 'supplemental' income-earner status (UNDP 1995). Third, when states reduce social and welfare services, it is primarily women who 'take up the slack' in their positioning as social reproducers. Hence, women find themselves burdened by increased demands on their food providing, emotional care-giving and responsibility for the ill and dependent. The above situations result in a further loss of women's control over resources and independence. For single women it may mean loss of the means to support themselves and the necessity of dependence on the patriarchal state; for married women, the effect may be to exacerbate dependence on and vulnerability to the power of the male breadwinner. In both cases, women lose autonomy/agency and are rendered structurally more vulnerable to abuses of power. At the same time, women's dependence sustains gender hierarchy more generally.

Finally, the state is complicit in maintaining gender hierarchy by not ensuring that women are treated as 'humans' with rights to physical safety in the workplace, even though the ICESCR promotes the right to work under favourable conditions. This right is often violated for both men and women (Chapman 1996). However, for women it is especially problematic insofar as sexual abuse is often considered a private issue rather than a public one. Therefore, sexual harassment and even assault and rape by employers may go unpunished. Women are especially vulnerable as domestic workers in a foreign country and as sex workers in a global climate of heterosexist misogyny (HRW 1995, 286–90). Human Rights Watch estimates that every year many thousands of young girls/women are lured, abducted or sold into prostitution (HRW 1995, 196). There is little state or international intervention in the trafficking of women, in part because (and in spite of extensive evidence to the contrary) prostitution is typically considered 'voluntary'. Here the growing business in sex tourism, the structural violence limiting women's choices and the increasing risks of deadly infection interact, rendering sex workers – voluntary or otherwise – tragically vulnerable (Pyne 1995).

With regard to social and cultural rights, state élites may draw upon the many cultural exemptions from CEDAW (Convention on the Elimination of All forms of Discrimination Against Women) to justify direct and indirect violence against women (James 1994). Culture becomes an ideological tool of oppression when deployed to legitimate women's subordination and/or objectification. Consider that the world's most powerful religions are without exception male dominated and heterosexist. They are responsible for some of the most tenacious and deeply held beliefs prejudicial to women. In this environment, and especially in the context of heightened fundamentalisms, it is no surprise that women are pressured, symbolically and materially, to assume traditional, dependent and male-serving identities. Similarly, sexual minorities are cast as diabolical, disruptive and in need of saving.

In short, state complicity in the devaluation of the feminine – whether in relation to formal or informal economic sectors – precludes protection of women under human rights law. Under conditions of structural violence, as constituted by gender hierarchy, the choice for most women 'is not between dependence on the state and independence, but between dependence on the state and dependence on a man' (Elson 1992, 38). Either option translates into a loss of agency for women *qua* women. And in particular, dependence on a man presupposes heterosexual coupling that precludes other forms of group reproduction, social relations and gender identities. Economic, social and cultural rights premised on public sphere activities and patriarchal authorities not only fail to challenge but too often exacerbate the structural subordination of women and the denial of women's rights.

## THIRD GENERATION RIGHTS: COLLECTIVE/GROUP RIGHTS

The third generation of rights, collective or group rights, are not specifically addressed by the UDHR or the subsequent International Bill of Rights

(James 1994, 566). This generation of rights seeks to preserve the integrity of a particular cultural, ethnic or indigenous group through the right of self-determination; claims are typically cast as resistance to the homogenizing and/or genocidal practices of colonization and/or centralization. In effect, subgroups draw upon the discourse of group rights to counter what is perceived as domination in the form of forced assimilation and cultural annihilation. Group rights are therefore predicated on and legitimized by emphasizing the cultural identity of the group rather than rights and identities of individuals (Charlesworth 1994, 75; Kiss 1995). This group emphasis is fundamentally at odds with the dominant liberal view that favours autonomous individuals as rights holders, which prompts considerable debate. Not surprisingly, a growing literature attempts to weigh the trade-offs between benefits to the group as a whole at the expense of harm to individuals within the group (e.g., subgroups based on ethnicity, class, gender, religion, sexual orientation, etc. (Kymlicka 1995; Glazer 1995; Green 1995; Young 1995). Of particular relevance here are feminist analyses arguing that emphasis on the collective is often detrimental to women as *individuals* (Jayawardena 1986; Charlesworth 1994; Young 1995; Peterson 1995; Pettman 1996; Yuval-Davis 1996). Moreover, as we argued earlier, women's subordination within heterosexist and male-defined groups denies women the status of personhood equal to that of male decision-makers and precludes primary identification with women *qua* women. Rather, the history of state making and its intra- and inter-group hierarchies has institutionalized male leadership and authority such that women's interests *qua* women are structurally subordinated to masculinist projects.

We frame our discussion by identifying three ways in which group rights are problematic for promoting women's rights, and concretize the discussion by focusing on the pending Draft Universal Declaration on the Rights of Indigenous Peoples (hereafter, the Draft Declaration). If passed by the UN, this would be the first international human rights 'law' to sanction group rights over individual rights, with important effects for the approximately 5,000 indigenous groups in the world constituting an estimated population of 300 million (Corntassel and Hopkins Primeau 1995, 346), over half of whom are women.

First, the normalization of masculinism/heterosexism prevents women *qua* women from constituting groups of their own, through which women might take advantage of group rights. This shapes women's options for self-determination, which we discuss below. Similarly, insofar as heterosexism is presumed in human rights documents, including those specific to group rights, sexual minorities cannot constitute 'appropriate' groups and are thereby precluded from the benefits of group rights. In terms of the Draft Declaration, spokespersons for indigenous collectivities are predominantly male, which suggests male dominance in these collectivities, as well as the absence of any groups premised on women's primary identification as/with women.

Second, due to their subordination within heterosexist groups, women do not enjoy the rights to self-determination emphasized in group rights. That is, under masculine/heterosexist leadership, women's interests and concerns are structurally marginalized in determining group strategies and goals. In effect, women give up their right to self-determination as individuals, or as a collectivity of women, in favour of self-determination of the group as defined by male élites. Consequently, although the group as a whole, including women within the group, may benefit from claims to self-determination, history suggests forcefully that women's interests (e.g., in reproductive rights, political representation, economic equality) will be treated as secondary. In short, self-determination of heterosexist groups has historically meant the particular realization of (primarily élite) men's selves and dreams.

As a corollary, individual women may be at risk if they are unable/unwilling to 'deliver' in terms of their primary reproductive role insofar as that constitutes their value and status. Indeed, the Draft Declaration is potentially problematic in this regard since it affirms that 'indigenous peoples are entitled to the recognition of the full ownership, control, and protection of their cultural and intellectual property' (Ewen 1994, 170, Article 29, Reprint of the Draft Declaration). It is important to bear in mind that this right is accorded to the group as a whole in relation to the state. Applied to intra-group relations, this article could be interpreted as a collective right to control, without any countervailing protection from the state, women understood to be the biological and cultural reproducers of the group, and sometimes identified as property.

In the face of cultural or physical annihilation, it is not surprising that groups promote their own reproduction and seek legal protections. Women also benefit from their group's survival, but under heterosexist social relations, women are especially burdened by responsibility for reproducing the group. Unlike men, women find themselves disciplined not only to bear children but to do so according to group-defined parameters that constrain women's reproductive choices (e.g., at what age, with whom and how frequently to bear children). Moreover, under heterosexism women are expected not only to bear but also to raise the children. On the one hand, heterosexist delegation of this work exclusively to women denies individual women freedom to make their own choices about heterosexuality and parenting. It marginalizes women from public sphere power and imposes heavy sanctions on women who resist conforming to masculinist expectations. On the other hand, men's withdrawal from child rearing and other care-giving activities has consequences for the psyches, emotional development, life styles, capacities, and decision making of adult men. In short, heterosexist group reproduction may serve to expand group numbers and sustain cultural traditions, and these may be highly desirable goals. But they come at a cost, not only to women, who suffer a loss of rights and self-determination, but also for men, whose experience of dominating also has its costs.

Again, this is not to argue that women reap no benefits from participation in male-defined groups. Nor do we intend to trivialize the importance of seeking protection for endangered groups. Our point is rather to insist that women's allegiance to masculinist collectivities has structural consequences, one of which is systemic and inevitable subordination of women's concerns. In other words, group rights predicated on heterosexist social reproduction contradict women's self-determination. The empirical evidence for this ana- lytical claim is visible in revolutionary and nationalist struggles, where gender equality has without exception been subordinated to masculinist group objectives.

Third, although women are subordinated to male leadership within groups, their membership in particular groups may position them favourably *vis-à-vis* women in other groups and thus contribute – however unintention- ally – to other women's oppression. That is, women's affiliations with male-defined groups implicate women in hierarchies structured by inter- group competition such that women are oppressors of, and oppressed by, women who are members of other groups. In short, group benefits may oppress women in other groups as groups compete for the right to self- determination. The Draft Declaration is here problematic. While it promotes the rights of *all* indigenous groups, it lends itself to supporting competition among groups by emphasizing *group rights*.

In terms of human rights discourse and practice, the Draft Declaration embodies the very notion that collective or group cultural rights should take precedence over individual rights. Should the Draft Declaration be passed, indigenous group rights will be formalized for the first time in international human rights law. This move is applauded by many, including women, but at the same time it is problematic for women, given their structural subor- dination in heterosexist collectivities.

## Conclusion

Whereas most feminist critiques of human rights focus on their andro- centrism – identifying human rights as men's rights – we have focused on their heterosexism. Rather than assuming the categories of men and women as timeless and unproblematic, we explored how these categories were *made* in historical time, and how that making normalized gendered identities and heterosexist practices that underpin existing human rights. Rather than simply adding 'women's rights' to existing 'human' rights, we explored how only men are human under heterosexist social relations, and how human rights are therefore problematic terrain for women and all who are stigmatized by association with the feminine.

Due to limitations of space – and the volume's intent – we have focused entirely on critique in this paper. But our intent is *not* to dismiss the progressive possibilities of human rights or denigrate activities in pursuit of rights. Our critique exposes numerous and interrelated problems in rights *given* their heterosexist framing. We believe that it is crucial to render that framing and its limitations *visible*. Only then can we adequately theorize and more effectively eliminate social hierarchies and their structural violence.

We also recognize, however, that we currently live *within* that framing. Therefore, women and men must pursue justice with the tools at hand, and rights are crucial tools in the face of state and structural violence.[17] In short, our argument is less to denigrate rights than to situate them in the context of heterosexist states and thereby reveal their limitations. They are important – indeed often life-saving – as available tools in contemporary battles against oppression and violence. We must, therefore, strategically deploy them. But their limitations are also literally deadly. If we do not simultaneously work to dissemble heterosexist oppression, we resign ourselves to perpetuating, not eliminating, direct and indirect violence against all who are 'othered' as feminine.

## Notes

1 Peterson wishes to thank Charlotte Bunch, Hilary Charlesworth, Riane Eisler, Stanlie James, Arati Rao and Sandra Whitworth for their inspiration and leadership in the theory/practice of human rights that empower women as well as men. She also thanks Patrick McGovern for his research assistance and gratefully acknowledges the support of a Research and Writing Grant from the John D. and Catherine T. MacArthur Foundation that enabled research for this article. Parisi wishes to thank Jeff Corntassel and Cindy Holder for their support and for many insightful discussions regarding rights.

2 In this paper, gender hierarchy describes systems of structural power that privilege men and that which is associated with masculinity over women and that which is associated with femininity. By masculine privileging we refer to men's appropriation of women's re/productive labour, their disciplining of women's bodies/sexuality, and their dominance in society's important institutions and in the production of ideologies, especially those that naturalize masculine dominance. Patriarchy is used narrowly to describe the absolute power of male heads of households over dependent family members; its broader meaning, as male dominance over women extended to society in general, is similar to gender hierarchy. Masculinism and heterosexism may refer to the system (masculine privileging) and/or to the ideology (naturalization) of gender hierarchy. We understand feminism *not* as the 'opposite' of masculinism but as theoretical/practical efforts to transform *all* oppressive hierarchies, such as classism, racism and imperialism, that are intertwined and naturalized by the dichotomy of gender and its denigration of femininity. Finally, our critique of heterosexism is

not an indictment of heterosexual relations *per se*; rather, we reject the systemic oppressions constituted by assuming heterosexuality as the *only* acceptable expression of sexuality and social relations.

3 Like every effort to illuminate, ours pays the price of selectivity. Our interest in exposing structural features of gender hierarchy/heterosexism has the effect of privileging generalizations that neglect, for example, differences among women and variations in how men and states participate in masculinist privileging. We are – and encourage the reader to be – aware of simplifications and distortions encouraged by such broad-brush analyses, but deem the risks of over-generalization less dangerous than the continued neglect of gender in even critical discussions of 'human' rights.

4 'Human civilization rests upon two pillars, of which one is the control of natural forces and the other the restriction of our instincts' (Freud quoted in Padgug 1989, 63).

5 The classic text here of course is Engels, *The Origin of the Family, Private Property and the State* (1972).

6 In particular, we cannot address the important differences among feminists themselves in regard to interpreting the category of sex and its relationship to gender.

7 The linear demands of writing text force us to adopt some organizational order in referring to components whose interaction is not characterized by linearity. Of necessity then, we present these components in the form of what might be conventionally understood as 'inner to outer levels' – as concentric circles, from the 'most individual/internal', etc. to the 'most global/largest social structure', etc. Such depiction imposes its own distortions, especially in regard to masking how symbol systems/language, etc. are 'large' structures that mediate/pervade all 'levels'. Similarly, we remind the reader that these 'levels' are mutually constituted and dynamic; in the argument we are making, neither the 'subject' nor the 'family' precedes the 'state'.

8 With Vickers, we emphasize that the development of gender hierarchy was neither 'necessary' nor 'inevitable' but represents one among numerous possibilities. Like states, racism and nationalism, gender hierarchy is a complex, contingent, historical development that is not reducible to 'nature'.

9 This is exemplified in western philosophy and political theory where man stands for the universal – the norm – and woman represents the particular – the other (e.g., Peterson 1990; Charlesworth 1994).

10 See, for example, Showstack Sassoon (1987); Yuval-Davis and Anthias (1989); Gordon (1990); Parpart and Staudt (1990); Watson (1990); Kandiyoti (1991); Peterson (1992); Sainsbury (1994); Brown (1995). Although most are critical of the masculinist history and practice of states, there is less agreement on whether and how to mobilize state power in support of feminist objectives. Especially in today's context of transnational capitalist forces – which shape the well-being of all of us but are not held accountable for their social effects – states remain the primary site of political accountability and welfare delivery. Because women and the children for whom they are responsible are particularly vulnerable to the effects of economic maldevelopment (within both 'First' and 'Third' worlds), states are singularly important reference points in struggles for equity and economic security. These complex issues have obvious relevance to the role of states in relation to human rights, but we can address only a portion of issues here.

11 Bahar (1996, 131) notes that the metaphor of three generations itself is controversial because it implies progress and hierarchy. For an excellent historical overview of how each Covenant, etc. has affected the development of women's rights see James (1994).

12 Bahar (1991) compellingly argues that NGOs such as Amnesty International help sustain the public–private split by focusing their attention on state abuse of individual rights.

13 'Studies from countries as diverse as Mexico, South Africa, and Bangladesh have found that partner approval is the single greatest predictor of women's contraceptive use' (Heise 1995, 242).

14 The main point is that the objectification of women and forced penile penetration as a violent act requires for its intelligibility the polarized identities and objectification of the feminine constituted by heterosexist ideology and practice. Stated differently, the willingness/desire to rape is not established by the presence of a (normally flaccid) penis but by the internalization of a masculine/heterosexist identity that promotes aggressive male penetration as an expression of sexuality and power. It is, presumably, the mobilization of some version of such an identity that renders rape a viable form of social control and violence. On this view, heterosexist masculinity is mobilized to sustain gender hierarchy *within* groups (e.g., domestic violence in 'private' and the threat/reality of rape in 'public' that prevent women's autonomy and equality) and to reproduce collective violence *between* groups (e.g., forced prostitution and mass rapes in war).

15 The UNDP (1995, 4) reports that there currently exists a global 'feminization of poverty' in that '70% of the 1.3 billion people in poverty are women'. The UNDP (1995, 36) also notes that the 'number of rural women living in absolute poverty rose by nearly 50% over the past two decades'. The increasing feminization of poverty is not only prevalent in developing countries but in industrialized ones as well. The UNDP estimates that 'in the United States ... while only 40% of the poor were women in 1940, 62% were women in 1980'.

16 See Scott (1995) for an in-depth feminist critique of the modernization programmes of the World Bank.

17 For feminist discussions of 'what is to be done' in support of women's rights as human rights, see for example Cook (Introduction 1994); Kerr (1993, especially Part 4); LaViolette and Whitworth (1994).

# References

Amnesty International (1994), *Breaking the Silence: Human Rights Violations Based on Sexual Orientation*, New York, Amnesty International.

Bahar, S. (1996), Human rights are women's rights: Amnesty International and the family, *Hypatia*, 11:1, 105–34.

Barry, K. (1995), *The Prostitution of Sexuality: The Global Exploitation of Women*, New York, New York University Press.

Binion, G. (1995), Human rights: a feminist perspective, *Human Rights Quarterly*, 17, 509–26.

Braidotti, R. (1991), *Patterns of Dissonance*, New York, Routledge.

Brennan, T. (1989), *Between Feminism and Psychoanalysis*, London and New York, Routledge.

Brown, W. (1995), *States of Injury: Power and Freedom in Late Modernity*, Princeton, Princeton University Press.

Bunch, C. (1990), Women's rights as human rights: toward a re-vision of human rights, *Human Rights Quarterly*, 12:4, 486–98.

Bunch, C. (1995), Transforming human rights from a feminist perspective, in J. Peters and A. Wolper (eds), *Women's Rights, Human Rights: International Feminist Perspectives*, New York and London, Routledge.

Butler, J. (1989), *Gender Trouble: Feminism and the Subversion of Identity*, New York, Rout-ledge.

Butler, J. (1990), Gender trouble, feminist theory, and psychoanalytic discourse, in L. Nicholson (ed.), *Feminism/Postmodernism*, London and New York, Routledge.

Caplan, P. (ed.) (1987), *The Cultural Construction of Sexuality*, London and New York, Tavistock.

Chapman, A. R. (1996), A 'violations approach' for monitoring the International Covenant on Economic, Social, and Cultural Rights, *Human Rights Quarterly*, 18, 23–66.

Charlesworth, H. (1994), What are 'women's international human rights'?, in R. Cook (ed.), *Human Rights of Women: National and International Perspectives*, Philadelphia, University of Pennsylvania Press.

Charlesworth, H. (1995), Human rights as men's rights, in J. Peters and A. Wolper (eds), *Women's Rights, Human Rights: International Feminist Perspectives*, New York and London, Routledge.

Charlesworth, H., C. Chinkin, and S. Wright (1991), Feminist approaches to international law, *American Journal of International Law*, 85, 613–45.

Collier, J. F. and M. S. Rosaldo (1981), Politics and gender in simple societies, in S. Ortner and H. Whitehead (eds), *Sexual Meanings*, Cambridge, Cambridge University Press.

Cook, R. (ed.) (1994), *Human Rights of Women: National and International Perspectives*, Philadelphia, University of Pennsylvania Press.

Copelon, R. (1994), Intimate terror: understanding domestic violence as torture, in R. Cook (ed.), *Human Rights of Women: National and International Perspectives*, Philadelphia, University of Pennsylvania Press.

Corntassel, J. J. and T. Hopkins Primeau (1995), Indigenous 'sovereignty' and international law: revised strategies for pursuing 'self-determination', *Human Rights Quarterly*, 17:2, 343–65.

de Lauretis, T. (1987), The female body and heterosexual presumption, *Semiotica*, 67:3–4, 259–79.

Donnelly, J. (1993), *International Human Rights*, Boulder, Westview.

Dorf, J. and G. Careaga Perez (1995), Discrimination and tolerance of difference: interna-tional lesbian human rights, in J. Peters and A. Wolper (eds), *Women's Rights, Human Rights: International Feminist Perspectives*, London and New York, Routledge.

Eisenstein, Z. R. (1981), *The Radical Future of Liberal Feminism*, Boston, Northeastern University Press.

Eisler, R. (1987), Human rights: toward an integrated theory for action, *Feminist Issues*, 7:1, 25–46.

Elshtain, J. B. (1991), *Public Man, Private Woman: Women in Social and Political Thought*, Princeton, Princeton University Press.

Elson, D. (1992), From survival strategies to transformation strategies: women's needs and structural adjustment, in L. Beneria and S. Feldman (eds), *Unequal Burden: Economic Crises, Persistent Poverty, and Women's Work*, Boulder, Westview Press.

Engels, F. (1972), *The Origin of the Family, Private Property, and the State*, New York, Pathfinder.

Ewen, A. (ed.) (1994), *Voice of Indigenous Peoples*, Santa Fe, NM, Clear Light Publishers.

Flax, J. (1989), *Thinking Fragments: Psychoanalysis, Feminism, and Postmodernism in the Contemporary West*, Berkeley, University of California Press.

Foucault, M. (1978), *History of Sexuality, Vol. 1*, trans. Robert Hurley, New York, Random House.

Freud, S. (1978), *The Standard Edition of the Complete Psychological Works of Sigmund Freud*, J. Strachey (ed.), London, Hogarth Press.

Glazer, N. (1995), Individual rights against group rights, in W. Kymlicka (ed.), *The Rights of Minority Cultures*, Oxford, Oxford University Press.

Gordon, L. (1990), *Women, the State, and Welfare*, Madison, University of Wisconsin.

Grant, R. (1991), The sources of gender bias in international relations theory, in R. Grant and K. Newland (eds), *Gender and International Relations*, Bloomington and Indianapolis, Indiana University Press.

Green, L. (1995), Internal minorities and their rights, in W. Kymlicka (ed.), *The Rights of Minority Cultures*, Oxford, Oxford University Press.

Heise, L. L. (1995), Freedom close to home: the impact of violence against women on reproductive rights, in J. Peters and A. Wolper (eds), *Women's Rights, Human Rights: International Feminist Perspectives*, London and New York, Routledge.

Holmes, H. B. (1983), A feminist analysis of the Universal Declaration of Human Rights, in C. Gould (ed.), *Beyond Domination*, Totowa, NJ, Rowman and Allanheld.

Hosken, F. P. (ed.) (1981). Symposium: women and international human rights, *Human Rights Quarterly*, 3:2.

Human Rights Watch (1995), *Global Report on Women's Rights*, New York, Human Rights Watch.

Irigaray, L. (1985), *This Sex Which is Not One*, Ithaca, NY, Cornell University Press.

James, S. M. (1994), Challenging patriarchal privilege through the development of international human rights, *WSIF*, 17:6, 563–78.

Jayawardena, K. (1986), *Feminism and Nationalism in the Third World*, London and New Jersey, Zed Books.

Kandiyoti, D. (1991), *Women, Islam and the State*, Philadelphia, Temple University Press.

Kerr, J. (1993), *Ours by Right: Women's Rights as Human Rights*, London and New Jersey, Zed Books.

Kiss, E. (1995), Is nationalism compatible with human rights? Reflections on east-central Europe, in A. Sarat and T. R. Kearns (eds), *Identities, Politics, and Rights*, Ann Arbor, University of Michigan Press.

Kymlicka, W. (1995), *Multicultural Citizenship*, Oxford, Clarendon Press.

Lacquer, T. (1990), *Making Sex*, Cambridge, MA, Harvard University Press.

LaViolette, N. and S. Whitworth (1994), No safe haven: sexuality as a universal human right and gay and lesbian activism in international politics, *Millennium*, 23:3, 563–88.

Lerner, G. (1986), *The Creation of Patriarchy*, New York, Oxford University Press.

MacKinnon, C. E. (1989), *Towards a Feminist Theory of the State*, Cambridge, MA, Harvard University Press.

Mies, M. (1986), *Patriarchy and Accumulation on a World Scale: Women in the International Division of Labor*, London, Zed Books.

Olsen, F. E. (1985), The myth of state intervention in the family, *University of Michigan Journal of Law Reform*, 18:4, 835–64.

Ortner, S. and H. Whitehead (eds) (1981), *Sexual Meanings: The Cultural Construction of Gender and Sexuality*, Cambridge, Cambridge University Press.

Padgug, R. A. (1989), Sexual matters: on conceptualizing sexuality in history, *Radical History Review*, 20, 3–23.

Parpart, J. L. and K. A. Staudt (eds) (1990), *Women and the State in Africa*, Boulder, CO, Lynne Rienner Publishers.

Peters, J. and A. Wolper (eds) (1995), *Women's Rights, Human Rights: International Feminist Perspectives*, London and New York, Routledge.

Peterson, V. S. (1990), Whose rights? A critique of the 'givens' in human rights discourse, *Alternatives*, 15:3, 303–44.

Peterson, V. S. (ed.) (1992), *Gendered States: (Re)Visions of International Relations Theory*, Boulder, CO, Lynne Rienner Press.

Peterson, V. S. (1995), The politics of identity and gendered nationalism, in L. Neack, P. J. Haney and J. A. K. Hey (eds), *Foreign Policy Analysis: Continuity and Change in Its Second Generation*, Englewood Cliffs, NJ, Prentice Hall.

Peterson, V. S. (1996a), The politics of identification in the context of globalization, *Women's Studies International Forum*, 19, 1–2.

Peterson, V. S. (1996b), The gender of rhetoric, reason, and realism, in F. A. Beer and R. Hariman (eds), *Post-Realism: The Rhetorical Turn in International Relations*, East Lansing, Michigan State University Press.

Peterson, V. S. (1997), Whose crisis? Early and postmodern masculinism, in S. Gill and J. H. Mittleman (eds), *Innovation and Transformation in International Relations Theory*, Cambridge, Cambridge University Press.

Peterson, V. S. and A. Sisson Runyan (1993), *Global Gender Issues*, Boulder, Westview Press.

Pettman, J. J. (1996), *Worlding Women: A Feminist International Politics*, London and New York, Routledge.

Pyne, H. H. (1995), Aids and gender violence: the enslavement of Burmese women in the Thai sex industry, in J. Peters and A. Wolper (eds), *Women's Rights, Human Rights: International Feminist Perspectives*, New York and London, Routledge.

Rao, A. (1996), Home-word bound: women's place in the family of international human rights, *Global Governance*, 2:2, 241–60.

Romany, C. (1994), State responsibility goes private: a feminist critique of the public/ private distinction in international human rights law, in R. Cook (ed.), *Human Rights of Women: National and International Perspectives*, Philadelphia, University of Pennsylvania Press.

Sainsbury, D. (ed.) (1994), *Gendering Welfare States*, London, Sage.

Sanders, D. (1996), Getting gay and lesbian issues on the international human rights agenda, *Human Rights Quarterly*, 18, 67–106.

Schuler, M. (ed.) (1992), *Freedom from Violence: Women's Strategies From Around the World*, New York, UNIFEM.

Scott, C. V. (1995), *Gender and Development: Rethinking Modernization and Dependency Theory*, Boulder and London, Lynne Rienner.

Sedgwick, E. K. (1990), *Epistemology of the Closet*, Berkeley, University of California Press.

Showstack Sassoon, A. (ed.) (1987), *Women and the State*, London, Hutchinson.

Stanton, D. C. (ed.) (1992), *Discourses of Sexuality: From Aristotle to AIDS*, Ann Arbor, MI, University of Michigan Press.

Sullivan, D. (1995), The public/private distinction in international human rights law, in J. Peters and A. Wolper (eds), *Women's Rights, Human Rights: International Feminist Perspectives*, New York and London, Routledge.

Tambiah, Y. (1995), Sexuality and human rights, in M. A. Schuler (ed.), *From Basic Needs to Basic Rights: Women's Claim to Human Rights*, Washington DC, Women, Law & Development International.

Thomas, D. Q. and M. L. Beasley (1993), Domestic violence as a human rights issue, *Human Rights Quarterly*, 15, 36–62.

UNDP (1995), *Human Development Report*, New York, Oxford University Press.

United Nations (1991), *The World's Women: 1970–1990 Trends and Statistics*, New York, UN.

Vickers, J. M. (1990), At his mother's knee: sex/gender and the construction of national identities, in G. Hoffmann Nemiroff (ed.), *Women and Men: Interdisciplinary Readings on Gender*, Toronto, Fitzhenry & Whiteside.

Wallerstein, I. (1988), The ideological tensions of capitalism: universalism versus racism, and sexism, in J. Smith *et al.*, *Racism, Sexism, and the World-System*, New York, Greenwood Press.

Waring, M. (1988), *If Women Counted: A New Feminist Economics*, San Francisco, Harper.

Watson, S. (ed.) (1990), *Playing the State: Australian Feminist Interventions*, London, Verso.

Wittig, M. (1980), The straight mind, *Feminist Issues*, 1:1, 103–11.

Young, I. M. (1995). Together in difference: transforming the logic of group political conflict, in W. Kymlicka (ed.), *The Rights of Minority Cultures*, Oxford, Oxford University Press.

Yuval-Davis, N. (1996), Women and the biological reproduction of 'the nation', *WSIF*, 1/2, 17–24.

Yuval-Davis, N. and F. Anthias (eds) (1989), *Woman-Nation-State*, London, Macmillan Press.

# 7

# International financial institutions and social and economic human rights: an exploration

## Caroline Thomas

### Introduction

This chapter considers the possibility of delivering economic and social rights within the prevailing liberal economic structure. Despite the formal recognition of economic, social and cultural rights under international law, the dominant liberal discourse prioritizes the importance of civil and political rights. In an era when the changing structures of international relations make the realization of some dimensions of human dignity more difficult, an investigation into the future of economic and social rights is apposite.

A liberal philosophy underpins the process of global economic integration and the accompanying global reorganization of social relations. This dominant philosophy of economic and political liberalism finds practical application in the policies promoted by International Financial Institutions (IFIs) such as the World Bank, the regional development banks and the IMF. What are the outcomes of such policies? And in particular, how are the benefits distributed? Are these policies resulting in fundamental changes in the world order which privilege some actors and marginalize others? IFIs hold ideas of universality, and these are evident in a range of liberalization processes which they promote. How does this affect the status of social, economic and cultural rights, and the possibility of their realization? Do we encounter resistance to the attempted universalization of the liberal rights discourse?

The chapter has three sections. The first outlines the overarching context of globalization in which the later discussion of IFIs and social and economic rights is located. By focusing on inequality, this section reviews the achievement of social and economic rights after fifty years of official development policies aimed specifically at improving the standard of living of human beings and the economic status of 'developing countries'.

The second section assesses the relationship between the policies of IFIs and the achievement of social and economic rights in the 1980s and 1990s. To achieve this, consideration is given to the neoliberal ideas underpinning the policies of IFIs throughout this period. Then the results of the practical application of IFI policies are examined. This is followed by an evaluation of the responses of the IFIs, particularly the World Bank, to critics. The section ends by looking to the future, speculating on the fate of economic and social human rights in an environment characterized by the gradual withdrawal of the IFIs and the increasing role of private investors.

The third section of the chapter offers a brief examination of resistance to the universalizing trend of undermining the status of economic, social and cultural rights.

## Globalization and the fulfilment of economic and social rights

This section offers an overview of the wider context or structure in which we can locate and interpret the processes in which IFIs are engaged. The focus here is global economic integration. This is evident in the liberalizing trend of the Uruguay Round and more recently in the World Trade Organization. It is reinforced by the movement towards increased regional liberalization. The essence of this trend is captured by the term globalization, though the latter has ramifications beyond the purely economic.

Globalization as used here refers broadly to the process whereby power is located in global social formations and expressed through global networks rather than through territorially based states. The driver of this process remains contested in the literature, with broadly speaking two schools of thought: the first prefers a monocausal explanation, the second a multicausal one (Wilkin 1996, 228–31). This chapter is not the place to engage in that discussion. It will suffice to say that here globalization is understood as being driven by the latest stage of capitalism, wherein accumulation is taking place on a global rather than a national scale. In addition to the accumulation of capital, as classically understood, there is the accumulation of power in other forms, e.g., knowledge, military capability, regulatory capacity. These other accumulations can be identified across a wide spectrum, for example in the universal legitimacy accorded to western liberal social and political values, and in the human rights discourse. Global accumulation in all its aspects undermines the value of local diversity and legitimizes the dominant liberal agenda, presenting it as universal, 'natural' and common sense. Yet it is rooted in a local, essentially western, capitalist world view (Thomas and Wilkin 1997, 2).

The restructuring of the global economy through the globalization process has been driven and supported in the 1980s and 1990s by a neoliberal ideology. This ideology was evident in the administrations of Prime Minister Thatcher and Presidents Reagan and Bush. It rests on a particular conception of freedom, defined in terms of private power and the individual, to which is attributed universal validity (Wilkin 1996, 231–5). The corollary of freedom interpreted as a private good has been an attack on the public realm and associated ideas of collectivity and society.

This conception of freedom has gained great force in global society at the level of élites. However, the period over which it has been most systematically applied in practice has been characterized by widening inequalities within states and between states. This has led authors such as Wilkin to write of the contradiction in the 'new mythology' of private power and freedom (Wilkin 1996, 227). The appearance of extending individual choice and control over the products which capitalism successfully generates, belies increasing inequality and the resultant differential enjoyment of such benefits. A particular aspect of human rights, based on an individual's civil and political freedom, is being prioritized, while another, equally valid, the economic and social, is being marginalized.

Under international law, it is the duty of states to secure the human rights of their respective citizens (though not of non-citizens apparently – see Article 2(3) of the Economic, Social and Cultural Covenant) but the global economic structure increasingly renders the state less able to fulfil this duty. Globalization is privileging the private over the public sphere and over the commons. It is eroding the authority of states differentially to set the social, economic and political agenda within their respective political space. It erodes the capacity of states in different degrees to secure the livelihoods of their respective citizens by narrowing the parameters of legitimate state activity. The process of globalization is rendering it impossible for many states to exercise a basic minimum control over the domestic economy, and therefore it is directly undermining the state's ability to deliver social and economic rights to citizens (Mittelman 1996).

This is part of a wider process of redrawing hierarchical social relations in the world system. With the wide-ranging erosion of the regulatory capacity of the state, other actors influence entitlement and directly affect the delivery of economic, social and cultural rights. These include IFIs, the Group of 7, and non-state actors such as transnational corporations and banks. Such actors advocate the current development orthodoxy, that global welfare is maximized by economic growth, and the latter is best achieved through economic and political liberalization. The fulfilment of social and economic rights is most likely therefore within the context of the free market, as the wealth generated will trickle down through society and ultimately all will benefit.

In recent years a series of international fora have lent legitimacy to this development orthodoxy by neutralizing opposition via the incorporation of the language of criticism into mainstream free-market formulations (Graf 1992). The Brundtland Report of 1987 stressed the importance of further growth for sustainability; UNCED and Agenda 21 in 1992 promoted free-market principles for sustainable development; then at Copenhagen in 1995, the Poverty Summit legitimated further application of economic liberalization as the best economic policy to counter poverty and under-employment (Thomas 1997, 407).

Hand in hand with the promotion of liberal economics has gone the promotion of liberal political ideology and associated liberal interpretation of human rights. In the post-cold war era, there were optimistic assumptions about the possibility of 'western style' democratization across the world. Indeed one writer even remarked that 'What we may be witnessing is ... the end of history as such: that is, the end point of mankind's ideological evolution and the universalization of Western liberal democracy as the final form of human government' (Fukuyama 1989, 4). Latin America and Africa enjoyed some successes, and in other parts of the world, such as China, there were democratic challenges, albeit unsuccessful. Yet important questions arise about the progress of substantive rather than formal democracy (Gills, Rocamora and Wilson 1994). The latter, demonstrated, for example, through periodic elections, does not tell us whether there has been any significant change in empowerment of the general population and any general improvement in their experience of economic, social and cultural rights.

The liberal political discourse is thus related directly to rights discourse. In the post-Second World War period the USA has attempted the philosophical and legal legitimation of a set of internationally recognized human rights norms. Yet underlying this position are clear economic and political interests which result in the highlighting of civil and political over economic and social rights (Evans 1996). The success of this endeavour is such that human rights are assumed to refer to civil and political rights, and not to the full range of human rights, including the equally important economic and social rights.

The fulfilment of social and economic rights eludes over half of the global population. Development success is not reflected in societies at large. Despite adequate global per capita food availability, 800 million people are malnourished, 40,000 die every day from hunger and related diseases (International Commission on Peace and Food 1994, 104 and 106), and up to 1,000 million lack access to clean water or sanitation. Thirty per cent of the global labour force is under- or un-employed, and this in an era when global population is increasing rapidly. Such indicators are worrying, not least because the last fifty years has witnessed the growth of unprecedented official public development policies. And even though $250 billions have been transferred to developing countries through IFIs, poverty remains widespread. The realization of social, economic and cultural rights seems increasingly elusive for a significant proportion of the global population.

The current development orthodoxy, based on economic and political liberalism, is being sold as the best method for maximizing global welfare. Yet the evidence for such a claim is lacking, resting largely on the perceived absence of alternatives. The evidence against seems to be mounting. Is the market really capable of delivering economic and social rights for the majority of humanity, or might the majority be better served by a different balance between state, market and commons?

Neoclassical liberal economics does not assume any negative correlation between growing inequality and the achievement of economic and social human rights; indeed, quite the opposite. At the Royal Geographical Society's Presidential dinner in 1991, Prime Minister Thatcher said that 'It is our job to glory in inequality, and see that talents and abilities are given vent and expression for the benefit of us all' (see Ball and Jenkins 1996, 51). The theory was that the rich, enjoying the benefit of tax cuts, would invest their money and create new jobs. Wealth would trickle down and everyone would benefit. The enjoyment of economic and social rights would actually be enhanced.

Growing inequality continues to characterize the global social order. The 1996 UN Human Development Report shows quite clearly that the gap between rich and poor is widening within states and between them (UNDP 1996). James Gustave Speth of the UNDP said that 'An emerging global élite, mostly urban-based and interconnected in a variety of ways, is amassing great wealth and power, while more than half of humanity is left out' (Crossette 1996, 55). Over three billion people – more than half the people on the planet – earn less than $2 a day. Of course, if we group populations by territorial states, we find that the North–South disparity remains a central facet of the global order. However, this tells us nothing about distribution within the South or within the North.

Even supporters of the neoliberal approach have had to admit its failure to assist the world's poor, and have questioned its potential in this regard. For example, the *Financial Times* in the UK, despite praising the 'system of wealth creation ... now everywhere regarded as the most effective that humanity has yet devised', has had to concede that 'it remains ... an imperfect force ... [since] two thirds of the world's population have gained little or no substantial advantage from rapid economic growth' and even 'in the developed world, the lowest quartile has witnessed trickle-up rather than trickle-down' (*Financial Times* 1993). And in 1996, the OECD wrote that 'Future prosperity depends on reducing unemployment ... and, in some instances (reducing) growing inequalities in earnings and incomes' (quoted in Lean and Cooper 1996, 51–2).

Having outlined the broad consequences of neoliberalism for world economic integration and growing inequality, let us turn to the specifics of IFI policies and how they impact on the fulfilment of social and economic human rights.

## IFIs and economic and social rights

NEOLIBERAL IDEOLOGY AND THE IFIS

The IFIs understand the world through neoliberal tinted glasses. This has clear economic and political implications. Former World Bank President, Barber Conable, speaking of the 1980s, has asserted that:

> If I were to characterize the past decade, the most remarkable thing was the generation of a global consensus that market forces and economic efficiency were the best way to achieve the kind of growth which is the best antidote to poverty. (quoted in Cavanagh, Wysham and Arruda 1994, 3)

The IFIs define the discussion of appropriate remedial action in terms of economic growth through the unfettering of the market from government controls. They see this as developing hand in hand with political liberalization. For example, the Development Assistance Committee of the OECD sees 'a vital connection ... between open, democratic and accountable political systems, individual rights and the effective and equitable operation of economic systems' (OECD 1989).

Whereas the developed countries as a general rule pursued political liberalization after economic development, political liberalization is being promoted throughout the rest of the world as a forerunner, if not a prerequisite, of economic development. The IFIs have developed an interest in 'good governance', and it is not uncommon now for the World Bank, groups of donors and the Group of 7 to delay or withhold funds where political liberalization does not appear to be progressing in a manner they consider acceptable (Gillies 1996, 101–2; Leftwich 1994).[1] This is not without problems. The adverse consequences of economic liberalization can undermine the consolidation of democracy (Shaw and Quadir 1997; Walton and Seddon 1994). There are plenty of examples where economic liberalization has 'directly contributed to the descent into anarchy and civil wars' (Hoogevelt 1997, 176) as seen in Angola, Sierra Leone, Rwanda and Sudan. The universal application of a single view of democracy is also problematic (Barya 1993). Moreover, the fundamental logic of liberal democracy preceding economic development is questionable, as the authoritarian nature of the successful South East Asian Tiger economies makes clear (Leftwich 1993).

The IFIs promote the idea that the free market is the only alternative to centrally planned economies. It is presented as 'common sense' or 'natural' that we are now reaching the end of history, where the free market gains universal acceptance as the legitimate form of economic organization, with its attendant social and political relations. IFIs promote the ideal of the perfectly functioning free market, free of state interference or control, in which inequality is a good thing because it generates progress and wealth.

Wealth created by the rich will trickle down to the poor, as investment of the profits of the rich will lead to the creation of new jobs.

Since the early 1980s, the global network of IFIs has been the vehicle through which the Group of 7 industrialized states, and more particularly the USA, have promoted a particular conception of development throughout the rest of the world. This mission has been pursued with such a degree of success that by the mid-1990s, most of the world's leaders agree with it. This was shown clearly in the consensus at the Copenhagen Social Summit where governments agreed that free-market policies were the preferred way to tackle poverty and unemployment.

The policies of the IFIs are shaped by the belief of its most influential member, the USA, that participation in the global trade and finance systems is the best method to promote global welfare. It is interesting to ponder for a moment on the source of legitimacy of the IMF and World Bank. As key institutions pushing the notion of private power and individualism, they are not models of democratic representation, as Table 1 below reveals.

#### Table 1 Structure of voting in the IMF

| Country | Pop. (m.) | IMF executive vote (%) |
|---|---|---|
| USA | 246 | 19.11 |
| UK | 57 | 6.62 |
| Germany (FGR) | 61 | 5.78 |
| France | 55 | 4.80 |
| Japan | 122 | 4.52 |
| Saudi Arabia | 12 | 3.44 |
| Countries: 6 | 553 | 44.27 |

Rest of world: 187 countries; 3.7 billion pop.; 55.73 votes.

Ratio of rich country citizens' votes to poor countries: 5 to 1

Source: *Europa Handbook 1991.*

PRACTICAL APPLICATIONS: STRUCTURAL ADJUSTMENT

The primary goal of the IFIs is to facilitate the establishment of an environment in borrowing countries that will attract private capital, both domestic and foreign. This goal has informed their policies since the late 1970s, when liberal economic ideology underlay the decision by the Group of 7 to push a free-market approach to development via structural adjustment (Ould-Mey 1994). In the 1980s, however, the approach was institutionalized by the IMF and the World Bank as a debt management strategy. They applied adjustment programmes with increased vigour throughout much of the rest of the world. There was an unspoken agreement that adjustment and debt repayment would be rewarded by inflows of new finance and investment.

The IFIs went about restructuring the economies of the South, and the centrally planned economies. The aim was to make them more open to foreign investment and to free trade, and to roll back the state. Henceforth, the market, and not the state, was to be the motor of these economies, and ultimately the market would replace the state in determining entitlement to everything, including basic necessities such as food, education and health-care, transport. Clearly there is a fundamental incompatibility between economic human rights claims and the elevation of the free market as the determinant of a person's economic entitlement. Claims for economic sover-eignty, championed in the 1970s via the call for a new international economic order and also the Charter of Economic Rights and Duties of States (CERDS), also fell by the wayside.

Through adjustment programmes the IFIs oversaw the further opening up of national economies to foreign investment; the cutting of bureaucracies and of subsidies for food, health and transport; and the promotion of exports. National ownership and rights to indigenous resources, long a significant part of the struggle by the South to establish economic rights, was rendered illegitimate in the drive to privatization and in the push for unhindered foreign investment.

The private sector, not state or state-assisted development finance in-stitutions such as farmers' clubs, were henceforth to provide finance to the poor. This policy arose because of the influence of the US 'Ohio School' on World Bank policy (Hulme and Moseley 1996a, 3). Exponents of that school of development economics believed that it was impossible for any credit institution set up by governments to avoid damage to loan portfolios via loan write-offs and so forth. They argued that private-sector loans provided a solution to this problem. Thus the World Bank advocated the 'closure of existing Development Finance Institutions' (Hulme and Moseley 1996a, 4–6), hoping that the private sector would take up the slack.

EVALUATING THE SOCIAL AND ECONOMIC IMPACT OF ADJUSTMENT

The social and economic impact of adjustment has become a topic of heated debate over the last decade. There is broad acceptance that structural adjustment has resulted in contradictions in ensuing patterns of entitlement that have strained political systems and affected the fulfilment of social and economic rights. A consensus has emerged that there is a problem to be addressed, but opinion is bitterly divided as to the nature and extent of the problem and the appropriate path forward for achieving social and economic rights. Broadly speaking, we can divide opinion into two groups: the refor-mers and the transformers. The transformers identify equity-related problems with the neoliberal model of development promoted by the IFIs, but argue that reform is possible so that the orthodox trade-off between growth and equity can be avoided. Against this, the reformers argue that the neoliberal policies of the IFIs are beyond reform and are totally inappropriate in terms of meeting social and economic rights. Let us consider both positions.

The reformers accept the broad policy of adjustment, but want changes of detail, mainly to accommodate the gap between what works in theory and in practice. An example of this gap is provided by the operational results of the ideologically driven policy of privatizing loans to the poor.

The poor often do not have a point of entry into the private borrowing sector due to scarcity of investment funds and the risks of non-payment against which a lender cannot ensure, for example, the weather. The private sector naturally aims to limit its own risks. The poor therefore rely on public-funded or -backed development finance institutions.

> If ... a Malawian smallholder with two acres of maize, needing to borrow about half his average annual income for the previous five years in order to buy a 'green revolution package' of fertilizer, hybrid seed and a water pump, is unable to borrow from the state through a farmers' club, his alternative is often not to borrow it from a competitive network of informal moneylenders, but not to borrow at all. The same applies to most other poor African and Asian farmers and micro-entrepreneurs. (Hulme and Moseley 1996a, 4–5)

The reformers call for a softening of adjustment policies to make them more in tune with social reality, and in this instance favour some latitude for the traditional state-assisted development finance institutions.

The most influential voice for reform was heard in 1987 when UNICEF published the first official damning critique, edited by Cornia, and Jolly and Stewart entitled *Adjustment with a Human Face*. The report, based on ten country case studies, argued that adjustment to a changing world economy was necessary, but had to be designed in such a way as to ensure that the poor did not carry a disproportionate share of the adjustment burden. Adjustment programmes were deflationary in character and this led to growing poverty through depressed employment and real incomes; also there were direct negative effects of certain macro-economic policies on the welfare of particular groups (Cornia, Jolly and Stewart 1987, 288). Therefore growth-oriented adjustment had to be devised in a manner consistent with ensuring the protection of vulnerable groups in the short and medium term. Key problems to be addressed included: the short time horizon, insufficient finance, macro as opposed to sectoral and targeted policies; and the lack of explicit consideration of the effects of programmes on income distribution, the incidence of poverty and the health/nutritional status of particular groups (Cornia, Jolly and Stewart 1987, 288).

The report issued clear policy prescriptions for achieving adjustment with a human face (Cornia, Jolly and Stewart 1987, 291): more expansionary macro-economic policies, aimed at sustaining output, investment and human need satisfaction over a longer adjustment period; the use of meso policies to prioritize and restructure resources and activities in favour of the poor; sectoral policies aimed at restructuring within the productive sector to strengthen employment and raise productivity, for example, by focusing on small farmers; improving the equity and efficiency of the social sector; compensatory programmes; and monitoring the human situation.

The UNICEF report also advocated the explicit integration of human concerns into all negotiations about adjustment, and the adaptation of the negotiation process to accommodate this. Negotiations were usually confined to the Ministry of Finance of the country concerned plus representatives of the World Bank and the IMF. An input from ministries concerned with social sectors and from international organizations concerned with nutrition was vital in the negotiation of adjustment. However, it is possible that even this recommendation did not go far enough. The illustration of privatizing loans to the poor reveals that involvement of affected persons in the policy design process may yield better results. Indeed there is growing evidence that ownership of policies, whether at local or national level, makes implementation much easier.

Since the UNICEF report, various studies of adjustment have been undertaken or funded by organizations such as the World Bank and the OECD. Several independent analyses have appeared also, such as the work of Moseley, Harrigan and Toye (1991). Killick has reviewed the reformist literature emanating from the West, and draws the following conclusions. First, he argues that generalizations are difficult, because the issues are complex and the database is totally inadequate. Nevertheless, it is well documented that SAPs (Structural Adjustment Programmes) often put the poor at risk. SAPs are likely to impact very differently across different groups, with greater negative consequences for the urban rather than rural poor. The former rely more on subsidies, government services, employment opportunities, etc. The poorest people are marginalized and are therefore less at risk; the 'not quite so poor' stand to lose – or gain – the most. Killick believes that the negative effects of adjustment programmes have been exaggerated, and that many hardships attributed to adjustment are actually the result of pre-existing national economic crises rather than the subsequent adjustment package. Indeed Killick's survey of available data suggests that a concentration on SAPs diverts attention away from the more fundamental causes of poverty, primarily the distribution of assets and political power. This is a point to which we shall return (Killick 1994).

A transformist critique of IFI adjustment policies has been developed by several independent authors. Walden Bello's *Dark Victory* (1994) launched a damning critique of the whole adjustment endeavour. Similarly, Michel Chossudovsky has launched a trenchant critique. In 1996 he commented that:

Structural adjustment is conducive to a form of 'economic genocide' which is carried out through the deliberate manipulation of market forces. When compared to genocide in various periods of colonial history, its impact is devastating. Structural adjustment programmes directly affect the livelihood of more than 4 billion people. (quoted in Khor 1996, 17)

This critique has been sustained vigorously by Chossudovsky's recent publication: see Chossudovsky (1997).

The UN Commission on Human Rights Special Rapporteur, Danilo Turk, reporting on the human rights implications of SAPs, has taken a strong line. He notes that states have legal obligations to move towards fulfilling the economic, social and cultural rights of their citizens, but the increasing integration of the world economy undermines their ability to fulfil these obligations. In particular, he suggests that harm is done to the rights to work, to food, to adequate housing, to health, to education and to development (Khor 1996, 17–18).

The basic argument of the transformers is that the overarching policy of global economic integration via free-market policies, of which structural adjustment forms a part, cannot satisfy the economic or social rights of the majority of human beings or of states. The elevation of the private sphere, at the expense of public sphere or the commons, is a direct attack on these rights.

These critics claim that the IFIs, by organizing the restructuring of the world economy along *laissez-faire* lines, and by promoting the attendant liberal conception of freedom as private power, are helping reinforce and legitimize diverse forms of exploitation in the world economy and are legitimizing growing inequalities of health, income, employment opportunities, and so on. These inequalities reflect different social power, and are in essence concerned with class, gender and race/ethnic relations. Such growing inequality is regarded by transformer critics not as contingent, but rather as the necessary outcome of social relations in a world capitalist economy.

At a structural level, the liberal orthodoxy driving the policies of the IFIs in the 1980s and 1990s has supported the private sector and, by implication, a particular conception of civil and political rights. This is presented as expanding human freedom through better institutions of good government. The IFIs thus became interested in political conditionality. The emphasis on western-style democratic reform gives the illusion of empowering people: but without economic transformation the illusion could not be translated into anything more tangible.

At the level of process, transformers argue that the IFIs have not kept their side of the bargain, in that adjustment and debt repayment has not resulted in new flows of investment and credit from the developed world to the developing countries. Official overseas development assistance is falling (in 1996 ODA (Overseas Development Aid) from the OECD was $59 billion – the lowest figure in twenty-three years) and thus private finance is becoming proportionately more important. But in 1995 over two thirds of FDI reaching the developing world (38 per cent of the global total) went to just eight countries, while over half of developing countries received little or none (Brown 1996, 158). Brown has noted that '[p]rivate capital has not been pouring into sub-Sahara Africa where a child today is still more likely to go hungry than to go to school' (Brown 1996, 159). Moreover, even the influx of private capital cannot alone guarantee the safeguarding of economic and social rights: 'Even though private capital has been pouring into Latin America, one third of the population still has no sanitation and ten million children still suffer from malnutrition' (Brown 1996, 159). The transformers regard the transformation of social and economic structures as essential to the delivery of economic and social rights to humankind. While acknowledging the possible pitfalls of generalization, broadly speaking they prioritize a conception of sustainable development based on self-reliance, respect for nature, diversity, the local community, appropriate technology and so forth.

THE RESPONSE OF THE IFIs

How have the IFIs responded to the charges of the reformers and the transformers? Interestingly, they ignore the transformist critique, and respond only to the concerns raised by the reformers. Therefore remarks here are confined largely to assessing how far the IFIs have taken on board the possibility of, and need for, growth with equity via reformed lending policies which protect the vulnerable. The IFIs are interested in limited, piecemeal reform of the existing system, rather than in the fundamental restructuring advocated by transformists.

Prior to the 1987 UNICEF report, the IMF regarded the distributional impact of its programmes as a matter for government, not IMF, concern. Indeed, a review of thirty IMF stand-by programmes implemented during the 1960s and 1970s found that only one contained provisions to protect the poor against possible adverse consequences (Bird and Killick 1995, 33).

It appears that the UNICEF report resulted in pressure on the IMF for change, to which Fund Director, Camdessus, was fairly responsive. It is now more accepted by the Fund that the distributional aspects of its programmes are a matter that should concern Fund staff. Policy Framework Papers prepared in connection with structural adjustment programmes are required to 'identify measures that can help cushion the possible adverse effects of certain policies on vulnerable groups', and IMF missions commonly discuss distributional aspects of programmes with governments (Bird and Killick 1995, 33–4). In addition, social safety-net provisions are becoming more common, although so far these relate mainly to Eastern Europe.

The World Bank has a history of interest in poverty reduction. In the

1980s the neoliberal development orthodoxy shaped Bank attitudes to poverty reduction. The strategy shifted away from dedicated poverty reduction programmes in favour of structural adjustment programmes and policy reform.

By the mid to late 1980s, criticism of Bank policies in terms of negative effects on the achievements of social, economic and cultural rights was resulting in some changes at the Bank. Indeed, one author claims that since 1985, 'the Bank has experienced an institutional revolution that is still in process' (de Vries 1996, 66). The author attributes this directly to the activities of NGOs, which have pinpointed critical issues and put pressure on the Bank to change its policies. This, argues de Vries, has resulted in more attention on the role of women in development, environmental issues, local participation in project preparation and implementation, and greater attention to the poverty-SAP linkages.

In 1987, the Bank introduced a 'Social Dimensions of Adjustment' programme (Bird and Killick 1995, 34). Ghana's SAP was the first in Africa to formally integrate a 'Programme of Actions to Mitigate the Social Costs of Adjustment' (PAMSCAD), on the joint initiative of the government, the World Bank and UNICEF. This was deemed necessary because 'fiscal rationalization, involving the removal of subsidies and cost saving and cost recovery measures, affected health and education services' (ODI (Overseas Development Institute) 1996, Box 1). For example, fees were introduced into the health service and parental contributions to children's education were increased, at the same time as the number of public sector workers was cut and subsidies were withdrawn on certain agricultural inputs. Under the PAMSCAD, US$ 83 million were to be spent over two years on twenty-three projects in five areas: education, employment generation, community initiatives, basic needs of vulnerable groups and actions to help retrenched workers. A report in 1990 concluded that only eight of the twenty-three projects had made good progress. A recent assessment by the ODI suggests that no real integration of social dimensions into the SAP really took place, and the measures adopted addressed pre-existing social problems rather than problems induced by the SAP (ODI 1996, Box 1). Clearly the challenge of adjustment with a human face has not yet been met by the Bank or the government.

The 1990 World Development Report was dedicated to poverty reduction. Since then, we have seen a growing proportion of lending devoted to poverty reduction (15 per cent in 1992), plus 15 per cent to human resource development. It does appear that the IFIs are accepting that they have some responsibility for the impact of their policies on the vulnerable, even though they maintain that primary responsibility for helping such groups rests with governments. By 1996 the Bank was clear that while '[e]conomic growth remains the cornerstone of the Bank's strategy for reducing poverty ... many constraints prevent the poor from benefiting from the opportunities presented by growth' (World Bank 1996, 49). The Bank's answer was to remove such constraints, for example, by improving access of the poor to credit, specifically by encouraging microcredit in the cause of self-employment by the poor. All solutions therefore are drawn up within the neoliberal framework.

While changes in detail have occurred in the policy articulated by top Bank/Fund managers regarding poverty alleviation, there is scant evidence that this limited movement has filtered down to lower levels of their organizations or resulted in real changes in operational practice. Killick argues that the Bank and the Fund 'need to go further, for example, in making it a minimum programme requirement that essential social services to vulnerable groups be maintained and in setting specific safety-net provisions into the context of a broader anti-poverty strategy' (Bird and Killick 1995, 37).

At the broadest level, the resilience of the dominant liberal economic ideology even in the face of contrary evidence is surprising. A good example is provided by orthodox explanations of the remarkable growth of East Asian economies. The IMF and the World Bank emphasize that growth is dependent on further liberalization, and that the free market is the global panacea. However, the evidence presented in the World Bank's own study, *The Asian Economic Miracle*, suggests not only that the state played a leading economic role in the East Asian Tigers, but that it has been the central factor in the take-off of these economies (Bello 1997). Despite identification of the important role of state intervention, the Bank then argued this model would not be applicable elsewhere. The market held the day.

It is interesting to note that in 1996 several international institutions, including the World Bank and the OECD, seemed to have a change of heart. In that year, the OECD, so long a champion of wage inequality, *laissez-faire* policies, and the trickle down theory of economic growth, did a U-turn. It actually suggested that too much inequality can be bad for economic growth, and questioned the long-held assumption that wage inequality generates jobs and keeps unemployment low. Moreover, the OECD argued that: 'The future prosperity of OECD countries depends on reducing social and economic exclusion in the forms of high unemployment, non-participation in the labour market ... and in some instances, growing inequalities in earnings and incomes' (OECD 1996, 6).

World Bank and UNDP (United Nations Development Programme) data also seemed to suggest that countries with smaller gaps between the top and bottom of society performed better in the 1980s and 1990s. The East Asian Tigers, which have enjoyed far greater domestic equality than, for example, Latin American states, have had more sustained growth. The UNDP actually says there is a positive correlation between economic growth and income equality (UNDP 1996, 53–4). This is supported by a World Bank study of OECD countries. But the World Bank argues now that what matters is the nature of equality, in particular the ownership of assets like land and education (World Bank 1996, 47). The Human Development Report argues that 'a progressive redistribution of assets tends to boost growth because it has a broad, positive effect on people's incentives' (UNDP 1996, 52). A more equal distribution of land means more people have access to credit to invest, and thus the economy has a broader base, and poverty is simultaneously reduced as growth is increased.

The World Bank has just begun to examine differential impacts of policies on groups within states, and in some cases has disaggregated this by gender, ethnic group or region. Such studies are of very recent origin and there is no way of telling if they will result in fundamental reassessments by the Bank. The UNDP has also been engaged in this sort of disaggregation for a few years, with Human Development Reports disaggregating the human development index along racial, gender, regional and ethnic groups for the USA, Brazil, China, Egypt, Malaysia, Mexico, Nigeria, South Africa and Turkey. The Human Development Report 1996 shows that even to disaggregate in India by gender is insufficient, for there may be disparities in female capabilities among regions, ethnic groups or urban and rural areas (UNDP 1996, 34).

It is clear that the IFIs have responded to criticisms of structural adjustment, but their responses have been addressed to the critiques of the reformers, and not to those of the transformers. Their responses have been framed entirely within the context of the existing neoliberal framework, the application of which they continue to see as the solution rather than the problem. The balance between state and market has not tipped back even slightly in favour of the state, as the policies put forward to deal with the iniquitous results of growth are rooted squarely within the *laissez-faire* orthodoxy. Reliance on micro-credit to boost self-employment of the poor is a good example. While access to credit is important, just how many rickshaw drivers can Bombay sustain?

## IFIS, FOREIGN DIRECT INVESTMENT AND THE FUTURE OF ECONOMIC AND SOCIAL RIGHTS

IFIs have done an effective job in creating an enabling environment for FDI (Foreign Direct Investment) throughout the world. This is not surprising, given their original purpose. Article 2 of the World Bank's constitution, for example, identifies the promotion of private foreign investment as one of its fundamental purposes. As early as 1956, the World Bank set up its affiliate, the International Finance Corporation (IFC), to invest in private sector companies rather than governments. In 1988, the Multilateral Investment Guarantee Agency (MIGA) was set up to encourage the flow of FDI by providing guarantees of investments in private ventures in developing countries (ODI 1996, 2). In the 1980s and 1990s, the dominant ideology of neoliberalism permeating the IFIs led to a much greater emphasis on the role of the private sector in development. For example, the newest IFI, the

European Bank for Reconstruction and Development (EBRD) set up in 1991, is compelled to direct over 60 per cent of its lending to the private sector.

Having created an enabling environment for FDI particularly in the 1980s and 1990s, IFIs are in the process of a gradual withdrawal. The proportion of FDI, as opposed to IFI, money reaching the South is growing. Having dropped sharply after the 1982 debt crisis, private flows recovered in the 1990s, and by 1994 they surpassed both bilateral and multilateral flows. Over 70 per cent of resource flows to the developing countries in 1994 came from private market sources, another 22 per cent bilateral aid and only 6 per cent from IFIs. However, four fifths of private flows since 1990 have gone to only twelve developing countries, with the majority having no access to the market for finance (ODI 1996b, 5).

The private sector is becoming more influential in affecting the fulfilment of economic and social rights. This is a cause for concern, given that the constituency is shareholders and it is to them that the private sector, such as multinational corporations, are accountable. While their activities fundamentally affect life chances, they have no formal responsibility towards people in the way that governments do. They have no mechanisms such as public policy of governments to address people's needs even if they felt they had a responsibility and the authority to do so. The idea that basic needs can be met in, and economic and social rights protected in, the marketplace without the resources and authority of governments is fanciful.

The relationship between the organization of agriculture and the enjoyment of the basic human right to food provides a good example. The state has been displaced by agribusiness as the primary source of resources, ideas and authority in this area. Transnationals are superseding states in the production and marketing of food. A global agribusiness is instrumental in, and responsible for, the development of new social relations and new food insecurities (Saurin 1997). Moreover, since the early 1980s structural adjustment policies have given a boost to the undermining of the national organization of agriculture and food production already under way. So too has the aggressive pursuit of unilateralist trade policies by the USA, such as the invocation of free trade to legitimize prizing open the Korean agricultural market, which had traditionally been protected by the government (Bello 1997, 148). The result is an increasingly global organization of food provision and of access to food, with transnational corporations playing the major role.

The power of transnational corporations in global agenda setting was evident at the United Nations Conference on Environment and Development (UNCED) in June 1992. Most glaringly absent from the Rio output were guidelines – let alone regulatory policies – for transnationals. At the behest of the USA, all references to transnational corporations were removed from Agenda 21. Yet these actors are responsible for 70 per cent of world trade, and of course their activities have important social and environmental effects. Prior to UNCED, as part of Boutros Ghali's UN reforms, the UN Centre on Transnational Corporations had been dismantled. This body, under the lead of Sweden and the Group of 77, had been urging the formulation of internationally recognized guidelines to make transnationals more open and accountable. Thus the way was left open for these corporations to plead their own case for self-regulation. In this, they were successful. Yet there is a clear conflict at least in the short term between the profit motive/responsibility to shareholders, and socially and environmentally responsible corporate behaviour.

Economic liberalization and the private interests it supports received a boost with the conclusion of the Uruguay Round of trade negotiations. Areas previously excluded from GATT rules, such as trade-related intellectual property rights and investment measures, now came under its remit. This amounted to the further opening of southern economies to transnationals, financial and insurance industries based mainly in the North. This of course represented an increase in the power of the already powerful, and a further weakening of those already disadvantaged.

Particularly worrying at the moment is the discussion taking place within the OECD (to which the majority of developing countries do not belong) on a Multilateral Agreement on Investment (MAI). The aims of the MAI are higher liberalization in general, and specifically investment liberalization, investment protection and dispute settlement.

The matter of investment was discussed during the Uruguay Round, but rejected at the insistence of developing countries and confined to 'trade-related investment measures'. The EU and other countries such as the USA, Canada, Australia and Japan support the right of foreign companies to enter and establish themselves in any sector of the economy in any member country of the WTO, and to enjoy national treatment. The MAI will remove all remaining national policy tools for regulating foreign investment and Transnational Corporation (TNC) activities. It will 'guarantee generally free entry and establishment for foreign investors, full national treatment for established investments and high standards of investment protection' (Brittan 1995).

Martin Khor, of Third World Network, argues that an MAI would have serious effects on the ability of governments and people to exert a critical minimal control of their economies and social life. It would affect ownership patterns, the survival of local enterprises, employment opportunities and social and cultural life. It would directly impact on the achievement of social, economic and cultural rights of human beings and states (Khor 1996, 21).

## Counter-hegemony

A broad consensus (but not unanimity) has been achieved at government level on the appropriateness of current development policies of IFIs, on the larger picture of world economic integration in which IFI activity is embedded, and on the universal application of an essentially local, western neoliberal ideology underpinning all of this. However, there is mounting evidence of dissatisfaction from other levels of global society. We can detect a variety of resistance responses in different localities to the neoliberal vision. The purpose of development is being questioned, and this questioning is intimately bound up with the rights discourse.

The common thread running through the various examples of resistance is the rejection of neoliberal universalism, including ideas of economics, politics and human rights that support existing processes of hegemony or dominance. The neoliberal model of development pursued by the IFIs in the 1980s and 1990s is attacked not simply for failing to deliver benefits to significant sectors of society, but more fundamentally for its insensitivity to cultural specificity and regional and local diversity. The model is challenged for hindering, rather than facilitating, the achievement of social, economic and cultural rights for all humanity. This position is clear at the oft-referred to grassroots level, but it is evident at other levels also: at the national level in the domestic political arena, and sometimes at the state level in international politics where there is concern about the imposition of alien values and externally driven timetables for liberalization. Let us look at a few examples.

The model of development expounded by the IFIs has come in for sharp criticism from people experiencing the consequences of these policies (Rich 1994; Ekins 1992). Particular policies, such as the construction of large-scale dams, have evoked protest from those directly dispossessed by such 'development' (Pearce 1992), while at a broader level the IMF and World Bank have been the target of popular protest in several countries because of unpopular adjustment policies and conditionality. Grassroots resistance can take a wide variety of forms, from micro-scale to large-scale movements, making generalization difficult. What follows, then, is simply a small selection of examples from different places.

In 1996, the US grassroots organization Pastors for Peace successfully challenged the US embargo against Cuba (Ponvert 1997, 53). The embargo has been in place since 1960, and was tightened significantly in 1992 and 1996 with the Torcelli and Helms–Burton Acts. Now, not even food or medicine can go to Cuba without permission from the US government. Since the US government has not ratified the Convention on Economic, Social and Cultural Rights, it does not accept that its embargo contravenes international human rights law. The UN General Assembly has voted overwhelmingly against the embargo for three years in a row (Ponvert 1997, 53).

Following a ninety-four day fast by five members, and without the appropriate licence from the US government, Pastors for Peace delivered 400 computers to the Cuban health service. Baptist Minister Lucius Walker, founder of Pastors for Peace, remarked that:

> We have not and never will apply for a license under the terms of the US embargo, since the use of medical supplies as weapons against 11 million innocent Cubans is morally repugnant. Participation in the licensing process would be a *de facto* recognition of US policy, and as Christians and people of conscience, we are unable to do this. (quoted in Ponvert 1997, 53)

In India, peasant farmers have been protesting throughout the 1990s against pro-liberalization agricultural policies being pursued by the national and federal state governments since the 1991 World Bank/IMF adjustment package. In the South Indian state of Karnataka, for example, the state government, in line with trade liberalization policies, introduced a new agricultural policy and proposals to reform the land laws to facilitate the corporatization of agriculture in the state. This has provoked strong resistance from farmers' associations, NGOs, trade union leaders in the banking, insurance and transport sectors, environmentalists and other activists (Shiva 1995, 33). The Karnataka farmers' union has in Shiva's words 'been spearheading the movement against the entry of multinational corporations in agriculture' (Shiva 1995, 33).

The Karnataka peasant farmers' protests attack the short-term policy of export agriculture promotion, which is underpinned by the removal of land-holding ceilings for aquaculture, horticulture, floriculture and agro-based industries (Shiva 1995, 35). Shiva has highlighted five points on which protests focus, all of which have relevance to peasants globally, and ultimately have implications for the fulfilment of social, economic and cultural rights for all of humankind.

First, the new policy neglects the goals of sustainable agriculture and associated sustainable livelihoods by promoting unsustainable access to land, water and biodiversity. Second, it neglects food security, which is guaranteed in the Indian constitution as well as being in the UN Covenant, by diverting the natural resources on which it depends from local communities to the requirements of exports. Third, it promotes the myth of people's participation, while privatization, e.g., of water, moves control away from communities and small-scale farmers to large corporations. Fourth, it reverses previous gains in land reform, as evident in the recent amendment to the 1961 Karnataka Land Reforms Act. (The similar case of the reversal of land-holding policy in the Chiapas, Mexico, as a direct government response to globalization springs to mind here also (Renner 1997, 127).) Lastly, agricultural research is moved from the domain of public to private research, and therefore is driven by the profit motive rather than basic human need (Shiva 1995, 33–5). In the process, intellectual property rights are developing to the advantage of private corporations while the rights of farmers who have husbanded seeds over generations are being neglected.

The Karnataka peasant protests are accompanied by clear alternative policies drawn up by other activists such as the Indian Research Foundation for Science, Technology and Natural Resource Policy (RFSTNRP), for example, 'common intellectual rights' and 'community registry' (Shiva 1995, 35).

Resistance to economic liberalization is also occurring at the grassroots level in the East Asian region. The process is regarded as environmentally destructive and socially iniquitous, failing to tackle redistribution issues. Grassroots organizations in East Asia are articulating sustainable development based not on private property or public ownership, but rather on the commons, on equity, environmental sensitivity, community participation in transparent decision making, and small-scale, labour-intensive projects using appropriate technology (Bello 1997, 157–9).

An example of national level popular resistance to government-promoted policies supportive of globalization is offered by workers' strikes in South Korea, December 1996 to January 1997. The workers were protesting against new labour laws railroaded through the National Assembly at dawn, in the absence of opposition members. The laws would delay the authorization of multiple unions at the national level in South Korea to the year 2000 and would directly affect job security due to clauses regarding lay-offs. The government argued that these laws were designed to help improve the competitiveness of the nation's industries at a critical economic juncture. President Kim said these laws simply upgraded existing labour legislation to the standard of advanced countries.

As support for the strike grew, industrial workers were joined by white-collar workers, Buddhist priests, professors, Catholic priests, plus representatives of the International Confederation of Free Trade Unions. Under mounting domestic and international pressure, the government eventually backed down.

In South East Asia there is significant resistance by state élites to the perceived US timetable for global liberalization, and the style of liberalization. The South East Asian preference is for state-assisted capitalism and a sub-regional free-trade bloc. The regional government's actions reflect an attempt to dilute the importance of individuals and companies inherent in western liberal economics, and to elevate the importance of communities and nations or states. Bello's account of the response of the South East Asian governments to the USA's push for an Asia Pacific Economic Cooperation (APEC) Free Trade Area Initiative is instructive (Bello 1997, 151). Resisting further integration into a free-market system which the USA had been working for hitherto in its bilateral dealings with these states, they opted for a faster timetable for their own ASEAN Free Trade Area (AFTA), and with a Malaysian proposal to create the East Asia Economic group, a regional trade bloc that would exclude Australia, Canada, the USA and the Latin American countries.

The greatest significance of these various forms of resistance lies in the opening up of new political space in which essentially contested concepts like democracy, development and human rights are being aired. It is clear that the neoliberal agenda is the dominant agenda, but it does not have universal legitimacy, and it is not the only agenda. State socialism may have died a death, but alternative forms of organization exist, and others are evolving as a response to need. Politics never stands still, and with the rise of the new social protest movements global politics is taking on a new meaning.

## Conclusion

While acknowledging the important progress made in the development of international human rights law, we must not be lulled into a false sense of security that the mere existence and development of such law is enough: it is not (Evans and Hancock, forthcoming). Such rights must be fulfilled in practical terms. The widening inequalities accompanying economic liberalization cast doubt on the ability of the economically powerless to enjoy the substance, rather than simply the form, of economic and social rights within the liberal economic structure. Liberal democracy in an important sense may be hiding growing inequalities, and while equity is not cited in the UN Covenants on human rights as a human right, inequality clearly affects the relative ability to enjoy social and economic rights.

Policies pursued by the IFIs support a particular conception of liberalism that equates freedom with private power, diminishing the status of economic and social rights and eroding the potential for fulfilling them. As inequalities widen, some groups benefit in terms of their economic well-being, while others are marginalized. Through structural adjustment policies the IFIs have rolled back the power of the state throughout the South and the former Eastern bloc, and have affected the fulfilment of social and economic human rights of millions of people. They have opened states for foreign investment and the expansion of private power, and are now stepping back their involvement, their task well done. Foreign direct investment is becoming increasingly important. The central place of government in determining access to economic and social rights is gradually being diluted as entitlement is determined more and more by various transnational capitalist actors, such as those associated with the global agribusiness.

The IFIs have responded to a limited extent to reformist critiques by dedicated poverty reduction policies. However, if they continue the process of economic liberalization with the attendant reduction in the role of the state, it is questionable whether such dedicated policies can result in sustained improvement in the economic and social rights of the targeted groups. Ultimately what matters is the overall framework in which specific policies are applied. The current global economic structure cannot deliver economic and social rights for all humankind, no matter how much modification takes place at the level of process. We can adjust adjustment policies indefinitely, but this will not result in the delivery of the substance of social and economic rights for all.

Reflecting on the prescriptions made by the UNICEF Report in 1987, it is clear that even from the reformist viewpoint the fundamental expansionary macro-economic bedrock which reformers believe can sustain output, growth and human need satisfaction over the longer term has still not been put in place. The focus of IFIs remains on adjustment, rather than finance. The unspoken bargain that adjustment would be accompanied by new credit and investment has not held true; adjustment has taken place, but the additional finance has not flowed in.

It remains to be seen whether the new insights of orthodox institutions such as the World Bank and the OECD regarding equity as a support, rather than obstacle to growth, will be translated into real policy shifts which would stop the further diminution of social and economic human rights. It is unlikely, since the agenda of those institutions is largely shaped by other powerful actors who have yet to be persuaded.

While the reformers such as Killick point to the fundamental causes of poverty as lying outside of IFI policies, in the realms of distribution of assets and political power, they fail to address the way in which the processes represented in the activities of IFIs reinforce existing structures of dominance. Ultimately, it is not the IFIs which are to blame for the lack of fulfilment of social and economic rights for all humanity, but rather the broader structure of dominance within which the IFIs are embedded and the interests which those IFIs support.

It is doubtful whether the limited success of the South in the past in championing economic and social human rights can be sustained under the existing conditions of increasing globalization. International law is a legal code operating between states. This applies equally to the international law of human rights. Yet the institutions of globalization which are intimately involved in eroding social and economic rights, such as the multinational banks and transnational corporations, can operate largely outside of national regulation, and outside of international law pertaining to rights. The state is no longer able (if indeed it ever was) to secure such rights for its citizens, even assuming that it wants to (Evans and Hancock, forthcoming).

It was clear at the Copenhagen Social Summit, and at the various global conferences before and after, that alternative conceptions of the problem and of the solution exist. The parallel NGO forums have been the site for expression of alternative views. Yet while the language of the alternative schools has been incorporated into many of the mainstream policies, such as the emphasis on sustainable development, the substance of the alternative critiques has been largely ignored. Consequently, the possibility of meaningful self-determination by the majority of humanity, which at the most basic level depends on their realization of economic and social rights, continues to be undermined. In response, resistance to the orthodoxy increases across the globe, as social movements arise to protest against the universalization of essentially western values of economic and political liberalism and accompanying western conceptions of human rights.

## Note

1 It is worth noting that certain international bodies, such as the UNDP, question this logic – see the UN Human Development Report, 1996. The World Bank itself may be questioning it too – see World Bank World Development Report 1997: The State in a Changing World.

## References

Ball, G. and M. Jenkins (1996), Too much for them, and not enough for us, *Independent on Sunday*, 21 July, 51.

Barya, J. (1993), The new political conditionalities of aid: an independent view from Africa, *IDS Bulletin*, 24:1, 16–23.

Bello, W (1994), *Dark Victory: The US, Structural Adjustment and Global Poverty*, London, Pluto.

Bello, W. (1997), Fast-track capitalism, geoeconomic competition, and the sustainable development of challenge in East Asia, in C. Thomas and P. Wilkin (eds), *Globalization and the South*, Basingstoke, Macmillan.

Bird, G. (1996), The International Monetary Fund and developing countries: a review of the evidence and policy options, *International Organization*, 50:3, 477–511.

Bird, G. and T. Killick (1995), *The Bretton Woods Institutions: A Commonwealth Perspective*, London, Commonwealth Secretariat.

Bourguignon, F. and C. Morrisson (1992), *Adjustment and Equity in Developing Countries: A New Approach*, Paris, OECD.

Brindle, D. (1996), How Whitehall kept poverty off the agenda, *Guardian*, 31 December.

Brittan, L. (1995), A level playing field in Direct Foreign Investment, Communication Presented by the European Commission, Brussels (cited in LeQuesne (1996)).

Brown, M. (1996), Aid moves from the messianic to the managerial, *The World Today*, June, 157–9.

Cavanagh, J., D. Wysham and M. Arruda (1994), *Beyond Bretton Woods: Alternatives to the Global Economic Order*, London, Pluto.

CGAP (1996), The Consultative Group to assist the poorest: a micro-finance program, *World Bank CGAP Focus*, Note No. 1, October-April.

Chatterjee, P. and M. Finger (1994), *The Earth Brokers*, London, Routledge.

Chossudovsky, M. (1997), *The Globalisation of Poverty: Impacts of IMF and World Bank Reforms*, London, Zed Books.

Cornia, A., R. Jolly and F. Stewart (1987), *Adjustment With A Human Face*, Oxford, Oxford University Press.

Crossette, B. (1996), UN survey finds world rich-poor gap widening, *New York Times*, 15 July, 55.

de Vries, B. (1995), The World Bank's focus on poverty, in J. Griesgraber and B. Gunter (eds), *The World Bank: Lending on a Global Scale*, London, Pluto.

Ekins, P. (1992), *A New World Order: Grassroots Movements for Global Change*, London, Routledge.

Engberg-Pedersen, P., P. Gibbon, P. Raikes and L. Udsholt (1996), *Limits of Adjustment in Africa: The Effects of Economic Liberalization – 1986–94*, Oxford, James Currey/Heinemann.

English, E. P. and M. Mule (1996), *The African Development Bank*, London, Lynne Reinner/IT.

Evans, T. (1996), *US Hegemony and the Project of Universal Human Rights*, Basingstoke, Macmillan.

Evans T. and J. Hancock (forthcoming), International human rights law and the Challenge of globalization, *The International Journal of Human Rights*, Autumn 1998.

Falk, R. (1995), *On Humane Governance*, Cambridge, Polity.

Fukuyama, F. (1989), The end of history?, *The National Interest*, Summer, 3–18.

Gillies, D. (1996), Human rights, democracy and good governance: stretching the World Bank's Policy frontiers, in J. Griesgraber and B. Gunter (eds), *The World Bank: Lending on a Global Scale*, London, Pluto.

Gills, B., J. Rocamora and R. Wilson (eds) (1994), *Low Intensity Democracy*, London, Pluto.

Graf, W. (1992), Sustainable development ideology and interests: beyond Brundtland, *Third World Quarterly*, 13:3, 553–9.

Griesgraber, J. M. and B. G. Gunter (eds) (1996), *The World Bank: Lending on a Global Scale*, London, Pluto.

Hanlon, J. (1995), Putting power in voters' hands, *Third World Network*, December, 36–7.

Hoogevelt, A. (1997), *Globalisation and the Postcolonial World*, Basingstoke, Macmillan.

Hulme, D. and P. Moseley (1996), *Finance Against Poverty: Volume 1*, London, Routledge.

Hulme, D. and P. Moseley (1996a), *Finance Against Poverty: Volume 2: Case Studies*, London, Routledge.

International Commission on Peace and Food (1994), *Uncommon Opportunities: An Agenda for Peace and Equitable Development*, London, Zed Books.

Jacques, M (1996), New rich kids on the block, *Observer*, 21 July.

Kappagoda, N. (1995), *The Asian Development Bank*, London, Lynne Reinner Publishers.

Khor, M. (1996), Globalisation: implications for development policy, *Third World Resurgence*, 74, 15–22.

Killick, T. (1994), *Structural Adjustment and Poverty Alleviation: An Interpretative Survey*, London, ODI mimeo.

Kneen, B. (1995), *Invisible Giant: Cargill and its Transnational Strategies*, London, Pluto Press.

Lazare, F. and S. Marti (1996), Les Nations unies dénoncent la 'fracture sociale' mondiale, *Le Monde International*, 18 July, 2.

Lean, G. and Y. Cooper (1996), The theory was that as the rich got richer, we'd all benefit. But it hasn't worked, *Independent on Sunday*, 21 July, 52–3.

Leftwich, A. (1993), Governance, development and democracy in the Third World, *Third World Quarterly*, 14:3, 605–24.

Leftwich, A. (1994), Governance, the state and the politics of development, *Development and Change*, 25, 363–86.

LeQuesne, C. (1996), *Reforming World Trade: The Social and Environmental Priorities*, Oxford, Oxfam.

Marglin, F. A. and S. A. Marglin (eds) (1990), *Dominating Knowledge: Development, Culture and Resistance*, Oxford, Clarendon Press.

Mittelman, J. (ed.) (1996), *Globalization: Critical Reflections*, Boulder and London, Lynne Reinner.

Mosley, P., J. Harrigan, and J. Toye (1991), *Aid and Power: The World Bank and Policy-Based Lending, Vol. 1*, London and New York, Routledge.

Mosley, P., J. Harrigan and J. Toye (1991), *Aid and Power: The World Bank and Policy-Based Lending, Vol. 2*, London and New York, Routledge.

ODI (1996), Adjustment in Africa: lessons from Ghana, *ODI Briefing Paper*, 3.

ODI (1996b), Rethinking the role of the multilateral development banks, *ODI Briefing Paper*, 4.

OECD (1989), *Development Cooperation in the 1990s: Policy Statement by DAC Aid Ministers and Heads of Agencies*, Paris, OECD.

OECD (1996), *OECD Employment Outlook*, July, SG/COM/PUN(96)65, Paris, OECD.

Ould-Mey, M. (1994), Global adjustment: implications for peripheral states, *Third World Quarterly*, 15:2, 319–36.

Pearce, F. (1992), *The Dammed*, Kent, Mackays of Chatham Place.

Ponvert, P. (1997), Pastors for peace breach US trade embargo against Cuba, *Third World Resurgence*, 77/78, 53–5.

Renner, M. (1997), *Fighting for Survival: Environmental Decline, Social Conflict, and the New Age of Insecurity*, London, Earthscan.

Reno, W. (1995), Markets, war and the reconfiguration of political authority in Sierra Leone, *Canadian Journal of African Studies*, 29:2, 203–21.

Rich, B. (1994), *Mortgaging the Earth*, London, Earthscan.

Saurin, J. (1997), Organizing hunger: the global organization of famines and feasts, in C. Thomas and P. Wilkin (eds), *Globalization and the South*, Basingstoke, Macmillan.

Shaw, T. and F. Quadir (1997), Democratic development in the South in the next millennium: what prospects for avoiding anarchy and authoritarianism?, in C. Thomas and P. Wilkin (eds), *Globalization and the South*, Basingstoke, Macmillan.

Shiva, V. (1995), Indian farmers protest against pro-liberalisation agricultural policy, *Third World Network*, December, 33–5.

Simmons, P. (1995), *Words into Action: Basic Rights and the Campaign against World Poverty*, Oxford, Oxfam.

Thomas, C. (1997), Poverty, development and hunger, in J. Baylis and S. Smith (eds), *Globalization of World Politics*, Oxford, Oxford University Press.

Thomas. C. and P. Wilkin (eds) (1997), *Globalization and the South*, Basingstoke, Macmillan.

UNDP (1994), *Human Development Report, 1994*, Oxford, Oxford University Press.

UNDP (1995), *Human Development Report, 1995*, Oxford, Oxford University Press.

UNDP (1996), *Human Development Report, 1996*, Oxford, Oxford University Press.

Walton, J. and D. Seddon (1994), *Free Markets and Food Riots: The Politics of Global Adjustment*, Oxford, Blackwells.

Wilkin, P. (1996), New myths for the South: globalisation and the conflict between private power and freedom, *Third World Quarterly*, 17:2, 227–38.

World Bank (1993), *The Asian Economic Miracle*, Washington DC, World Bank.

World Bank (1996), *World Development Report 1995: Workers in an Integrating World*, Oxford, Oxford University Press.

# The future of human rights

# 8

# Human rights in a global age: coming to terms with globalization

*Anthony G. McGrew*

## Introduction

As Richard Rorty has observed, the idea of universal human rights is today a 'fact of the world' (Mullerson 1997). But as the new millennium beckons, the very processes of globalization which have facilitated this worldwide diffusion of the idea of rights are implicated in a growing challenge to the efficacy of the global human rights regime. For contemporary patterns of globalization are arguably transforming world politics and thereby the necessary conditions for further progress towards the substantive realization of, and adherence to, the principles of universal human rights. While much of the contemporary academic study of human rights remains fixated with the legal and institutional dynamics of the international human rights regime, the powerful forces of globalization, which are remaking the world, go largely unremarked inasmuch as for both idealists and realists alike 'progress in the field of international human rights remains substantially constrained by deep structural forces' for the 'states system remains essentially unchanged in the post Cold War world' (Donnelly 1993, 141). This contrasts dramatically with Ruggie's assessment that the present era is defined by a fundamental re-organization of international relations, propelled by processes of globalization, in which the form and the functions of the sovereign territorial nation-state are being redefined and reconstituted (Ruggie 1993). Under these conditions it may be the very transformation in the nature of state power, rather than sovereign statehood *per se*, which constitutes a hindrance to substantive progress in the achievement of human rights. In transforming state power, globalization provokes critical questions about the political and institutional conditions necessary for the advancement of human rights in a global age.

This chapter examines the contemporary form of globalization and its implications for the global human rights regime. It argues that globalization is implicated in a growing disjuncture between the principles of universal human rights (embracing civil, social, economic and political rights) and the substantive realization or promotion of such rights. This, in turn, suggests the need for a rethinking and regrounding of the human rights project to reflect the late twentieth-century 'global condition', recognizing that the era of 'big government', which nurtured and diffused the idea of rights, has disappeared along with the cold war politics which sustained it. Paradoxically, in an epoch of intensifying global interconnectedness, which intuitively might be expected to promote the cosmopolitan ideal underlying the Universal Declaration of Human Rights, the advancement of the human rights project confronts new and difficult obstacles generated by those very same processes of globalization.

## Globalization and universal human rights

Five decades on from the Declaration, the idea of rights seemingly has acquired the status of a 'global ideology', although one which is deeply contested. This ideology has become institutionalized in global and regional human rights regimes as well as in other functional domains of global governance, from the environment to trade. It has also been accompanied by a distinctive form of transnational mobilization and organization, as human rights NGOs and social movements have radicalized and globalized the politics of universal human rights. In this respect the politics of rights is no longer the sole preserve of diplomats and state authorities but involves a plurality of agencies: governmental, inter-governmental and non-governmental. This was evidenced at the UN World Conference on Human Rights in Vienna (1993) where some 2,721 representatives of 529 INGOs (International Non-Governmental Organizations), from every region of the world, virtually outnumbered the representatives of states (Boyle 1995). The global politics of rights is just one aspect of a more pervasive globalization of modern social life.

Globalization can be understood quite simply as the stretching, deepening and speeding up of global interconnectedness, i.e., the multiplicity of networks, flows, transactions and relations which transcend the states and societies which constitute the contemporary global system. Consider the following:

- Over $1 trillion flows across the world's foreign exchange markets every day; well in excess of fifty times the size of world trade and dwarfing the collective foreign exchange reserves of the world's richest states;
- In 1960 there were 70 million international tourists; by 1995 there were nearly 500 million;
- Multi-National corporations (MNCs) now account for between 25–33 per cent of world output, 70 per cent of world trade and 80 per cent of international investment; in 1992 the top 100 multinationals controlled sales almost equal in size to the world's largest economy, the USA;

- In 1993 the UN calculated that there were 28,900 citizen, or non-governmental, organizations with an international dimension compared with 176 at the turn of the century;
- Global warming, ozone depletion and deforestation constitute environmental catastrophes with potentially worldwide ramifications;
- By 1990, 95 per cent of the world's nations were in the global trading system while world trade has more than doubled since the 1950s and become increasingly important to national economic survival in the majority of states;
- At the turn of the century it took days, sometimes weeks, for telegraph communications to reach the Indian sub-continent; today e-mail traverses the same distance in minutes, if not seconds – the world is 'shrinking'.

Globalization reflects the 'stretching' of social, political and economic activities and practices across national frontiers with the consequence that events, decisions and actions in one continent impact upon communities and nations a continent away. Associated with this 'stretching' goes a 'deepening' enmeshment of the local and the global, compromising the boundedness of the modern state and eroding the boundary between the inside/outside, the domestic and the foreign. This deepening is linked with a developing cognitive awareness of, or sensitivity to, the global domain such that though 'everyone has a local life, phenomenal worlds for the most part are truly global' (Giddens 1991, 87). Underpinned by worldwide infrastructures of transport and communication, globalization therefore expresses a qualitative shift in time/space relations – the fundamental coordinates of modern social life – which Harvey refers to as 'time-space compression' (Harvey 1989, 240). In this 'shrinking world' the 'truth of experience no longer coincides with the place in which it takes place' (Jameson quoted in Harvey 1989, 261), since sites of power and the subjects of power may be continents apart while the speed of modern communications links distant locales or events in almost real-time interactions. As social relations come to transcend national boundaries, political, social and economic space is prised away from its rootedness in the territorial nation-state. In this respect, globalization contributes to the 'de-nationalization' of territorial space and so problematizes the modern institution of sovereign statehood based upon the principle of exclusive territorial rule. This growing interconnectedness generates a dense and regularized multi-layered patterning of transnational flows, networks and relations which cumulatively generate a global structure of opportunity and constraint embodying its own systemic logic (Robertson 1992; Axford 1995). For instance, the cumulative pattern and dynamics of global financial flows influences the scope which individual governments have to conduct an autonomous macro-economic policy.

Accordingly, globalization involves something more than simply flows and connections between nation-states and national territorial boundaries and may be defined as a *structural shift in the spatial organization of socio-economic and political activity towards transcontinental or inter-regional patterns of relations, interaction and the exercise of power* (Goldblatt, Held, McGrew and Perraton, forthcoming). In effect, processes of globalization define the ordering and re-ordering of 'relations of domination and subordination among all regions of the world' (Geyer and Bright 1995, 1,047). In this respect globalization necessarily involves the organization and exercise of social power on a transnational and inter-continental scale.

In an increasingly interconnected global system the exercise of power through the decisions, actions or inaction of agencies on one continent can have significant consequences for nations, communities and households on other continents. This 'stretching' of power relations means that sites of power and the exercise of power become increasingly distant from the subjects or locales which experience its consequences. Inequality and hierarchy are therefore deeply inscribed in the very processes of globalization. States, communities and nations are differentially enmeshed in global and transnational flows and networks. Patterns of inclusion and exclusion mediate access to sites of power while the consequences of globalization are unevenly experienced. Political and economic élites in the world's major metropolitan areas are much more tightly integrated into, and have much greater control over, global networks than do the subsistence farmers of Burundi. Globalization therefore has to be conceived as a dialectical process producing both global fragmentation and global integration such that it simultaneously destroys and reinforces social solidarities both within the same locale and between different parts of the globe.

Of course globalization is not unique to the late twentieth century but there are distinctive aspects to its contemporary *historical form*. These include its multidimensional character – economic globalization, cultural globalization, political globalization and legal globalization, etc. – and a heightened consciousness, mediated by electronic forms of communication, of the 'global condition'. Moreover, highly developed worldwide infrastructures of communication and transportation deliver a historically unprecedented potential for new kinds of intensive, as well as regularized, global interactions and associations but within the context of a highly regulated and institutionalized global order. Moreover, contemporary patterns of globalization define the global system's contours which exhibits a high level of 'systemness' such that events, decisions and actions in one part of the world can very rapidly acquire worldwide ramifications while webs of global interconnectedness lock together (in highly complex ways) the fate of peoples and communities in remote corners of the globe. As Nierop notes 'Virtually all countries in the world, if not all parts of their territory and all segments of their society, are now functionally part of that larger [global] system in one or more respects' (Nierop 1994, 171).

Contemporary globalization implies a world in which many of the traditional assumptions, institutions and practices of 'modern' international relations are being destabilized and in which 'political space' is being restructured and reconstituted. For Giddens, contemporary processes of globalization are historically unprecedented, producing new patterns of inclusion and exclusion in the global political economy and requiring governments to adapt to a world in which there is no longer a clear distinction between the foreign and domestic, internal and external affairs (Giddens 1990; Giddens 1996). Globalization is also associated with a new geometry of world power relations. The old North-South hierarchy is rapidly deconstructing as globalization, modernization and a new global division of labour transform the architecture of world order such that the 'familiar pyramid of the core-periphery hierarchy is no longer a geographic but a social division of the world economy' (Hoogvelt 1997, xii). To talk of North and South, or First World and Third World, is to overlook the ways in which globalization has recast traditional patterns of inclusion and exclusion between countries by forging new patterns which cut across and reach deeply into all the countries and regions of the world. North and South, First World/Third World are no longer 'out there' but nestled together 'right here' in all the world's major cities. Rather than a pyramid a more apt analogy would be a three-tier structure of concentric circles, each cutting across national boundaries, representing the élites, the contented and the marginalized respectively (Hoogvelt 1997). This recasting of patterns of inclusion and exclusion presents distinct challenges to the protection and advancement of human rights across the globe.

Such challenges are compounded by the form in which globalization is reconstituting or 're-engineering' the power, functions and authority of the national governments. While not disputing that states still retain the ultimate legal claim to 'effective supremacy over what occurs within their own territories' this is juxtaposed, to varying degrees, with the expanding jurisdiction of institutions of international governance and the constraints of, as well as the obligations derived from, international law. Complex global systems, from the financial to the ecological, connect the fate of communities in one locale to the fate of communities in distant regions of the world. Sites of power and the subjects of power may be literally, as well as metaphorically, oceans apart. A new 'sovereignty regime' is displacing traditional conceptions of state power as an absolute, indivisible, territorially exclusive and zero-sum form of public power. As Held remarks, 'Sovereignty itself has to be conceived today as already divided among a number of agencies – national, regional and international – and limited by the very nature of this plurality' (Held 1991, 222). Accordingly, sovereignty is best understood as 'less a territorially defined barrier than a bargaining resource for a politics characterized by complex transnational networks' (Keohane 1995, 17). In this context the form and functions of the state too are being adapted as governments seek coherent strategies for engaging with a globalizing world. Diverse trajectories are being followed from the neoliberal competitive state model, through the developmental state, to the catalytic state (government as facilitator) models. Rather than globalization bringing about the 'end of the welfare state' it has encouraged a spectrum of adjustment strategies. While the power of national governments is not necessarily being diminished by globalization it is nevertheless being reconstituted 'around the consolidation of domestic and international linkages' (Weiss 1998, forthcoming).

This is not to argue that territorial boundaries retain no political, military or symbolic significance but rather to acknowledge that, conceived as the primary spatial markers of modern life, they have become increasingly problematic in an era of intensified globalization. Sovereignty, state power and territoriality thus stand today in a more complex relationship than in the epoch during which the modern nation-state was forged and the post-war era during which the idea of human rights took hold. Indeed, globalization is associated not only with a new 'sovereignty regime' but also with the emergence of powerful new non-territorial forms of economic and political organization in the global domain, e.g., MNCs, transnational social movements, international regulatory agencies, and so on. The modern institution of territorially circumscribed sovereign rule appears somewhat anomalous juxtaposed with the transnational organization of many aspects of contemporary economic and social life. Globalization, in this account, is therefore associated with a transformation or, to use Ruggie's term, an unbundling of the relationship between sovereignty, territoriality and state power (Ruggie 1993; Sassen 1996). In this regard the contemporary global system can no longer be conceived as purely state centric or even primarily state governed. On the contrary, the present global system is best conceived as a hybrid form constituted by and through the interactions of states and non-territorial agencies and forces. As such, in adapting to the forces of globalization in the coming decades, 'we can expect to see more and more of a different kind of state taking shape in the world arena, one that is reconstituting its power at the centre of alliances formed either within or outside the nation-state' (Weiss 1998, forthcoming).

As Clark argues, in part the 'so-called contemporary crisis of the state is a product of its shouldering the political costs of globalization in comparison with the golden era of ... the 1950s and 1960s, when growth seemed universal and permanent, [and] globalization was politically cost-free' (Clark 1997, 202). This was the era of 'embedded liberalism', 'state socialism' and 'post-colonial states' in which faith in the power of the state and its capacity to engineer progress reached its zenith. In this context the global diffusion of the idea of human rights (especially economic and social rights) and their formal institutionalization in notions of citizenship took a great leap forward encouraged by the expansion of the welfare state, decolonization and the cold war climate of ideological competition. The role of 'big government' in managing and mediating the adverse impact of global economic competition on its citizens was central to the protection and promotion of economic and social rights in the West and the East. With the intensification of globalization in the 1980s and the end of the cold war, the conditions that were once conducive to promoting and advancing social and economic rights (strong states and welfarism) are increasingly compromised, such that the very notion of rights is increasingly contested on normative, practical and political grounds. Paradoxically, while there is growing scepticism, even within the wealthiest societies, that government, in an era of intensifying global economic competition, can protect or promote social and economic rights, the idea of civil and political rights, according to Fukuyama, appears to have acquired global primacy (Fukuyama 1992). Of course these are not unrelated developments but rather reflect the contradictions inherent in contemporary patterns of globalization.

## Disjunctures[1]

The demise of the cold war and the intensification of globalization might at first appear to enhance the prospects for the widening and deepening of the global human rights regime (Clark 1997; Mullerson 1997). Human rights are no longer caught up in the East-West conflict, while in a more interconnected world order the domestic policies of states, such as their human rights record, acquire significant global impacts and thus are no longer 'considered to be exclusively internal matters' (Mullerson 1997, 31). But globalization does not necessarily signal a new and more progressive era for the advancement of universal human rights. On the contrary, its consequences are highly ambiguous and contradictory. In particular, contemporary patterns of globalization are associated with a set of growing disjunctures between the global diffusion of the idea of universal human rights and the social, political and economic conditions necessary for their effective realization. For, under conditions of intensifying globalization, the capacity of states and the global human rights regime to ensure compliance with established norms of social, economic, civil, political and cultural rights is significantly eroded. These disjunctures are evident in respect of: the realization of rights; the diplomacy and politics of rights; and the normative foundations of rights.

### THE REALIZATION OF UNIVERSAL HUMAN RIGHTS

The twentieth century has witnessed an unprecedented global diffusion of the idea of rights. As Donnelly observes, 'The universality of the Universal Declaration and the Covenants is now the real starting point for discussion' (Donnelly 1993, 146). Ratification of, and accessions to, global and regional human rights regimes and instruments have increased while, to date, there have been no abdications or withdrawals (Rosas 1995).[2] The global machinery of surveillance and monitoring, in the form of the UN human rights regime, is reinforced by an evolving set of regional regimes and mechanisms for the adjudication and enforcement of rights. Thus not only has there occurred a globalization of the idea of rights but also a consequent institutionalization of human rights. The treatment by states of their citizens is potentially open, as never before, to a level and form of international monitoring and scrutiny which has no historical parallel. Moreover, the recent 'third wave' of global democratization has contributed to the consolidation and extension of the human rights discourse such that rights and democracy have become hegemonic narratives of the 'global condition'. But whereas the idea of rights has spread, this has not necessarily been accompanied by greater universal observance of rights. For the existence of a global machinery of rights is, by itself, no necessary guarantee of the substantive realization of universal rights. Indeed, globalization is implicated in a significant disjuncture between the universalization of the idea of rights and the global observance of human rights.

While the initial euphoria of the post-cold war era promised the prospect of greater 'progress' in the realization of human rights the historical record is somewhat less than positive (Clark 1997; Mullerson 1997). From East Timor, Somalia, Rwanda and Haiti to the former Yugoslavia, atrocities and abuses of rights represent the return of barbarism. Although in some regions, such as Latin America and Eastern Europe, there has been some progress in the entrenchment and recognition of rights in many other regions, despite the spread of democracy, the conditions for the realization of rights are much less secure (Christie 1995; Panizza 1995). In part this is due to the reassertion of nationalism, ethnicity and the politics of identity – arguably in some contexts a reaction against more intensive globalization – which create a fractured and hostile political environment not conducive to the consolidation of democracy and rights. As Hobsbawm notes, nationalism in the contemporary period has acquired a quite different, and reactionary, form to that of the emancipatory nationalism of the nineteenth century which was strongly associated with the struggle for national democratization (Hobsbawm 1990). The global diffusion of democratic values may be a necessary condition for more effective observance of human rights but, as Beetham concludes, it is not sufficient in itself to ensure that goal (Beetham 1995).

Globalization, as the earlier discussion has noted, is associated with processes of global integration and fragmentation, and creates global patterns of hierarchy and stratification. This unevenness, according to Keohane, Brown and others, is contributing to a bifurcation of the global system into 'zones (not necessarily regions) of compliance' with international and global norms and 'zones of instability' in which conflict, poverty and authoritarianism undermine, but do not completely eradicate, the basis of such compliance

(Goldeier 1992; Brown 1995; Keohane 1995). This is not a return to a simple North–South, modern–traditional, advanced–industrializing, analysis of the world system, but represents a more complex characterization which recognizes differentiation within and across the world's global regions. The significance of this argument for human rights resides in the conclusion that the effective conditions for the realization of rights in different parts of the global political economy have become significantly interrelated by and through the logic of globalization. For instance, the global economic restructuring associated with the emergence of a new international division of labour and the globalization of neoliberal economic orthodoxy has had enormous consequences, both North and South, for the effective realization of social and economic rights. On the one hand it has led to the mobilization of workers, labour movements and communities, both North and South, in the defence of and struggle for their rights. On the other hand fierce global economic competition places significant constraints upon what governments and employers are willing to concede (if anything at all) such that, many would argue, the global prospects for economic and social rights are worsening rather than improving (Beetham 1995).

This is compounded by the fact that in the last two decades the intensity of economic globalization, and associated restructuring of national economies, have fuelled growing inequality within and between nations (Hoogvelt 1997). There is a widening of the gap between rich and poor societies, and the rich and poor within states, which varies in degree in the different regions of the world (Bradshaw and Wallace 1996). In 1996 the total wealth of the world's richest 300 individuals was equal to that of the entire 25 per cent of the world's poorest (UNDP 1996). The share of the poorest 20 per cent of the world's peoples has declined from 2.3 per cent of global income in 1960 to 1.1 per cent in 1994 while, over the same period, the top 20 per cent saw their incomes increase from thirty times that of the poorest to a staggering seventy-eight times (UN Development Programme 1997, 9). Economic globalization, compounded in the South by structural adjustment programmes, is implicated in their growing social polarization on both a global and domestic scale. Within societies it fragments national and local communities, as some reap its rewards others bear its costs and some survive on its margins. This is nowhere so evident as in the citadels of global finance where foreign exchange dealers in the City can earn in a week what the office cleaners earn in a year. This social polarization is associated with an erosion of social solidarity, disillusionment with established forms of politics, depoliticization, and direct challenges to hard won social and economic rights (Cox 1996 and 1997). But this challenge to social and economic rights is connected to the more general problem of 'state capacity' in the context of contemporary economic globalization.

The institutions and procedures of the global (and regional) human rights regime lodge the responsibility for the observance and implementation of rights with states or governments. This follows logically from the state centric, sovereignty bound, international society approach to human rights upon which the regime is constituted. But it also in part reflects the post-war (and cold war) political context in which the human rights project developed; the era of 'big government' and a belief in the capacity of the state to deliver welfare and 'progress'. In the 1990s, even among the world's richest nations the capacity of governments to 'deliver' social and economic rights, as the national debates over welfare policy everywhere demonstrate, is subject to powerful constraints. While in most parts of the world, post-colonial states have never acquired the capacity or resources to ensure the realization of such rights, globalization has contributed to this erosion of state capacity since it locks states into global networks and systems which directly and indirectly affect the lives of their citizens but over which no single state can, by itself, exert effective control. Only through cooperation with other states is it be possible to re-establish some capacity for effective governance. But, as Zurn suggests, 'since the rise of international governance is slower than the process of globalization, the loss of effectiveness of national politics is not adequately replaced by effective international institutions. This causes a substantial deficit in the capacity to govern in all issue-areas' (Zurn 1995, 156). This has obvious implications for the practice and realization of rights.

This erosion of state capacity and state autonomy raises serious questions about the ability of states, in the context of contemporary globalization, to deliver upon their human rights responsibilities, most especially in the economic and social domains. This is compounded by the weakness of the implementational machinery of regional and global human rights regimes (Donnelly 1993). While globalization may have contributed enormously to making human rights 'the idea of our time' its consequences for the practice, or substantive realization, of such rights appears much more ambivalent.

THE 'NEW' POLITICS AND DIPLOMACY OF UNIVERSAL HUMAN RIGHTS
'The defence of human dignity knows no boundaries' observes Emilio Mignone, a famous Argentinian human rights campaigner (quoted in Brysk 1993, 281). Human rights activists, such as Mignone, vigorously reject the notion of the nation-state as a bounded political space within which political authorities can treat their citizens as they so desire. Moreover, as Mullerson observes, in a more interconnected world 'the domestic characteristics of states and internal developments in those states affect international relations much more directly. Hence the increase in the importance of human rights in foreign policy' (Mullerson 1997, 181). But states still aggressively seek to defend their sovereignty in this domain. Human rights is one domain in which the clash between the assertion of sovereign political power and alternative, transnational principles of political community, authority and legitimacy is

most acute and politically visible. This clash of political principles has been conditioned by the nature of contemporary globalization which has created the infrastructural conditions of a 'global civil society' which makes feasible political action 'at a distance' (Giddens 1990). One consequence of this has been a growing disjuncture between the 'old' legal and institutional politics of human rights and the 'new' global politics of rights based upon contestation of state power and republican notions of empowerment.

The contemporary human rights regime consists of overlapping global and regional institutions and conventions. At the global level, human rights are firmly institutionalized in the International Bill of Human Rights, which comprises the UN Declaration and the several conventions on civil, political and economic rights adopted predominantly in the 1960s and 1970s. These were complemented in the 1980s by the Convention on the Elimination of Discrimination against Women and the Convention on the Rights of the Child. The UN Commission on Human Rights (UNCHR) is responsible for policing this system and bringing to the attention of the UN Security Council persistent abuses. In addition, the International Labour Organization (ILO) regulates the area of labour rights. Within most of the world's global regions there is an equivalent legal structure and machinery. In the case of Europe the European Commission on Human Rights (ECHR), the European Court of Human Rights and the Conference on Security and Cooperation in Europe (CSCE) oversee human rights issues and adjudicate abuses. Beyond Europe, in Africa the Banjul Charter and in the Americas the Organization of American States (OAS) Inter-American Committee on Human Rights have similar functions.

Within these institutional arenas the politics of rights is often defined in terms of traditional inter-state politics. Thus the politics of rights has to be balanced with a sober awareness of institutional and international power politics. Maintaining institutional consensus and agreement may therefore on many occasions become a more overriding objective than pursuing the advancement of rights or particular cases of alleged abuse. Even the UN Vienna Conference on Human Rights in 1993 did not escape from this kind of politics. Moreover, within much of the UN machinery of human rights, the advancement of rights is often equated solely with institutional and procedural reform, the expansion of human rights law, and expansion of human rights machinery. Of course these are not unimportant issues or irrelevant strategies for achieving the progress of human rights. However, together they represent a particular form of institutional politics which is being contested by a form of human rights politics energized by the activities and concerns of social movements seeking to make states more accountable for their actions (Shaw 1994; Goodman 1996).

To talk of a global politics of contestation (or empowerment) is shorthand for the explosive growth of human rights movements and associated NGO activity within the global system. Since the 1970s 'both the number of human rights NGOs and the level of their activity has increased dramatically' (Donnelly 1993, 14). There are now over 200 US NGOs associated with human rights issues, a similar number in the UK and across Europe, and expanding numbers of such organizations across the Third World. The significance of these NGOs is not simply that they monitor and publicize human rights abuses, but that they also campaign on specific causes and, combined, form a global network of human rights organizations. As a result, human rights have not only been incorporated into the national foreign policy postures of many states – the Dutch section of Amnesty International (AI) drafted the human rights provisions of the Dutch government's 1979 White Paper on foreign policy – but they 'now play a part in the decision about the legitimacy of a state in international society' (Vincent 1986, 13).

Social movements, within and beyond the human rights domain, now play an increasingly significant role in national and global politics. Their power arises from the capacity to mobilize public and political opinion around specific 'life issues', such as the environment, gender, rights, and so on, in combination with flexible organizational structures, and a repertoire of tactics for campaigning or influencing societal and institutional agendas (Tarrow 1994). In the human rights field NGOs represent a distinctive kind of social movement in that they promote rights for humanity as opposed to specific sectional or promotional interests. But it is not just social movements that have influence, since growing interconnectedness has meant that business and other groups have been forced to acknowledge the connection between their own corporate policies and the rights of others thousands of miles away. Under local and domestic political pressures many US businesses in 1995, such as Levi Strauss and Macy's, among many others, cancelled contracts with companies in Burma because of its human rights record while local governments in New York and California cancelled contracts with US companies doing business there (Mullerson 1997, 33).

Within the human rights domain the activities of social movements and NGOs have sought to contest and redefine the politics of human rights. Among other activities, this involves monitoring and publicizing human rights abuses, mounting global campaigns against specific regimes and lobbying to achieve specific institutional or legal reforms. Strong transnational solidarities and identities have been formed such that Boyle remarks that one of the most significant outcomes of the Vienna Conference in 1993 'was the depth of common understanding on the level of values, on goals and required policies, expressed by the human rights activist from both the South and the North of the world' (Boyle 1995).

Human rights NGOs have also lobbied for strengthening the linkage between human rights and other global policy domains, such as development, trade policy, environmental issues, aid and telecommunications in the desire to improve the prospects for the realization, as opposed to simply the legislation, of rights. This 'issue-linkage' has been especially evident in respect of the proposed WTO 'social charter'. Similarly at the Beijing Women's Conference in September 1995 human rights activists and women's groups from around the world cooperated in launching campaigns and educational programmes to improve the prospects for women's rights in the next decade. Through these diverse strategies – coalition building, issue linkage, challenging the established rights agenda – NGOs have sought to contest the 'statist' politics of human rights and to connect the agenda of 'life politics' in the North to the agenda of 'emancipatory politics' in the South. How successful they are in furthering the realization of human rights is difficult to establish by any objective measure. But as Brett concludes, 'Given the inherently political nature of human rights work, it is not surprising that many governments continue to have reservations about the role of human rights NGOs; indeed, this might be seen as a measure of their success' (Brett 1995).

This 'new' politics of human rights has also spurned a 'new' kind of diplomacy. Rather than the diplomacy of rights being conceived as the sole preserve of governments, there is a growing tendency for states to act as 'catalysts' in a coalition of other states, business organizations and NGOs (Hocking 1996). The promotion and protection of rights thus becomes a shared activity. The concerted campaign in the mid 1990s to establish an International Criminal Court, in which some governments acted as catalysts for a broad global coalition of states, international organizations and a diverse array of NGOs, business and citizens groups from across the globe, proved highly successful in achieving its objectives.

The 'global politics' of rights is evidence of an evolving infrastructure of a global civil society – that global 'space of uncoerced human association and also the set of relational networks – favoured for the sake of family, faith, interest, and ideology – that fill this space' (Walzer 1995, 1). Politics within global civil society is not concerned with the capture of state power so much as empowering citizens and holding states, and other global agencies, accountable for their actions (Scholte 1993; Shaw 1994). In a limited sense it is concerned with the democratization of world order. But it would be naïve to assume that, in the context of human rights, NGO activity is necessarily always benign or a substitute for an effective international implementational machinery. For the very conditions which facilitate benign NGO activity also have encouraged intense global counter-reactions in the form of fundamentalist and other movements which seek to contest the liberal or western project of human rights. Despite the hyperbole of his 'clash of civilizations' thesis, Huntington is probably correct in asserting that human rights is today the critical faultline in an emerging cultural contestation of western globalization and hegemony (Huntington 1996). The 'new politics' of human rights is therefore far from benign but increasingly becoming a domain of conflict and struggle between competing value systems and cultures brought into intense interaction by the processes of globalization. In this respect the dialectic of globalization generates both conflict and cooperation, as well as harmony and discord, in the 'new' politics of human rights.

## THE NORMATIVE FOUNDATIONS OF UNIVERSAL HUMAN RIGHTS

As the preceding discussion has concluded, the states system is today deeply embedded in a wider global system of socio-economic relations and networks. But the normative foundations of human rights are effectively predicated upon the 'reality' of an 'international society' of states (Donnelly 1993). The dynamic of contemporary globalization suggests the emergence of a significant disjuncture between the idea of human rights rooted in an 'international society' of states, and the normative foundations of rights in a world of global flows and connections. A globalizing world calls for a global ethic insofar as taking seriously 'the idea that we are inhabitants of one world means accepting that a wholly new approach to moral questions is required' (Graham 1997, 157). Indeed, since the inauguration of the Declaration in 1948, the cosmopolitan idea of universal human rights has existed in tension with the communitarian principles of international society. Contemporary globalization has intensified, and given new meaning, to this normative disjuncture through its challenge to the fundamental organizing principles of international society, i.e., territoriality and sovereign statehood.

There is a curious anomaly between the manner in which much of the human rights literature exhibits a fixation with the morality of humanitarian intervention while the routine 'interventions' of global financial and economic markets in the economic affairs of states is assumed as 'normal'. This anomaly is symptomatic of the hegemony in human rights discourse of the 'international society' approach and its failure to come to terms with the way in which state autonomy is routinely violated by the existence of global flows and relations. Globalization highlights the ways in which relations between the state and the citizen are not simply determined by endogenous factors but rather are conditioned by the intersection of domestic and external forces. Whereas in 1948 the notion of universal human rights may have presented a rather unique challenge to state authority to determine its own domestic arrangements, in the context of contemporary patterns of globalization, it no longer appears so anomalous. This is not to argue that states are no longer animated by the intrusions of human rights concerns into domestic affairs, since most remain aggressively protective of their remaining autonomy in this domain. Indeed, it may be the very weakness of the global human rights regime which encourages states to assert that autonomy in a confrontational manner; one which most would not countenance in their dealings with, for example, global financial markets.

The human rights literature is replete with discussions of the inherent tensions between sovereignty and intervention, universalism and particularism, and cosmopolitanism and communitarianism in attempts to ground the practice of universal rights in a coherent moral and philosophical system (Vincent 1986; Donnelly 1993). An attempt at partial resolution of these tensions (reflecting the hegemony of realism within the discourse of human rights) is evident in the principles and institutional practices of existing global and regional human rights regimes. But the intensification of globalization invites a critical questioning of this orthodoxy most especially in respect of its acceptance of: states as largely autonomous moral communities; the cultural and moral relativism of rights; and the priority accorded to the claims of sovereignty over international responsibilities and duties.

Writing some years ago, Charles Beitz sought to defend a conception of rights which recognized the interdependence of humanity (Beitz 1986). His argument is that the intensification of economic interdependence undermines the notion of the state as an autonomous moral community and the Hobbesian view of the world upon which the orthodox conception of rights rests. While notions of international society presuppose the idea of a 'national community of fate' – a community which rightly governs itself and determines its own destiny – this premise is fundamentally contested by the scope and intensity of contemporary patterns of globalization. Today, decisions and actions in one part of the world very rapidly acquire worldwide ramifications. In addition, sites of political action or decision become linked through rapid communications and media reporting into complex networks and cascades of decision making and political interaction. It is no longer self-evident that 'national communities – exclusively 'programme' the actions, decisions and policies of their governments and the latter by no means simply determine what is right or appropriate for their citizens alone' (Held 1991, 202). In conditions of chronic globalization, the fate of communities in very distant parts of the globe may be linked through complex networks and abstract systems which create moral connections between the agents and the subjects of social action irrespective of political or territorial boundaries.

But the possibility of moral connections does not by itself create a single moral universe. For there are indeed quite different conceptions of: what constitutes rights, the priority accorded to different types of rights and the entire project of human rights. But the philosophical and political debate about universalist and particularist interpretations of rights is itself conducted in a global setting. This was evident at the Vienna Conference in 1993 at which Islamic and Asian delegations mounted a sustained critique of the universalist presumptions of the UN Human Rights regime but falling well short of outright condemnation. As Halliday observes, in the case of Islam the response to the debate on universal human rights is fragmented (Halliday 1995). There is no single Islamic response, nor is there an outright rejection of universal rights but a rather more complex position. Cultures, like nations, are not 'value containers' but 'value spaces' which are defined and articulated in an increasingly global context. This is not to argue that globalization is a homogenizing force since it is equally as associated with cultural diversity and the reinvention of tradition (McGrew 1992). What it does suggest, at the very least, is the need for some critical re-examination, from within the discourse of human rights, of what Brown and others regard as a false dichotomy between universalism and particularism (Scholte 1993; Brown 1995; Halliday 1995).

In his study of 'global society' Martin Shaw argues that the international society of states cannot be understood separately from the global social relations in which it is immersed (Shaw 1994, 130). But while 'global society' is integrated through abstract systems, networks and connections, defining a social totality in a systemic sense, it is far from normatively integrated and exhibits a vast diversity of values, ways of life and consciousness of the 'global condition'. The existence of a global system may be a necessary condition of the emergence of a sense of global community but it is not by itself a sufficient condition. In this sense globalization does not preordain the arrival of a global community within which the progress of universal rights might be guaranteed. But it does imply the co-existence of communitarian and cosmopolitan approaches to human rights in as much as 'communitarian values are operationalized within a cosmopolitan framework. Local interpretations can evolve within a safety net of global norms' (Booth 1995, 342; Goodman 1996). In this sense globalization contests the conventional dichotomy between communitarianism and cosmopolitanism expressed in the orthodox discourse of universal rights. Furthermore it suggests the need for rethinking the normative foundations of rights to reflect a 'global ethics' for a 'global age'.

## Rethinking human rights

Ulrich Beck, the prominent sociologist, calls for 'the reinvention of politics' to meet the challenges posed by the emerging global social order (Beck 1997). While globalization may not quite demand the 'reinvention' of universal human rights the disjunctures explicated in the previous section suggest that, at the least, some rethinking of human rights is called for. A strong precedent for this exists in the expanding literature concerned with the predicament of liberal democracy under conditions of contemporary globalization; a literature which seeks to reconstruct modern democratic theory to fit with new historical circumstances (Held 1995; Axtmann 1996; Connolly 1996; Gray 1996; McGrew 1997 and 1997a). It is a literature which has significant implications for the contemporary debate about human rights in that it confronts directly the consequences of globalization for established conceptions of liberal democracy which, as a system of political rule, is rooted primarily in the institution of the territorial sovereign nation-state. There are obvious intellectual connections between the rethinking of democracy and the rethinking of rights since discourses of rights and democracy are intimately related. In as much as globalization problematizes the institution of sovereign statehood it presents a challenge both to liberal democracy and the progress of universal human rights.

In respect of universal human rights, globalization presents several distinctive challenges which need to be addressed. First, insofar as it contributes to eroding the autonomy and capacity of states to pursue economic strategies conducive to the substantive realization of economic and social rights, it undermines the principle of the state as the guardian or guarantor of such rights; a principle which is implicit in the functioning of global and regional human rights regimes. In their study of Western states, Garret and Lange conclude that under conditions of globalization 'governments no longer possess the autonomy to pursue independent macroeconomic strategies effectively, even if they were to seek to do so' (Garrett and Lange 1991). If states are increasingly constrained in this respect serious consequences follow for the fulfilment of their obligations in respect of economic, social and welfare rights. In these circumstances a fundamental question is posed: what alternative agencies or agents have the capacity or duty to realize such rights claims? Put more crudely, if under conditions of economic globalization, even states committed to the observance of universal human rights find it increasingly difficult to ensure the protection of social, economic and welfare rights, how can such rights be assured and by whom? Of course this is not to exaggerate the consequences of economic globalization since as many studies have shown its impacts upon state autonomy are significantly mediated by domestic institutional structures, state strategies and domestic political coalitions (Milner and Keohane 1996). Nevertheless for many peoples in the South, economic globalization constitutes a fundamental constraint upon the substantive realization or implementation of economic and social rights. In these circumstances, if states cannot protect such rights in the face of global market forces who or what can?

Second, in connection with the implementation of human rights, globalization presents a direct challenge to the efficacy and legitimacy of the existing global human rights machinery. For, as Zurn notes, the discourse of rights has been associated with processes of individualization (the ideology of individual self-determination) (Zurn 1995). Where this has taken root it sits uneasily alongside a 'globalizing' world in which, as Sandel puts it, the scale of modern social and economic organization invites a 'fear that, individually and collectively, we are losing control of the forces that govern our lives' (Sandel 1996, 3). Where globalization impacts upon rights most acutely, especially in the sphere of social, economic and environmental rights, the limited effectiveness of international mechanisms of enforcement contributes to the erosion of the legitimacy and efficacy of human rights regimes more generally. For as Zurn observes, the expanding gap between the acceleration of societal globalization and the capacity of international regimes, such as the human rights regime, to respond effectively results in 'an increasing inability of democratically elected leaders to sell international agreements at home' (Zurn 1995, 154). But equally the failure of international institutions to prevent abuses of human rights contributes further to general scepticism about the efficacy of the global human rights regime.

Third, if globalization is associated with the emergence of a new 'sovereignty regime' this poses important questions for the existing international law of universal human rights which is predicated upon traditional notions of sovereignty as an illimitable and indivisible form of public power. In particular it raises questions of the conditions under which the international law of human rights could evolve in the direction of a more cosmopolitan form, namely not simply law between states but law which was enforceable across and within states (Archibugi 1995). As discussed in other contexts, the development of a more cosmopolitan law of rights may be an essential requirement of the effective enforcement of civil, political, economic and social rights under conditions of globalization (Held 1995).

Fourth, the emergence of a 'global civil society', spurred by processes of globalization, is far from benign in respect of the politics of human rights. Inequalities of resources and access to sites of power have to some degree distorted the global politics of rights in the sense of greater priority and visibility on global agendas being given to civil and political rights. The global politics of rights is thus structured in a way which tends to reflect dominant western interests and this too is reflected in the institutional politics of rights regimes. Moreover a 'global civil society' also implies the transnational presence and mobilization of reactionary social forces which contest the very idea of rights. This is compounded by the growing salience of inter-civilizational conflicts over universal human rights. Thus while globalization may unleash progressive political energies, along with a politics of contestation, it is also signally implicated in a resurgence of 'culture wars' and a reactionary politics of, what Connolly calls 'homesickness' or, 'a nostalgia for a time when a coherent politics of place could be imagined as a real possibility for the future' (Connolly 1991).

Finally, there is, as noted above, a curious contradiction between the contemporary globalization of social life and the normative discourse of rights which is couched largely in the language of an international society of states. Under conditions of globalization that orthodox language of rights is itself made problematic and a new 'global ethics', in which alternative normative principles more relevant to a 'global age', such as global citizenship, human dignity or a duty of 'care', is called for (Rosenau 1992; Linklater 1996; Evans 1997; Governance 1995; Robinson 1997). Such a 'global ethics' involves the identification of how, in a less state centric world, rights and duties might be founded and alternative normative principles upon which ethical behaviour might be justified (Graham 1997).

Globalization is associated with significant challenges to the human rights project as conventionally conceived. But it would be sheer hyperbole to draw the conclusion that it extinguishes the possibility of progress in the extension and deepening of human rights. Rather, as this chapter has sought to argue, its record is somewhat more ambiguous and contradictory. Nevertheless, it has also stimulated a vibrant dialogue about the nature of rights and the nature of democracy in the contemporary global order and the kinds of normative principles and institutional structures necessary to the effective realization of both (Beetham 1995; Cochran 1995; Dryzek 1995; Falk 1995; Held 1995; Axtmann 1996; Frost 1996; Linklater 1996; Evans 1997). In this respect the most pressing issue confronting the guardians of the human rights project is how to marshal the forces of globalization in order to ensure the advancement of human rights and justice in the new millennium.

## Notes

1 The notion of disjunctures is borrowed from the work of my colleague David Held (Held and McGrew 1993).
2 But not all states have acceded to all the Covenants.

## References

Albrow, M. (1996), *The Global Age*, Cambridge, Polity Press.
Amin, S. (1996), The challenge of globalization, *Review of International Political Economy*, 2, 216–59.
Archibugi, D. (1995), Immanuel Kant, cosmopolitan law and peace, *European Journal of International Relations*, 1:4, 429–56.
Axford, B. (1995), *The Global System*, Cambridge, Polity Press.
Axtmann, R. (1996), *Liberal Democracy into the Twenty-first Century: Globalization, Integration and the Nation-State*, Manchester, Manchester University Press.
Beck, U. (1997), *The Reinvention of Politics*, Cambridge, Polity Press.
Beetham, D. (1995), What future for economic and social rights?, *Political Studies*, 48 (Special Issue), 41–61.
Beitz, C. (1986), *Political Theory and International Relations*, Princeton, Princeton University Press.
Booth, K. (1995), Dare to know, in K. Booth and S. Smith (eds), *International Relations Theory Today*, Cambridge, Polity Press, 328–50.
Boyer, R. and D. Drache (eds) (1996), *States Against Markets*, London, Routledge.
Boyle, K. (1995) Stock-taking on human rights: the World Conference on Human Rights Vienna 1993, *Political Studies*, 43 (Special Issue), 79–96.
Bozeman, A. (1984), The international order in a multicultural world, in H. Bull and A. Watson (eds), *The Expansion of International Society*, Oxford, Oxford University Press.
Bradshaw, Y. W. and M. Wallace (1996), *Global Inequalities*, London, Pine Forge Press, Sage.

Brett, R. (1995), The role and limits of human rights NGOs at the United Nations, *Political Studies*, 43 (Special Issue), 96–111.

Brown, C. (1995), International political theory and the idea of world community, in K. Booth and S. Smith (eds), *International Relations Theory Today*, Cambridge, Polity Press, 90–109.

Brysk, A. (1993), From above and below – social movements, the international system and human rights, *Comparative Political Studies*, 26:3, 259–85.

Bull, H. (1977), *The Anarchical Society*, London, Macmillan.

Burbach, R., O. Nunez, *et al.* (1997), *Globalization and its Discontents*, London, Pluto.

Buzan, B. (1997), The Asia-Pacific: what sort of region, in what sort of world?, in A. G. McGrew and C. Brook (eds), *The Asia-Pacific in the New World Order*, London, Routledge.

Callincos, A., J. Rees, *et al.* (1994), *Marxism and the New Imperialism*, London, Bookmarks.

Cammilleri, J. A. and J. Falk (eds) (1992), *The End of Sovereignty: The Politics of a Shrinking and Fragmented World*, Aldershot, Edward Elgar.

Christie, K. (1995), Regime security and human rights in southeast Asia, *Political Studies*, 43 (Special Issue), 204–19.

Clark, I. (1997), *Globalization and Fragmentation*, Oxford, Oxford University Press.

Cochran, M. (1995), Cosmopolitanism and communitarianism in a post-Cold War world, in J. Macmillan and A. Linklater (eds), *Boundaries in Question*, London, Frances Pinter, 40–53.

Connolly, W. E. (1991), Democracy and territoirality, *Millennium*, 20:3, 463–84.

Connolly, W. E. (1996), *The Ethos of Pluralization*, Minneapolis, University of Minnesota Press.

Cox, R. (1981), Social forces, states and world orders, *Millennium*, 10:2, 126–55.

Cox, R. (1996), Globalization, multilaterlism and democracy, in R. Cox (ed.), *Approaches to World Order*, Cambridge, Cambridge University Press, 524–37.

Cox, R. (1997), Economic globalization and the limits to liberal democracy, in A. McGrew (ed.), *The Transformation of Democracy? Globalization and Territorial Democracy*, Cambridge, Polity Press.

Crawford, J. (1994), *Democracy in International Law*, Cambridge, Cambridge University Press.

Deudney, D. (1996), Binding sovereigns: authorities, structures, and geo-politics in Philadelphian systems, in T. J. Biersteker and C. Weber (eds), *State Sovereignty as Social Construct*, Cambridge, Cambridge University Press, 190–239.

Donnelly, J. (1993), *International Human Rights*, Boulder, CO, Westview Press.

Dryzek, J. S. (1995), Political and ecological communication, *Environmental Politics*, 4:4, 13–30.

Evans, T. (1997), Democratization and human rights, in A. McGrew (ed.), *The Transformation of Democracy? Globalization and Territorial Democracy*, Cambridge, Polity Press, ch. 6.

Falk, R. (1995), Liberalism at the global level: the last of the independent commissions?, *Millennium*, 24:3, 563–78.

Fawcett, L. and A. Hurrell (eds) (1995), *Regionalism in World Politics*, Oxford, Oxford University Press.

Frank, A. G. and B. K. Gills (eds) (1996), *The World System*, London, Routledge.

Frost, M. (1996), *Ethics in International Relations*, Cambridge, Cambridge University Press.

Fukuyama, F (1992), *The End of History and the Last Man*, London, Hamish Hamilton.

Garrett, G. and P. Lange (1991), Political responses to interdependence: what's 'left' for the left?, *International Organization*, 45:4, 539–65.

Geyer, M. and C. Bright (1995), World history in a global age, *American Historical Review*, 100:4, 1034–60.

Giddens, A. (1990), *The Consequences of Modernity*, Cambridge, Polity Press.

Giddens, A. (1991), *Modernity and Self-Identity*, Cambridge, Polity Press.

Giddens, A. (1996), Globalization – A keynote address, *UNRISD News*, 15, 4–5.

Gill, S. (1995), Globalization, market civilization, and disciplinary neoliberalism, *Millennium*, 24:3, 399–424.

Gilpin, R. (1981), *War and Change in World Politics*, Cambridge, Cambridge University Press.

Gilpin, R. (1987), *The Political Economy of International Relations*, Princeton, Princeton University Press.

Goldeier, M. M. J. M. (1992), A tale of two worlds: core and periphery in the post-cold war era, *International Organization*, 46:2, 467–91.

Goodman, J. (1996), *Social Movements and Global Politics: Labour Rights and Globalization*, Deakin University, Australia.

Goodman, J. (1997), The European Union: reconstituting democracy beyond the nation-state, in A. G. McGrew (ed.), *The Transformation of Democracy? Globalization and Territorial Democracy*, Cambridge, Polity Press, ch. 8.

Gordon, D. (1988), The global economy: new edifice or crumbling foundations?, *New Left Review*, 168, 24–65.

Governance, C. O. G. (1995), *Our Global Neighbourhood*, Oxford, Oxford University Press.

Graham, G. (1997), *Ethics and International Relations*, Oxford, Blackwells.

Gray, J. (1996), *After Social Democracy*, London, Demos.

Halliday, F. (1995), Relativism and universalism in human rights: the case of the Islamic Middle East, *Political Studies*, 43 (Special Issue), 152–68.

Harvey, D. (1989), *The Condition of Postmodernity*, Oxford, Basil Blackwell.

Held, D. (1991), Democracy, the nation-state, and the global system, in D. Held (ed.), *Political Theory Today*, Cambridge, Polity Press.

Held, D. (1995), *Democracy and Global Order*, Cambridge, Polity Press.

Held, D. and A. McGrew (1993), Globalization and the liberal democratic state, *Government and Opposition*, 28:2, 236–83.

Hirst, P. and G. Thompson (1996), *Globalization in Question*, Cambridge, Polity Press.

Hobsbawm, E. (1990), *Nations and Nationalism since 1780: Programme, Myth, Reality*, Cambridge, Press Syndicate of the University of Cambridge.

Hocking, B. (1996), *Catalytic Diplomacy*, Leicester, Centre for Diplomatic Studies.

Hoogvelt, A. (1997), *Globalization and the Postcolonial World – The New Political Economy of Development*, London, Macmillan.

Huntington, S. P. (1996), *The Clash of Civilizations and the Remaking of World Order*, New York, Simon and Schuster.

Hurrell, A. and N. Woods (1995), Globalization and inequality, *Millennium*, 24:3, 447–70.

Jackson, R. H. and A. James (1993), The character of independent statehood, in R. H. Jackson and A. James (eds), *States in a Changing World*, Oxford, Oxford University Press, 3–26.

Jameson, F (1991), *Postmodernism or the Cultural Logic of Late Capitalism*, London, Verso.

Keohane, R. (1995), Hobbes's dilemma and institutional change in world politics: sovereignty in international society, in H. H. Holm and G. Sorensen (eds), *Whose World Order?*, Boulder, CO, Westview Press, 165–86.

Keohane, R. O. and H. V. Milner (eds) (1996), *Internationalization and Domestic Politics*, Cambridge, Cambridge University Press.

Krasner, S. (1993), Economic interdependence and independent statehood, in R. H. Jackson and A. James (eds), *States in a Changing World*, Oxford, Oxford University Press.

Krasner, S. (1995), Compromising Westphalia, *International Security*, 20:3, 115–51.

Linklater, A. (1996), Citizenship and sovereignty in the post-Westphalian state, *European Journal of International Relations*, 2:1, 77–103.

Linklater, A. and J. Macmillan (1995), Boundaries in question, in A. Linklater and J. Macmillan (eds), *Boundaries in Question*, London, Pinter, 1–16.

Lyons, G. M. and M. Mastanduno (eds) (1995), *Beyond Westphalia? State Sovereignty and International Intervention*, London, Johns Hopkins University Press.

McGrew, A. (1992), A global society?, in S. Hall, D. Held and T. McGrew (eds), *Modernity and Its Futures*, Cambridge, Polity Press.

McGrew, A. G. (1997), Democracy beyond borders? Globalization and the reconstruction of democratic theory and practice, in A. McGrew (ed.), *The Transformation of Democracy? Globalization and Territorial Democracy*, Cambridge, Polity Press.

McGrew, A. G. (1997a), The globalization debate: putting the advanced capitalist state in its place, ECPR 26 February to 3 March, Bern, Switzerland.

Milner, H. V. and R. O. Keohane (1996), Internationalization and domestic politics, in R. O. Keohane and H. V. Milner (eds), *Internationalization and Domestic Politics*, Cambridge, Cambridge University Press.

Mullerson, R. (1997), *Human Rights Diplomacy*, London, Macmillan.

Murphy, A. B. (1996), The sovereign state system as political-territorial ideal: historical and contemporary considerations, in T. J. Biersteker and C. Weber (eds), *State Sovereignty as Social Construct*, Cambridge, Cambridge University Press, 81–121.

Nierop, T. (1994), *Systems and Regions in Global Politics*, London, John Wiley.

Ohmae, K. (1990), *The Borderless World*, London, Collins.

O'Brien, R. (1992), *The End of Geography: Global Financial Integration*, London, Pinter.

Panizza, F. (1995), Human rights in the processes of transition and consolidation of democracy in Latin America, *Political Studies*, 43 (Special Issue), 168–89.

Pattie, C. J. (1994), Forgetting Fukuyama: new spaces of politics, *Environment and Planning*, 26:7, 1007–10.

Perlmutter, H. V. (1991), On the rocky road to the first global civilization, *Human Relations*, 44:9, 902–6.

Robertson, R. (1992), *Globalization – Social Theory and Global Culture*, London, Sage.

Robinson, F. (1997), Rights, relationships and responsibilities: the limits of a human rights approach to international ethics, ISA, Toronto, 18–23 March.

Rosas, A. (1995), State sovereignty and human rights: towards a global constitutional project, *Political Studies*, 43 (Special Issue), 61–79.

Rosenau, J. N. (1990), *Turbulence in World Politics*, Brighton, Harvester Wheatsheaf.

Rosenau, J. N. (1992), Citizenship in a changing global order, in J. N. Rosenau and E. O. Czempiel (eds), *Governance without Government*, Cambridge, Cambridge University Press, 272–94.

Ruggie, J. (1993), Territoriality and beyond, *International Organization*, 41:1, 139–74.

Sandel, M. (1996), *Democracy's Discontent*, Cambridge, MA, Harvard.

Sassen, S. (1996), *Losing Control? Sovereignty in an Age of Globalization*, New York, Columbia University Press.

Scholte, J. A. (1993), *International Relations of Social Change*, Buckingham, Open University Press.

Shaw, M. (1994), *Global Society and International Relations*, Cambridge, Polity Press.

Tarrow, S. (1994), *Power in Movement: Social Movements, Collective Action and Politics*, Cambridge, Cambridge University Press.

UN Development Programme (1997), *Human Development Report 1997*, Oxford, Oxford University Press.

Vincent, J. (1986), *Human Rights and International Relations*, Cambridge, Cambridge University Press.

Walzer, M. (1995), The concept of civil society, in M. Walzer (ed.), *Toward a Global Civil Society*, Providence, RI, Berghahn Books.

Weiss, L. (1998) (forthcoming), *State Capacity – Governing the Economy in a Global Era*, Cambridge, Polity Press.

Zurn, M. (1995), The challenge of globalization and individualization, in H. H. Holm and G. Sorensen (eds), *Whose World Order?*, Boulder, CO, Westview Press.

# 9

# The Third World and human rights in the post-1989 world order

*Johan Galtung*

### Three concepts: 'Third World', 'human rights' and 'post-1989'

This chapter will attempt to analyse the current world from three angles at the same time: the Third World, human rights and the post-1989 situation. Fifty years have passed since the Universal Declaration of Human Rights was passed by resolution of the United Nations General Assembly in 1948, and soon-'post-1989' will have completed its first decade. At the time the Declaration came into being, most of the countries of the Third World were engaged in a bitter struggle against colonial exploitation, including the demands for self-determination and economic, social and cultural rights. However, accepting Kwame Nkhrumah's term 'neo-colonialism' or not, statehood self-determination and the achievements of international law on human rights have not relieved the misery of many millions living in the Third World. Indeed, while there is still much talk about narrowing the poverty gap between the First and Third Worlds, the last decade has seen the decline of the ex-socialist world to levels of misery close to those already experienced in the Third World for the bottom half of society.

This chapter explores the three concepts and their three relationships. One conclusion is that even if human rights in general, and the Covenant on Economic, Social and Cultural Rights in particular, were really implemented, economic and social conditions in most Third World countries would continue to decline. Human rights are generally understood as individual rights, and may be used to rescue individuals from repression and misery. But they are guaranteed by states, and the rights of states are being eroded from without and within by globalization and privatization. The Charter of Economic Rights and Duties of States (CERDS), is dead. Hence, the problem to be discussed is whether, given the current conditions, states in general, and the Third World states in particular, are in a position to implement the human rights they have ratified.

It will be suggested here that two measures would ease the plight of the Third World: *globalization of human rights*, with joint world responsibility for their implementation, and *cultural equality in human rights*, to protect Third World cultures from further cultural and political erosion.

But first some introductory remarks to define the three concepts, or ideas, under discussion here.

The *Third World* will be conceived of here as the lower class of states in the world inter-state system. 'Class' is then conceived of in terms of four forms of power, namely:

- political power: the power to decide over others;
- military power: the power to invade/intervene/force others;
- economic power: the power to exploit others; and
- cultural power: the power to implant norms/values in others.

A strong definition of 'Third World' would be countries not members of the world upper-class 'clubs' (such as the Security Council, NATO, EU, OECD, G8), *and* invaded/intervened by such countries, *and* exploited by them through trade relations across vast gaps in degree of processing (raw materials against processed goods), *and* being receivers, not senders of culture. A weaker definition would substitute *or* for *and*; but we shall stick to the strong definition. By analogy, a true 'First World' is not decided over, not invaded, not exploited, not influenced by others. No such country exists, however, so here a weaker definition may be more appropriate. This also allows for a 'middle class' Second World, sometimes on top, sometimes at the bottom. This middle-class concept in global stratification differs from the cold war use of 'Second World' (meaning socialist countries), which was intended to describe a sphere of Russian domination both inside and outside the Soviet Union.

Thus, the conceptualization of the 'Third World' used here is broader than the economistic term 'less developed countries' (LDC). It is the bottom class of the state system. Whether this class of countries is organized and capable of solidarity, joint action, is not of the essence. In a still feudal world system, the 'most developed' overlords will continue to see the Third World as being in 'their' zones of influence. To change this, power relations must be altered. This can be done by acquiring upper-class power resources; joining the upper-class club that decides, invades, exploits and brainwashes lower-class states (countervailing power, 'power over others'), or by becoming more autonomous, through self-determination, defensive defence, equitable trade and dialogue (self-reliance, 'power-over-oneself') (Galtung 1980, 61–79).

A *human right* is a triadic construction with a norm-sender in the 'international community' (United Nations General Assembly, UNGA), norm-receivers in the state system (Member States), and individuals as norm-objects, thus linking international and municipal (domestic) law. The construction is vertical, state-centred, even stato-cratic. It is a system for the protection of individuals, with special emphasis on categories like women and children. The major human rights instruments, together constituting the International Bill of Human Rights, are the Universal Declaration of Human Rights, the two major Covenants (ICESCR and ICCPR and the Optional Protocol to the ICCPR). By signing and ratifying human rights instruments a state makes itself doubly accountable: to the UN organs and to their own citizens. Groups of individuals are protected, with nations, not gender, generation and class as norm-objects.[1] Thus, there is a right to national self-determination, but not to gender, generation and class self-determination.

The western historical stamp on the process whereby a bourgeois class replaced the power of a clergy by faith, and an aristocracy by birth, is unmistakable. Human rights became a major part of the world system, internalized in millions of individuals and to some extent institutionalized within and between states. But this does not mean that some, or most of the rights generated and promoted by western civilization are universal or even generally acceptable. However, as argued elsewhere (Galtung 1994), the contributions of non-western civilizations to universal rights have not (yet) been considered.

A basic justification for the claim that human rights are universal would be that they serve to meet human needs for survival, well-being, freedom and identity (Galtung 1996, Introduction). Justification of universal human rights by trying to universalize western historical processes as if they were *per definitionem* on behalf of humanity, smacks of colonialism. Rooting the justification in the norm-production process (UNGA) is not much better.

There is a problem, however. Human needs are met at the *individual* level, *in* human individuals.[2] But satisfying individuals may not change the class structure of the *state* system. Moreover, using western rights only will reinforce the cultural dimension of the massive power asymmetry in the world.

The *post-1989 world order* is characterized by a 'single superpower' capable of pursuing 'globalization/privatization' in the fields of *cultural power*, particularly in the organization of the media; and of *economic power*, with very high mobility for products and all production factors, except labour, facilitating the operation of transnational corporations, and the spread of US products. In short, a steeper hierarchy of states. This puts the relative position of the USA and the Soviet Union during the cold war into sharper focus, in several ways:

- the Soviet Union's bid for parity relative to the USA provided countervailing power, visible in such things as the UN veto system and the military system of balance of terror;
- the fear that people, groups of people, countries and groups of countries might favour the Soviet Union made the USA less ideologically fundamentalist in its exercise of power;

- the Soviet Union championed decolonization from western powers, but then established its own Third World class in Eastern Europe.

The demise of the Soviet Union has laid the world open for the United States to pursue its 'manifest destiny' to universalize the 'American Dream' in such instruments as NAFTA in the western hemisphere and NATO expansion, the WTO and the other institutions for globalization in the whole world.[3] In the cold war period, the Third World faced two northern fundamentalisms, to some extent cancelling out each other. In the post-1989 order, the South is exposed to only one fundamentalism and, predictably, responds with fundamentalisms of its own.

The days of balancing one superpower against the other, of extracting more aid from one by threatening to lean towards the other, are gone for the time being, although new power centres may emerge.[4] All this at a time when human needs are not met, as amply documented by UNDP Human Development Report publications.[5] With capital using increasingly productive technologies, permanent work positions are lost to contracts, long term or short term, and to unemployment.[6] With the state losing tax revenue because firms and jobs are exported, instruments for the redistribution of welfare are lost, in both the First and the Third World.[7]

## Three relationships and their consequences

### THIRD WORLD AND HUMAN RIGHTS

If the Third World concept is located in the state system, and the human rights idea is essentially individual oriented, and intra-state more than inter-state, then the Third World-human rights relationship is problematic. Improving the human rights situation, even along many dimensions of human rights, does not make a state immune to decision making, intervention, exploitation and penetration from the outside. The exclusive clubs for First World states continue. Military intervention may take place precisely because of human right deficits created by being at the bottom of the world community of states. Threats of withdrawal of 'most favoured Nation' status and political/economic sanctions are part of world politics, but not to be directed against the western pinnacle.[8] On top of all of this comes the massive cultural transfer built into the essence of the human rights formula, as it is composed today (Galtung 1994, ch. 1).

In short, even if human rights were realized for individuals by implementing the 1966 Covenants, the class structure of the state system might continue unabated, or even be strengthened.[9] On top of this comes, of course, the question of whether and how the human rights tradition can be helpful at all in meeting basic individual needs in Third World countries, given the penetration from the First World globalization and weak, inefficient, often corrupt states as norm-receivers. If we think of the Third World in the classical sense as less developed countries (LDC), even with L = least, then it is difficult to see how basic material needs can be met when the employment structure eliminates rather than creates positions with sufficient wages, at the same time as the state has less resources available to manage the redistribution. It is also worth noting that the main norm-sender in the state system, the USA, has not ratified the ICESCR.[10]

## THIRD WORLD AND POST-1989

The Third World and post-1989 globalization/privatization relationship is characterized by state power being eroded by making borders so porous that almost anything can enter. A Third World journalist working for the local CNN bureau is the closest the Third World seems to come to a new international communications order. The language spoken is an old colonial language. In some countries, like the Great Lakes region in Africa, the problem today may be which colonial language. A future with schooling over the Internet from metropolitan centres seems near, in line with the globalization of the post-1989 era.

Economic penetration not only substitutes foreign colas and tinned food for local beverages and foodstuffs, but – by buying land – gradually eliminates the age-old subsistence sector. The state, having entered the Faustian deal summarized in the World Trade Organization (WTO), has rendered itself impotent outwardly through globalization, and inwardly through privatization (except for a short period living off the proceeds from the sales of publicly run utilities). The problem is no longer that Third World states are at the bottom of the cultural and economic power hierarchies, but whether Third World states can continue to exist economically and culturally at all.

But this is less true for military power and political power. As other sectors shrink, the military budget increases relatively and absolutely. Some of that power may be used to discipline a restive population, some to fight with neighbours over such scarce resources as water. Some power may one day be directed against metropolitan powers, but unpredictable terrorism is more likely given power asymmetry. Democracy and human rights may make the political power of a Third World state more legitimate, but with the economy globalized, in the hands of the TNCs, and money privatized in countries with shrinking public sectors, relatively speaking, there may be less resources available to alleviate misery.[11]

## HUMAN RIGHTS AND POST-1989

The relationship between human rights and globalization-privatization is itself being globalized-privatized by the many NGOs in human rights in general, and by Amnesty International in particular. The state serves as a mail box for complaints from below (people, NGOs) and above (the UN

Human Rights Commission). With the funds for *l'état provident* seriously curtailed *l'état gendarme* looks more naked and brutal. Thus, even First World states will no longer be able to provide the free education, free health services, unemployment benefits and pensions to which people have become accustomed. Serious cut-backs to these services seem inevitable. Third World states will provide even less of what little they currently provide.

With enormous funds accumulating in the private sector, national and transnational, the question is whether we are in for *la corporation providente.*[12] But, so far, it looks rather as if corporate funds are searching for even more profit by switching from the real to the finance economy, speculating, and in the process pushing the Dow beyond the 8,000 level. What might happen would be globalization not only of education, but of other basic needs, with giant health corporations and pension funds in search of global markets, for those who can afford the fees. The local jobless, whether they lost permanent positions or contracts, would reach enormous proportions.

However, given the mobility of products and factors, except for labour, the Achilles heel of the whole system is the mass of people not only without permanent positions, but even without short-term contracts. If they are estimated at one billion or more (10 per cent of that in China alone), then the problem of policing becomes a major one. The FBI does that job for the USA, Schengen is the EU equivalent, Japan is an island far away, and other rich pockets will probably also be transformed into fortresses. The human rights situation for those on the outside will be abysmal. Ultimately, after much suffering, this may have the consequence that the focus of nationhood will shift 'away from issues of sovereignty and self-determination toward global human rights independent of national boundaries' (Anderson 1997).

## The next step: globalized human rights

But then the lighter side: if so much of the rest of the world is globalized, why not also human rights? What follows are some explorations of what that might mean to that fascinating, once upon a time highly innovative, triadic construction.

For human rights to meet human needs in the context of globalization and privatization, the form of the human right, and some of the content, will have to be reconsidered. There will still be three parties, norm-senders, norm-receivers and norm-objects, for that is in the very conception of a norm, although two of them – perhaps all three – may coalesce. Consider the following:

- as *norm-sender*, a democratized United Nations with an elected United Nations People's Assembly (UNPA), a UN Parliament;[13]
- as *norm-receiver*, a nexus of actors, including IGOs, regions, states, communes, TNCs, NGOs, all pledging with their signatures;

- as *norm-objects*, individuals, but also categories of individuals (women, children, those in misery) and some groups (families, tribes), depending on local circumstances, see Galtung (1994).

If the present system is, to a large extent, stato-cratic, then this system would be less so. UN parliamentarians would enter less as state representatives than as global citizens from that state constituency; and the UNPA could gradually become the norm-sender rather than the UNGA. The norm-receivers would be more diverse, distributing the task of seeing to it that human right norms are implemented in a more globalized, and also privatized manner. And the norm-objects would also be more diverse, opening for collective rights of various kinds. There would be a universal nucleus, but room for regional variation.

## Another next step: global citizenship

To be a citizen implies rights but also duties to a central authority. Countries may be high or low on rights and/or duties, but among the 200 or more countries, the global population and the world as a whole do not figure, so there are no global citizens, neither *de facto*, nor *de jure*. Citizens have duties to their own state, not to other states, nor to the world. There may be regional citizens, however, like 'Europeans',[14] meaning citizens of a member state of the European Union, and a million or more different types of municipal citizens; but no global citizens. To some people this has been so unsatisfactory that they have responded to globalism long before any world state has come into being. For example, attempts have been made to create world religions (Baha'i), world languages (Esperanto), and world citizenship with world passport (Garry Davis),[15] but so far none has been universally recognized.

The simplest way of thinking about global citizenship is the way we think about any citizenship in the modern world. We assume a codified social contract defining the relation between ruler and ruled, the ruled being citizens, not merely subjects. The rulers exercise power inside a society in the four forms familiar to the world state system mentioned earlier:

- *political*/decision-making power: you do because it was decided;
- *military*/coercive/stick power: you do or else you will suffer;
- *economic*/contractual/carrot power: you do and you will benefit;
- *cultural*/normative power: you do because you know it is right.

These forms of power are successful, bringing about compliance, if the ruled are submissive, frightened, dependent or weak on identity. If the ruled are autonomous, fearless, self-sufficient and have a strong identity, power-from-above will not be effective. The latter is probably the type of soft citizenship any democracy needs (local, national, regional or global) to become dynamic. But some less democratic rulers may prefer the former, 'governable', type, and aim at a (very) hard citizenship at the cost of a non-participatory population.

Which of the two types is needed for global citizenship? The answer given here is in favour of soft global citizenship as opposed to the hard approach. This means global citizenship with a lot of local autonomy, fearlessness, self-sufficiency and identity. But what would a global citizen expect from a world central authority? Here are four formulations, using the four forms of power:

- a global citizen would have reasons to expect that his opinion matters, and has an impact on how world society is run;
- a global citizen would have reasons to feel protected against major violence, in the triple sense that all will be done to transform conflicts before they enter a violent stage; that all will be done to contain violence should it occur; and that violence exercised by a world central authority will be minimal;
- a global citizen would have reasons to expect that consistent efforts are made to provide a livelihood for all, generally by providing gainful employment for all, with an income sufficient to provide for basic material needs;
- a global citizen would have reasons to expect that the world is a home where his/her basic non-material or spiritual needs are met. Local communities may create their own meanings out of old or new cultural material, with no right to impose that meaning on others, but including a duty to engage in dialogues with others about their meanings.

Some countries already provide these conditions, particularly those characterized by democracy, security, welfare and tolerance. The question is whether a country could serve as a model for the world as a whole, taking the step from globalized rights to global citizenship. There has to be a legal, institutional basis that could combine soft governance with the (reasonable) expectations mentioned above.

More concretely, the expectations could be translated into increasingly concrete entitlements and duties, relative to a UN-based world central authority for soft global governance (Galtung 1980, 341–52):[16]

- a global citizen is *entitled* to free expression of how a world society should be run, to be free to assemble, and to representation through a free and secret ballot in something like a United Nations People's Assembly; and the *duty* to participate in elections;
- a global citizen is *entitled* to protection against violence in the sense that all will be done to transform conflicts before they become violent, that violence is contained, that violence exercised by a world central authority will be minimal; and has the *duty* to serve in peacekeeping by peaceful means, either in a military or civilian capacity;
- a global citizen is *entitled* to a decent livelihood through access to gainful employment with income sufficient to provide for basic material needs; and the *duty* to pay global taxes;
- a global citizen is *entitled* to a cultural identity based on old and new cultural

material, with no right to impose his identity on others, but with a *duty* to show respect when engaging in dialogues with others about their meanings and identities.

This is all within the human rights tradition,[17] but articulates human duties in addition. In the stato-cratic system these duties were taken for granted. The duty to *vote* for a world central authority assembly like a United Nations People's Assembly, to *serve* in peacekeeping forces, to *pay* global taxes and to *relate* to other cultures in a spirit of respect and curiosity would assume their place alongside the rights.

This is still for the future, but perhaps a less distant future than people believe. Thus, TNCs may one day wake up and discover that strong NGOs capable of organizing consumer strikes have entered the global marketplace, perhaps backed by world central authorities. Of course, if organized groups are to impress anybody by refusing to purchase, consumers must have the necessary resources, which the poor do not have. Therefore, the poor would be disenfranchised through lack of financial resources and unable to gain a voice in the global economy once again.

## And one more step: cultural equality in human rights

The number of those suffering starvation in the world is increasing, but, it may be argued, the Third World does not live by bread alone. Like everywhere else there is a spiritual, cultural dimension. Much of that has a human rights angle, as the human rights tradition tends to favour one type of culture at the expense of others. One way of entering this problem would be to explore culture by means of a very simplified dichotomy: 'I-cultures' (mainly western) v. 'we-cultures' (mainly non-western); related to Panikkar's distinction between knots and nets (Panikkar 1982).

Typical of an I-culture is the emphasis on that Western construction, the individual, free to make decisions, uncoerced by social ties. If the individual adheres to values of altruism and solidarity, then this is by free choice. The outcome is society as a stage for individuals, strong or weak, active or passive, good or evil, enacting their will in regulated manners. The individual is the sum of what is inside the individual, by nature and nurture, and society is the sum of those individuals. Biological death is the end of individuals unless reincarnation is granted (Hinduism), or eternal life (Christianity, Islam).

In we-cultures, individuals come densely packed in a web of social relations; a 'we', a tribe, a clan, families (extended or nuclear), friends, neighbours, colleagues in organizations and associations and in nations and states. Individuals can be seen as the sum of these social relations. With no social relations the individual is (socially) dead. Social death may come before biological death (banishment, ostracism) or coincide with it. It may also come after biological death, for example, when the person no longer lives in the mind of anybody alive. Lastly, it may never come, perhaps because a person is always remembered or is reborn (Buddhism). Solidarity with 'we', even altruism, is normal. Ego-assertiveness, as a free-standing individual at anybody's expense, is an anomaly. Too much assertiveness may lead to social death and ostracism, such as found in primitive and traditional societies or smaller communities everywhere, e.g. Japan. While there are pockets of we-culture in modern societies, the postmodern society is particularly anomic and very dominated by I-culture (Galtung 1996a).

The dialectic between I-cultures and we-cultures is an indelible part of the human condition. At the individual level the dialectic comes as a personal dilemma between the freedom of the 'I' and the solidarity with the 'we'. At the social level there will be forces favouring one or the other horn of this dilemma, for example, a dominant I- or we-culture attempting to suppress instances of we- or I-culture living on the periphery.[18] Christian cultures are afraid of Muslim minorities, seen as collectivities threatening the social order. Islamic countries may find organized Christian minorities chaotic and unpredictable in their individualism. At the world level this is the struggle between nations and states dominated by I-cultures and we-cultures, a theme very well known in the present world,[19] where, as mentioned, most I-cultures are in the First World and most we-cultures in the Third World.

Take democracy as one example. There is no doubt that the practice of formal *debate* is a perfect, potentially elegant, practice for competitive individuals, out to corner an opponent in a verbal duel, *schlagfertig* (note the language of violence), epitomized by the Oxford Union. And there is no doubt that a *vote* can be very divisive, polarizing a collectivity into sub-collectivities. Criss-crossing divisions may be even more fragmenting and atomizing than polarization along the same faultline, dividing one 'we' always into the same two 'we's'.

Generally, debates and votes divide. On the other hand, the *dialogue* may unify, preserving the we-culture in a joint search for solutions, through shared brain-storming (Galtung 1988). The *consensus* (as opposed to the vote) may solidify it further. And, again no doubt, consensus can also serve as a basis for democracy in the sense of rule with the consent of the ruled.[20]

Take human rights as another example. Basic needs are ultimately satisfied in individuals, but (basic) rights can also apply to collective norm-objects. Human rights law derived from western law and I-culture in general, would use individuals as norm-objects (an important exception being the collective right of self-determination). Given the major imbalance in favour of I-culture, is it fair to demand that all we-cultures follow suit?

Take the Salman Rushdie case. That *The Satanic Verses* is a blasphemous book is obvious to a Muslim true believer. Sacrilege has been committed against key symbols of a we-culture, leading to a fatwa, mobilizing the faithful to come to the rescue of the faith, the cement of that culture, even to the point of killing Rushdie. That a fatwa in such serious matters does not respect secular trivialities as national borders and jurisdictions is also obvious. Christians would probably have come to a similar conclusion some centuries ago. That all of this is in stark contradiction with the *individual* freedom of expression enshrined in the I-culture is equally obvious. How do we identify a positive transformation of this conflict?

Take the case of sects, presently a major concern in the USA, Germany, Japan and, above all, in France, where secularism is a state faith and sects seen as a challenge to that faith/authority. Sects are islands of we-culture in seas of I-culture. As such they serve important integrative functions in individualizing, postmodern societies, suffering from anomie/atomie.[21] No doubt they often have totalitarian aspects, the step from total (*intégriste*) to totalitarian being short. This may show up as psycho-social manipulation of members, social and financial exploitation, contempt and rejection of surrounding society, authoritarian/hierarchical structures with no real debate, splitting of family, friends, colleagues and distancing from community, political parties, country, state.[22] It should be noted that entering from an I-culture is an easy individual decision whereas exiting from the sect, a we-culture, is difficult. It is a rupture with a *corpus mysticum*, a social death of the individual, and partial death of those left behind.

Take the debate pitting the West against Malaysia-Singapore, argued articulately by Prime Minister Mahathir and ex-Prime Minister Lee Kuan Yew.[23] The Confucian-based argument privileges we-culture over I-culture; as fostering not only economic growth, but also economic distribution. But who are 'we'?

If 'we' stands for the family/clan then the net result might be a limitation of the right of divorce, an enforcement of the solidarity with the family, extended and/or nuclear, in short, not so different from the US concept of 'family values'. But there may also be an important economic implication limiting individual and egoistic market behaviour in favour of family/clan, in other words constraining the individual as a juridical person. In practice 'family values' may reinforce patriarchy, and the rule of parents, but does not have to do so. Rather, it points in the direction of family we-logic rather than an I-logic for market behaviour, which may be problematic from the point of view of Western, economistic fundamentalism.

If 'we' stands for the nation/state then a Pandora's box of problems opens up. The norms of the state are known as laws, breaking the law as crime (and keeping the law as 'discipline'), enforcing the law as punishment. Privileging we-culture implies strict and public reinforcement since the crime is against the public 'we', not against an individual self, or God. The public cannot witness twenty years of time/freedom punishment being meted out to the criminal on a day-by-day basis. But they may witness physical punishment events like public whipping and beheading.[24] But what if the 'crime' is freedom of expression, having a direct Internet access abroad, even one carrying non-family values? And, what if those who demand this access are actually collectivities, like families? One 'we' against the other?

Finally, take the general case of Christianity v. Islam, a struggle that has lasted almost 1,400 years (from the start of Islam in AD 622), and particularly the last 900 years (from the Declaration of the Crusades 27 November 1095). A general thesis would be that Islam (but more the Shi'a than the Sunni versions) would be more of a we-culture, and Christianity (but more the Protestant than the Catholic and orthodox versions) more of an I-culture. I-culture fragments humanity more, we-culture less.

But Christianity also segments humanity more than Islam, dividing life into compartments. For example, in Christianity detaching political life from religious life is legitimized through the idea of giving to Caesar what is Caesar's and to God what is God's (in Protestantism *Die Zwei Regimenten*). Detaching economic life from religious life also came as the result of a historical process, an important event being the Church capitulating to capital in no longer opposing interest (1495). Military life was detached through nationalism, fighting for the nation rather than for God. Gradually, religious life became a narrow segment of the human condition, as one segment after the other became secularized. Finally came the attack on faith itself, substituting reason, through the Enlightenment.[25]

Not so in Islam. Islam is *intégriste*, insisting on integration, not segmentation. Human beings should be seen in their totality, human action and relations should be the same. The religious is in all political, economic and military life: not nuclear weapons but Islamic nuclear weapons; war is in the name of the faith; economic transactions are religious rituals; priests are politicians and politicians are priests (*shari'a*). Islam and secularization are incompatible; it is one or the other. A demand on Islam to 'secularize' is tantamount to launching a new crusade.

To clarify this further, have a look at some important social processes. Once upon a time humanity, probably lived in holistic we-cultures, the way we usually picture a nomadic tribe (Redfield 1995). Another word would be undifferentiated, a humankind with individuals barely distinguishable except by their trivial biological borders, and with no division of labour except by trivial gender and age borders. Imagine a similar image of an 'undifferentiated' nature, not divided into 'realms' of animals, plants and minerals with all the subdivisions, nor with borders defining the property of persons or nations. Then imagine that these two undifferentiated sets coalesce, that even borders between humankind and nature become unclear, like the border between the body and the air it breathes.

And then introduce differentiation, some kind of mitosis, in this undifferentiated whole. Humankind is separated from nature. Humankind is then subdivided into 'juridical persons' (some individual, some collective) defined as actual or potential *owners*, and both humankind and nature are subdivided into parts that can be *owned* (owned human individuals are called slaves, family members can be owned by the *pater familias*, owned peoples are called colonies). Connect these differentiated sets through the introduction of one relation, *dominium*, ownership, relating owner and owned. A human being is now defined by how much he owns rather than by how many others he relates to. And personal and social growth start yielding to economic growth; the use of property to create even more property.

Then follow two thousand years of differentiation, with fragmentation of human society and segmentation of everything, eagerly pursued by sciences, including geometry for measuring and drawing lines on *geo*, and arithmetic to measure the values of the owned. Market transactions are based on equal for equal.

I am, of course, describing a process related to Roman law, another pillar of western civilization. By what right, except might, can a fragmentation and segmentation culture be imposed on a solidarity and integration culture? Or vice versa?

Take the Roman law doctrine of *res comunis = res nullius*, what is owned by everybody ('in common') is owned by nobody, a principle used to justify land-grabbing in the colonies. Lines were drawn, owner-owned relations were established (those over slaves and colonials), including the right to destroy (kill) them. One logic was imposed on another, justified by seeing differentiation as evolutionary, as the characteristic of higher species as opposed to undifferentiated, primitive protozoa. This type of thinking is probably still prominent.

The argument made in the context of cultural struggle is not so much over any primacy of ownership as over the primacy of differentiation. The thesis is that just as there are limits to growth there are also limits to differentiation.[26] Segmentation may lead to the lack of steering known as anomie, a deep sense of confusion, being exposed to incompatible demands from different segments, not only in society but inside oneself, especially between the sacred and secular sectors.

In Europe this is exacerbated by giving the human soul to the Church and the human body to state, capital and civil society. With dissolution of the social fabric through fragmentation, atomie sets in, a state of atomization into individual atoms. Groups will grow, delinquent or sectarian, with solidarity and integration, in search of social fabric. But just as detaching the individual atom from a social molecule is dramatic, re-embedding the individual in a non-fragmented, non-segmented collectivity is also dramatic because of the conflict between I- and we-cultures. The price for security inside a we-group is often conflict with the surrounding I-culture, with the possibility of insecurity.

Are there solutions to these gigantic problems? Are all of them one way or the other rooted in the contradiction between I-cultures and we-cultures? The contradiction is at three levels:

- as an existential dilemma inside millions, billions of people;
- as a sociopolitical problem inside intolerant societies;
- as a geopolitical problem between (groups of) societies.

More particularly, are there solutions inside the framework of human rights, as they stand, or as they could be improved?

All we can do here is indicative, using the seven examples as points of departure.

*I-cultures* versus *we-cultures*: the basic point is to recognize and respect their existence and their dialectic, their *yin/yang* relation, at least in our present world, and any world relatively similar to the present. If freedom and identity are among the basic human needs, then people will strive to satisfy them. To strive for individual freedom is easy within an I-culture, to strive for collective identity is easy within a we-culture. But how about both, and at the same time? Easy if one of the cultures tolerates the other, easy in a mixed culture. Somehow to be a member of two worlds has to be a human right. The implication of this idea will then be explored in the points to follow, as they are all variations on the same theme.

*Democracy*: there is no reason to believe that debates and dialogues, voting and consensus, exclude each other in any absolute sense. The leaders of a party need a dialogue among themselves to clarify the issues they want to present to the public for debate; people may then carry that dialogue further. What is missing today is more respect for the dialogue culture, and for we-cultures where dialogue/consensus, or moves in that direction, may be more appropriate as a basis for democracy.

*Human rights*: the implication is more recognition of 'group rights', meaning the rights of certain categories of human beings (women, children; old people); the rights of groups of human beings (families, clans; how about habitats?); and the right to live in unorthodox communities (cooperatives, sects). Improvements in the recognition of group rights must, however, remain compatible with I-culture rights, like the right not to be a member, to withdraw, to change allegiance. But such rights do not come about by themselves. No recognition will come forth without struggle; for the rights of I-cultures inside we-cultures, and we-cultures inside I-cultures.

*Salman Rushdie*: Salman Rushdie claimed freedom of expression in defence of his actions, and in the process probably hurt the collective identity of the thousands, maybe millions. One of the formulations used in the Biel Declaration of 27 November 1995[27] *To End the Crusades: A Peace Declaration*, may be useful: 'we ask followers of both religions not to abuse the freedom of speech when speaking and writing about the other religion'. In other words, there are limits to the freedom of expression, preferably self-imposed. There are sensitivities that should be respected. Not to do so is verbal violence hurting and harming the soul, even if the body remains unmolested.

The formula is problematic, to put it mildly. Anyone may claim that his/her identity has been hurt when collective symbols have been attacked, doubted or rule out, for instance, the burning of the flag (the US parallel to the Rushdie case even if this is not understood in the USA). One possible way out might be to recognize the right of a collectivity claiming hurt to launch a libel action, where the truth or relevance of an allegation could be tested and the intention to hurt or harm examined. The problem will not go away by choosing one horn of the dilemma: unlimited freedom of individual expression, unlimited control in the name of collective sensitivity.

But what of the fatwa against Rushdie? The argument against cannot be based on extra-territoriality, on Rushdie not living in Iran. The long arm of Israel caught up with Eichmann in Argentina in 1967; and that of the USA with Noriega in Panama in 1989. The merits of the cases differ, but with justice-across-borders in common. The Inquisition did not respect borders either,[28] but the argument that its days are over is based on the supposition that western history is synonymous with universal history. There is even an underlying assumption of synchronicity: Islam is 'behind' and should catch up. The idea that western time constitutes universal time is an assumption as intolerable as it is intolerant, as if Islam has no right to its own track through history. History is seen as a train with the western engine pulling the other wagons on a track selected by a western engineer. However, those who continue to accept such assumption may be in for some surprises.

A better argument against the fatwa would invoke human rights against cruel and unusual punishment, directed at both capital punishment and the terrorist unpredictability of its mode of execution. The problem with this argument is the number of states, some with high prestige in the international community, with capital punishment on their statutes. They would prefer arguments that focus on Islam or extra-territoriality.

*Sects*: in principle this is relatively well covered by human rights: 'freedom of assembly' guarantees the right to enter a sect, as do the 'freedom of thought' and the 'freedom of expression' give the right to leave. An explicit 'freedom of disassembly', however, would have been useful.[29] Modern societies should be grateful to sects for offering a home for some of the countless homeless in societies with growth-torn fabrics. But individuals wanting to leave might need the support of an SOS system. Sects are not extra-territorial regardless of the truth they claim: they are accountable to the laws of the land and of the world, such as human rights. The solution lies in a more symmetric attitude to I- and we-cultures, not automatically favouring one over the other.

*The West* versus *the rest* (at least Malaysia-Singapore): a case could be built on similarities between sects and families/clans. The latter are major centres of brainwashing, and entry is even more easy, by the sheer fact of birth. Exit is even more difficult, and not even by death in some cases. Would it be possible both to recognize families/clans as *ipso facto* juridical persons and at the same time guarantee an individual's right to leave, constitute or join another juridical person? A culture so destructive of social fabric as the West, and in addition relatively blind to the significance of that factor, should enter this heavily mined moral/legal territory with care and humility. And so should cultures unwilling to relinquish their hold on individuals, using social fabric, i.e., social ties exactly as that, to tie them. As in the case of sects, there is a need for much rethinking and reformulating.

How about the nation and the state? Much of what has been said about sects and families/clans above can also be said about nations: entry by birth, exit never. Even within an overriding I-culture the nation defines a we-culture, offering protection in return for loyalty. There are sensitivities, and those who challenge sensitivities may have to suffer the consequences.

The state is different: citizenship may be acquired (only rarely bestowed), and may be relinquished (and sometimes withdrawn). The rights to citizenship is a 'we-right', the freedom of expression is an 'I-right'. The problem is that we need both rights, and that seriously limits the right of the state to limit the freedom of expression and assembly across borders. Unless, that is, the state can argue that a specific content is conducive to criminal acts, like the West argues in connection with drugs and child pornography. Advertising (the right to know) drugs and child pornography is not protected by the freedom of expression (and rightly so, most will probably agree); advertising arms and tobacco is protected (and wrongly so, many would probably agree). All four can cause enormous destruction and suffering for the 'we'; all four can bring enormous income to the 'I'. What is the more important task of the state, to protect the freedom of expression of some individuals or the livelihood of people in general? Obviously both, but the human rights tilt in favour of the individuals.

*Christianity* versus *Islam*: the inability of Christianity and Islam, the two largest religious communities, and with the singularist claim to exclusive truth and the universalist claim to universal validity, to live in peace is a bad omen for a humanity about to enter the third millennium. They both have to accommodate the other with mutual respect and dialogues.

The present author has on some occasions organized dialogues between Christians and Muslims, encouraging both to articulate what they fear most, and what attracts them most, in the other religion.[30] What they fear most is quickly said: the status of women in Islam (AlMunajjed 1997), and doctrines of holy wars imputed to both religions (in fact, holy wars are neither Biblical, nor Koranic). What they admire most takes more time to surface, especially for the Christians. But some Christians refer to the we-culture of Islam, a tightly spun identity not torn by doubts and diversities. And that I-culture aspect is exactly what some Muslims admire in Christianity: the freedom to choose interpretations, including the freedom to choose secularism.

In this there is no argument to the effect that Islam should be more permissive of secularism and Christianity less. The argument would be at the individual level in terms of the right to exit and the right to (re-)enter. Neither Islam, nor Christianity, can be reduced to the sum of adherents and their beliefs. Nor can it be reduced to the interpretations held by the powers that be. For the true believers these are revealed messages, even an entire religion in the case of Islam.[31] For others they are highly complex systems of belief undergoing some change but probably in the periphery more than in the core of the doctrine. That debate is outside the realm of human rights. But human rights should guarantee the right of entry and exit.

## Conclusion: the three concepts revisited

What are the conclusions emerging from this exercise?

First, the Third World is in deep crisis because sovereignty and statehood are eroding. But this is the crisis of the state system in general; the states yielding upward to IGOs, regions and super-states, downward to local communities including cities and sub-states, sideward to NGOs, TNCs.

Second, globalization today takes the form of a single-peaked state system with very weak bottom layers; in its place will have to come global governance making states accountable to elected representatives, bringing in IGOs, NGOs, TNCs, and the local communities; in short, a variety of global actors.

Third, this will change the structure as well as the content of human rights; making human rights less stato-cratic, more global and geared to human needs all over the world.

Last, along that line, a concept of global citizenship will have to take shape; if the state cannot care for its citizens, then the world will have to care for global citizens with the help of all global actors including what remains of states.

In other words, the assumption is not at all the unimpeded continuation of neoliberal expansion in the interest of the First World. The world, like anything human, is dialectic: any *actio* will meet its *reactio*. Democracy as a way of organizing a polity will sooner or later reach the global level, and the First World will then run up against a very hard fact: the First World represents a small minority of the world's peoples. The First World has globalized the media and business, but in doing so it has also globalized people's communication (the Internet), people's businesses (e.g., direct barter across borders) and people's actions (consumer strikes). The forces from which many powerful actors try to escape in their domestic dealings, like organized labour, women or consumer organizations may reappear in a much stronger form at the global level. Globalized human rights, global citizenship and world dialogue over how to reconcile I-cultures and we-cultures may dominate the agenda sooner than the First World envisages. And sooner or later a more humane world might even come into being, even under globalization/privatization.

## Notes

1  Of course, the basic principle of international law to establish valid title to territory is effective occupancy. But both 1966 Covenants state in their Article 1 that 'All peoples have a right to self-determination. By virtue of that right they freely determine their political status and freely pursue their economic, social and cultural development.' A very strong and contested statement. Nothing similar exists for gender, generation and class.

2  To meet human needs membership in a group may be a necessary condition; only very few individuals are known to survive as hermits. Groups can provide protection against violence and death as well as a livelihood for well-being. And membership in a group may be crucial for a sense of identity, for most; just as non-membership may be crucial for a sense of freedom, for some. But the satisfaction, the very process of meeting a need, is inside the individual body, mind and spirit however much the collectivity may be instrumental.

3  Thus, the former chairman of the US Joint Chiefs of Staff, Colin Powell, still possibly a presidential candidate, argued in August 1995 that 'America had been created by divine providence to lead the world', *International Herald Tribune*, 31 August 1995.

4  The most likely one right now would be centred on China, and the predictable US posture is already expressed in Bernstein and Munro (1997). In bad 'international relations' theory (a misnomer, what is meant is inter-state theory, of inter-nation theory there is very little) the two biggest powers are supposed to be on a collision course. They may collide, they may not. A far better theory is expressed in the African proverbs, 'when elephants fight, the grass suffers' and 'when elephants make love, it is still the grass that suffers'. The reader will have understood that the present author sees self-reliance as a far more promising road for the Third World, but that has not been the road travelled except for parts of East Asia.

5  Published annually by the United Nations Development Programme, New York.

6  With more producers and higher productivity, supply will quickly outstrip demand. Either the number of workers, or the number of hours they work, will have to yield, in the first case leading to unemployment, the second to contracts rather than positions. Unfortunately, the word 'job' is used to cover both positions and contracts where the former has a connotation of solidity, with a living wage, and the latter a connotation of fragility (referred to as flexibility in global NewSpeak), and no living wage. It is worth pointing out that the Covenant on Economic, Social and Cultural Rights stipulates in Article 6, in connection with the right to work, fair wages to ensure a decent living for employees and their families. Evidently, fragmenting the working life into contracts places the whole burden on the employee.

7  For an analysis of this process during the Thatcher-Major years in Britain, see Hutton (1995, ch. 1).

8 One implication being, of course, that some may try to correct what they see as a justice deficit with terrorist means.

9 Countries with a good record of meeting basic human material needs – Cuba and Nicaragua in the western hemisphere and Libya and Iraq in the Middle East – have certainly been exposed to asymmetric power in the world state system. Some might even argue that implementing basic human needs was among the factors triggering the ire of the First World.

10 Moreover, what the states ratifying the Covenant actually agree to, according to Article 2, is to 'take steps, with a view to achieving progressively the full realization of the rights'. The rights have been described as programmatic, as expressions of intentions.

11 Latin American, African and South Asian countries should be watched with this in mind; Muslim and Confucian/Buddhist countries having distribution more built into their belief systems.

12 A model would be the classical Japanese company taking care of the welfare of its employees.

13 This is described in some detail as a background paper for the Commission on Global Governance prepared by the author.

14 A term resented by other Europeans like 'Americans' for US citizens is resented by the inhabitants of Mexico, Central and South America. To use the name of the whole for the part is bound to create problems.

15 A US former GI, operating out of Paris from the late 1940s, establishing a file of world citizens.

16 Actually, the system of norm-senders and norm-receivers indicated above would have the UN as a nucleus, but be much more complex and much less peaked. Again the model would be the good country where the state shares responsibility for the welfare of the citizens with a complex diversity of other actors.

17 Particularly the admirable formulation in Article 28 of the Universal Declaration, 'Everyone is entitled to a social and international order in which the rights and freedoms set forth in this Declaration can be fully realized'.

18 In Western democracies the struggle against sects might serve as one example; in communist countries with (often imposed) we-culture, individualistic dissidents may serve as an example.

19 It is not the whole story, but a significant part of the story of the relation between a self-assertive West on the one hand, and the Muslim world, the Hindu world and the Buddhist-Confucian world; with Catholic and orthodox Christianity having some kind of in-between position.

20 Democracy v. dictatorship may correlate with I-culture v. we-culture, after all, the democratic way of organizing political power is rooted in Protestant countries. But a we-culture country like Japan has been both, so has an I-culture country like Germany. A better question might be what kind of democracy or dictatorship? One answer might be: an I-culture might be predisposed to a debating/voting democracy, and to an authoritarian dictatorship; a we-culture to a collectivist dialogue/consensus democracy, and a totalitarian dictatorship.

21 Anomie = normlessness, or rather absence of compelling norms. Atomie = fragmentation, atomization, dissolution of social fabric; see Galtung (1996a). Sects certainly offer compelling norms, and they offer intense interaction, 'social fabric' in other words.

22 The list is taken from the answer by Soka Gakkai-Germany (SGI-D) to the first question of the Enquête-Kommission 'Sog. Sekten und Psychogruppen' of the German Parliament: 'How would you define a "sect"?' SGI-D mentions these characteristics

and shows how they do not apply to SGI-D. It is worth noting how these characteristics apply to the most important sect in today's world: the nation. The original
list of themes was composed by a French parliamentary commission.

23 For a standard western presentation of Singapore, see Buruma (1995); or an interesting rebuttal, also critical of Singapore, see Devan (1996). Devan's point is that
much of the authoritarianism of Singapore stems from a western technocratic/social-
ist model. For a very balanced view in this debate, see Diokno (1997). However, to
refer to these values and rights as 'Asian' is wrong: Asia is a mixture of I-cultures
and we-cultures, and the Confucian-Buddhist mix picked up by both Mahathir and
Lee is East Asia, including some parts of South East Asia.

24 An I-culture sees this as cruel; it is actually another idiom.

25 Of course the Enlightenment started much earlier than the seventeenth to eighteenth
centuries. One way of conceiving of secularization would be as follows: bring the
transcendental world into the empirical world. Thus, religious paradise becomes
ideological utopia (with Christian utopias as a transition formula); religious hell
becomes intensified, total warfare and torture (with Christian Inquisition as a transition formula); eternal life becomes if not eternal at least longer life spans through
healthcare; illumination becomes general education, etc.

26 A book crying to be written.

27 Organized by the Swiss Academy for Development (SAD) on the occasion of the
ninth centenary of the Declaration of the Crusades 27 November 1995; available
from SAD, Lindenhof, Bözingen Str. 71, CH–2500 BIEL/BIENNE, Switzerland.

28 Of course, the clerics of the Catholic Church constructed one Christianity overriding
the borders drawn by man, meaning aristocrats. It is difficult to see that Islam does
not have as much of a right to a similar construction of the world as the states to
defend themselves against such terrible implications and to enter into dialogue with
Islam to limit the exercise of power. But to argue that Islam has to accept western
world views is cultural neo-colonialism.

29 This is a general critique of many human rights formulations, like the right to work,
but not the right to non-work, the right to vacation but not the right not to take a
vacation, the right of assembly but not the right of dis-assembly, non-assembly. The
rights designate active, positive activities as rightful; they do not focus on abstention
from these activities.

30 For instance the meeting mentioned in note 6.

31 In the Qur'ān, Alla'h is revealing the Truth through the prophet; in the Bible there
are messages from God, e.g., through Abraham, Moses and Jesus Christ.

## References

Al Munajjed, M. (1997), *Women in Saudi Arabia Today*, London, Macmillan.

Anderson, W. T. (1997), 'Denizens': the weakening of national citizenship, *Global Times*,
May/June 1997, 6.

Bernstein, R. and R. H. Munro (1997), *The Coming Conflict with China*, New York, Knopf.

Buruma, I. (1995), The Singapore way, *New York Review of Books*, 19 October.

Devan, J. (1996), The Singapore way, *New York Review of Books*, 6 June.

Diokno, M. S. I. (1997), A Filipino perspective of the Asian values debate on human rights,
paper given at a workshop, Human Rights and Asian Values, Nordic Institute of Asian
Studies, Copenhagen.

Galtung, J. (1980), *The True Worlds: A Transnational Perspective*, New York, Macmillan/The
Free Press.

Galtung, J. (1988), Dialogues as development, in *Methodology and Development*, Copenhagen, Ejlers, 68–92.

Galtung, J. (1994), *Human Rights in Another Key*, Cambridge, Polity Press.

Galtung, J. (1996), *Peace By Peaceful Means*, London, New Delhi, Thousand Oaks, SAGE.

Galtung, J. (1996a), On the social costs of modernization: social disintegration, Anomie/atomie and social development, *Development and Change*, 27:2, 379–413.

Hutton, W. (1995), *The State We're In*, London, Jonathan Cape.

Panikkar, R. (1982), La notion des droits de l'homme, est-elle un concept occidental?, *Diogenes*, 120, 87–115.

Redfield, R. (1995), *The Little Community*, Chicago, University of Chicago Press.

Rushdie, S. (1988), *The Satanic Verses*, London, Viking.

Vidal, J. (1997), *McLibel: Burger Culture on Trial*, London, Macmillan.

# Index

'n.' after a page reference indicates the number of a note on a page.